"Santa Clara County 2000," updated for the millennium, gives a snapshot of the county and its cities as they leave one era and move into another.

School Rankings, including the latest academic rankings (STAR test) for public schools, college placements by high school, SAT scores, a directory of private schools — they are all inside.

Community profiles. Home prices, rents. Descriptions of cities, towns and neighborhoods.

Santa Clara 100 years ago. The headlines, the prices, the hot topics of the day.

The perfect guide for parents or people shopping for homes or apartments or just interested in finding out more about Santa Clara County, its schools and its communities.

"Santa Clara County 2000" describes the local weather.

Hospital services and medical care. Directory of hospitals.

Child Care. Directory of infant-care and day-care centers. Most popular names for Santa Clara babies.

Places to visit, things to do.

Local Colleges and Unemployment Figures.

Vital statistics. Population, income and education by town. Republicans and Democrats. Presidential votes. Crime, history, trivia and much more.

McCormack's Guides, edited by former newspaper reporters and editors, was established in 1984 and publishes the most popular general-interest guides to California counties. For a list of our other guides and an order form, see the last page.

Publisher and editor Don McCormack formed McCormack's Guides in 1984 to publish annual guides to California counties. A graduate of the University of California-Berkeley, McCormack joined the Contra Costa Times in 1969 and covered police, schools, politics, planning, courts and government. Later with the Richmond Independent and Berkeley Gazette, he worked as a reporter, then editor and columnist. McCormack writes city profile articles for the real estate section of the San Francisco Examiner.

Researcher and writer Mary Jennings is a native Californian who holds a Diversified Liberal Arts degree from Saint Mary's College in Moraga. She has worked for many years to improve residential support services for adults with developmental disabilities. Mary now brings her data management and writing experience to publishing.

Maps illustrator Louis Liu, a Bay Area resident for 12 years, has a B.A. in Teaching English as a Second Language. He loves art and enjoys drawing and painting. Louis attended Los Medanos College and the Academy of Art College in San Francisco, where he majored in illustration. He is now the art director of Tartan Sports in Hayward, a golf equipment manufacturer and wholesaler. To contact Louis, please call (925) 779-0394 or e-mail: louisliu@jps.net.

Ad graphics by Pyramid Productions, Martinez, California

Many thanks to the people who write, edit, layout and help publish McCormack's Guides: Allan, Don, Jack, John V., Krista, Mary J., Colleen, Farhad, John S., Katie, Mark, Mary T., Talita.

DISCLAIMER

Although facts and statements in this book have been checked and rechecked, mistakes — typographical and otherwise — may have occurred. Census data, test scores and other information have been updated to the time of publication using cost-of-living figures, mathematical averaging and other tools, which by their nature must be considered estimates. This book was written to entertain and inform. The authors, the editors and the publisher shall have no liability or responsibility for damages or alleged damages arising out of information contained in the "Santa Clara County 2000" edition of McCormack's Guides.

Indexed

ISBN 1-929365-10-1

SANTA CLARA COUNTY 2000

Edited by Don McCormack

3211 Elmquist Court, Martinez, CA 94553
Phone: (800) 222-3602 & Fax: (925) 228-7223
bookinfo@mccormacks.com • www.mccormacks.com

Contents

On the cover:
Lockheed Martin, a leader in space technology and exploration.

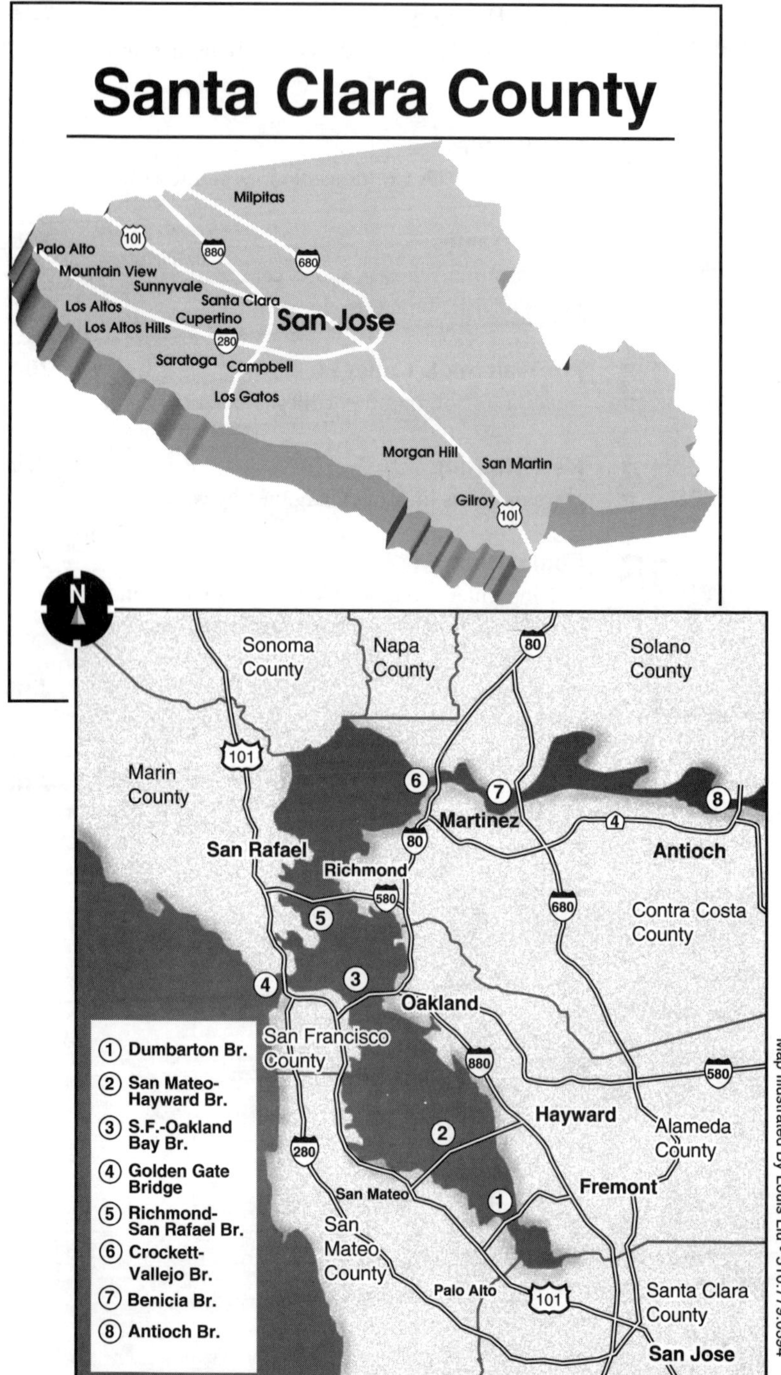
Santa Clara County
Milpitas
101
880
680
Palo Alto
Mountain View
Sunnyvale
Santa Clara
Los Altos
Cupertino
San Jose
Los Altos Hills
280
Saratoga
Campbell
Los Gatos
Morgan Hill
San Martin
Gilroy
101
N
Sonoma County
Napa County
80
Solano County
101
Marin County
6
7
8
Martinez
4
80
San Rafael
Antioch
Richmond
580
5
680
Contra Costa County
4
3
Oakland
1 Dumbarton Br.
2 San Mateo-Hayward Br.
3 S.F.-Oakland Bay Br.
4 Golden Gate Bridge
5 Richmond-San Rafael Br.
6 Crockett-Vallejo Br.
7 Benicia Br.
8 Antioch Br.
San Francisco County
880
580
Hayward
2
Alameda County
280
Fremont
San Mateo
1
San Mateo County
Palo Alto
101
Santa Clara County
San Jose
Map Illustrated By Louis Liu • 510.779.0394

Chapter 1

SANTA CLARA COUNTY *at a Glance*

ONE OF THE MOST DYNAMIC REGIONS ON THE PLANET, Santa Clara County started 1900 with 60,216 residents and will finish with about 1.7 million, the most populous county in Northern California.

Its weather is mild, its crime low, its delights many, its rents depressing, its home prices astronomical (among the highest in the U.S.), its opportunities dazzling and mixed. Almost every month some firm blasts to a new high in the stock market and another firm lays off hundreds.

Santa Clara, inspired intellectually by Stanford University, is the birthplace of Silicon Valley, the grouping of cities and industries that over the last 60 years has revolutionized, through computers and technology, how we think and communicate with one another, and how we solve problems.

Rectangular in shape, Santa Clara covers 1,316 square miles, smaller than Delaware, slightly larger than Rhode Island. There are two Santa Claras: one the county, encompassing everything; the second, a city, one of the largest in the county. San Jose, 909,602 residents, is the biggest and most populous city in the county. Monte Sereno, 3,443, has the fewest people.

Palo Alto, which adjoins Stanford, is the brainiest town; Los Altos Hills, the richest; San Jose, increasingly, the most dynamic and becoming recognized as the political leader of the region; Gilroy, in July, the most odoriferous. The town has become famous for its garlic festival.

Most people reside on the flatland of the Santa Clara Valley, which stretches from the Bay down to beyond Gilroy, the southernmost city. If you want a home with a view, generally you have to head for the hills and mountains that border the bay and the valley.

In housing and style, Santa Clara favors the suburban tract and the steadiness of the middle class. Crime rates, even in the larger cities, run in ranges on the low side of what's typical for suburban communities.

Single homes outnumber apartments 372,293 to 188,621 or two to one. Santa Clara has its mansions and its estates but the typical home is that old American workhorse, the three-bedroom unit (census and state figures).

Santa Clara County Population

City or Area	Male	Female	'90 Total	'99 Total
Campbell	49%	51%	36,048	39,871
Cupertino	50	50	40,263	47,668
Gilroy	49	51	31,487	39,071
Los Altos	48	52	26,303	28,488
Los Altos Hills	50	50	7,514	8,247
Los Gatos	48	52	27,357	30,274
Milpitas	53	47	50,686	64,325
Monte Sereno	49	51	3,287	3,443
Morgan Hill	50	50	23,928	31,896
Mountain View	51	49	67,460	75,201
Palo Alto	49	51	55,900	61,189
San Jose	51	49	782,248	909,062
Santa Clara	51	49	93,613	102,682
Saratoga	49	51	28,061	31,255
Stanford*	58	41	18,097	N.A.
Sunnyvale	50	50	117,229	132,940
Countywide	51	49	1,497,577	1,715,374
California				33,773,466

Source: Census for 1990 figures and Demographic Research Unit of the California Dept. of Finance for 1999 estimates. Stanford is located just outside Palo Alto city limits. **Key**: NA (not available).

Rarely does the humidity discomfort or the thermometer drop below freezing. Rain confines itself to the winter and snow to the tops of the local mountains, of which Copernicus, 4,360 feet, is the highest.

On the down side, Santa Clara and much of coastal California straddle active faults. Earthquakes are not a matter of if, but a matter of when. For sound advice on earthquakes, read the first section of the local phone directory.

Among California's 58 counties, Santa Clara is number two in median income, $69,873 (joint tax returns, 1997). Marin is first with $80,253.

Sports, Activities, Things to Do

Stanford and two other universities greatly enrich cultural life. Movies, opera, plays, pop and rock, professional and collegiate sports, ballet, symphonies, a children's musical theater, classes of all descriptions, performances by top-notch entertainers — in Santa Clara County you can find them all. Almost every year some new cultural ornament presents itself. What you can't find, nearby San Francisco and Oakland usually can provide.

In sports, San Jose is home to the only professional ice hockey team in Northern California, the Sharks. San Jose also fields teams for professional soccer and minor league baseball. Professional football (the Forty Niners and the Raiders) and baseball (the Giants and the Athletics) and basketball (the Warriors) are within a short drive. Just about every town offers the usual smorgasbord of Little League, softball, football, swimming, gymnastics, aerobics, tennis and so on. Among children, soccer is turning into the most

Average Household Income

City	1990	1995	*2000
Campbell	$59,746	$61,600	$65,100
Cupertino	89,142	97,200	111,800
Gilroy	57,831	58,300	62,300
Los Altos	122,204	137,600	160,200
Los Altos Hills	215,293	260,400	285,400
Los Gatos	97,453	110,100	128,800
Milpitas	74,096	81,000	93,500
Monte Sereno	164,745	198,000	240,700
Morgan Hill	75,292	77,500	84,800
Mountain View	60,618	64,100	73,700
Palo Alto	83,522	90,000	103,700
San Jose	63,439	65,300	73,100
Santa Clara	60,521	61,700	67,000
Saratoga	137,236	151,600	177,600
Sunnyvale	64,813	66,300	76,600
Remainder	84,721	95,500	110,200
Countywide	70,262	73,800	83,300

Source: Association of Bay Area Governments, *"Projections* 98." Average income per household includes wages and salaries, dividends, interest, rent and transfer payments such as Social Security or public assistance. Based on 1990 Census data and annual increases in the Consumer Price Index. *Projections.

popular sport. Parks, large and small, are scattered throughout the county. San Francisco Bay is in the county's back yard but rarely is it used for swimming (too cold; current comes from the Arctic.)

Yosemite, Lake Tahoe and the snow country are about six hours to the east. Most residents live within 60 minutes of the fishing boats of Half Moon Bay and the waves of the Pacific.

Because of the mild weather, outdoor sports run almost year round. Many people delight in gardening and hiking and cycling. Indoors, many a night is spent tinkering with this or that machine or computer.

Silicon Valley More a Frame of Mind

Silicon Valley is a term more indicative of a frame of mind than a geographic location but it used to have fairly precise borders, generally Palo Alto to south San Jose. Now high-tech firms (Sun, Oracle) have jumped over the county line into Redwood City and Menlo Park, and on the east side of the Valley and across the Bay, into Milpitas, Newark, Fremont, San Ramon, Livermore and Pleasanton, and even up to (gasp!) Berkeley and Richmond.

To work in Silicon Valley is to profess an interest in, often a passion for, high-tech. Here is where Stephan Wozniak, between raids on his parents' refrigerator, built the first Apple computer. And where his first partner, Steve Jobs, with the IMAC, is turning Apple around.

Here is where Stanford grads David Packard and Bill Hewlett, using the latter's master's thesis, built in a Palo Alto garage an audio oscillator. Their first

The South Bay

SANTA CLARA COUNTY

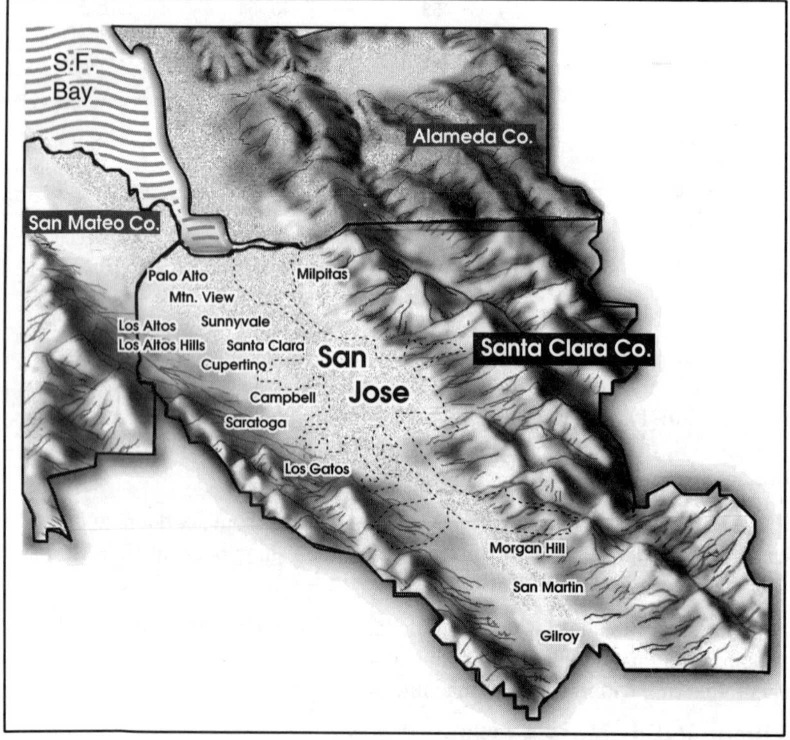

Map Illustrated By Louis Liu • 925.779.0394

customer, Walt Disney, ordered eight for the soundtrack of "Fantasia." Hewlett-Packard is now one of the biggies in high-tech research, development and manufacturing. Here also is where other firms pursue the golden breakthroughs, the ideas that will transform the ways of multitudes and nations.

Growth Pains

Paradise? Close, but not quite. The freeways are wide and plentiful but inadequate to handle the number of vehicles. In the last decade, the county added 202,506 people, a number equivalent then to the population of nine of its 15 cities. Many are the fights over development. If you strip away other fights — schools, traffic, taxes, services, rents, home prices — you will find underneath a county that is running hard to keep up with a growing population.

Religion in Santa Clara County

Denomination	Churches	Members	Total
African Methodist Episcopal Zion	1	234	309
American Baptist	11	2,353	2,910
Assembly of God	48	7,077	10,532
Baptist General Conference	5	798	987
Baptist Missionary Association	1	44	54
Catholic	52	NA	368,611
Christian & Missionary Alliance	5	1,010	1,383
Church of Christ	13	2,165	2,678
Disciples of Christ	3	406	606
Christian Reformed	4	422	657
Church of Christ, Scientist	12	NR	NR
Church of God (Anderson, Ind.)	3	133	267
Church of God (Cleveland, Tenn.)	7	363	449
Church of God (7th Day)	1	49	69
Church of God (Prophecy)	2	72	89
Church of Jesus Christ, Latter-day Saints	57	NA	23,595
Church of the Nazarene	14	1,742	2,269
Church of Christ	15	1,736	2,267
Congregational Christian	1	52	64
Conservative Baptist	12	NR	NR
Cumberland Presbyterian	2	141	182
Episcopal	19	7,038	9,953
Evangelical Free	4	619	795
Evangelical Lutheran	26	8,717	11,866
Free Methodist	5	202	343
Free Will Baptist	1	87	108
Friends	2	181	271
Mennonite Brethren	6	574	710
Greek Orthodox	2	NR	NR
Independent Fundamental	1	NR	NR
Foursquare Gospel	7	599	741
Lutheran-Missouri Synod	12	3,965	5,184
Mennonite General Conference	1	50	75
North American Baptist	1	64	79
Open Bible Standard	3	NR	NR
Orthodox Church in America	1	NR	NR
Pentecostal Church of God	7	214	566
Pentecostal Holiness	5	1,677	2,074
Christian Brethren	2	290	425
Presbyterian (USA)	26	9,078	11,228
Presbyterian Church in America	5	162	251
Primitive Baptists	1	8	10
Reformed Church in America	1	337	422
Romanian Orthodox Episcopate	1	NR	NR
Salvation Army	4	320	340
Seventh-day Adventist	18	4,754	5,880
Southern Baptist	45	17,103	21,153
Syrian Antioch	1	NA	400
Unitarian-Universalist	4	865	1,154

Religion in Santa Clara County

Denomination	Churches	Members	Total
United Church of Christ	12	3,393	4,197
United Methodist	32	13,463	16,651
Wisconsin Evangelical Lutheran	3	816	1,161
Jewish*	13	NA	32,000
Independent, Charismatic*	5	NA	9,760
Independent, Non-Charismatic*	7	NA	9,550
Santa Clara County totals	552	105,394	579,833

Source: Glenmary Research Center, Atlanta, Ga. **Key**: Churches and temples (Number in the county); Members (Communicant, confirmed, full members); Total (All adherents); NA (Not applicable); NR (Not reported). *Estimates. Our apologies to Muslims and members of other religions, we have not been able to obtain numbers on these groups.

Many schools score high but a good number do not. In recent years, voters in most local school districts have approved construction bonds or funds to improve instruction. After years of beggaring its schools, the state of California, thanks to the thriving economy, is putting up billions to lower class sizes and make other improvements. But the results may take a while to show themselves. The prudent parent will take an active interest in a child's school.

Crime is low, not nonexistent. You should always take precautions. In 1998, homicides in Santa Clara County totaled 44. By contrast, San Francisco, with less than half the population, recorded 69 homicides.

The Loma Prieta quake in 1989 scared holy hell out of thousands, killed dozens and caused damage in the millions. But few residents quit Santa Clara County and the population keeps growing. In sum, the good, the promising, the delightful, far outweigh the bad and the ominous.

A Changing Ethnic Mix

The county is changing from predominantly Caucasian — or in the local lingo: Anglo — to minority-majority. The sum of all minorities outnumbers or will soon outnumber Caucasians. This is often stated in a way that implies that minorities form a bloc that votes, thinks and acts in concert. They don't. A man from the highlands of Vietnam may have little in common with a man descended from people who roamed the highlands of Scotland. But he also may have little in common with a fellow recently arrived from the Mexican desert.

Santa Clara by mid Year 2000 should have, the state estimates, 842,643 Caucasians, 426,883 Asians, 425,918 Hispanics, 62,625 African-Americans and 5,153 American Indians.

Women and Minorities in Seats of Power

Women have discovered what men always knew: It is fun to give orders, command attention and respect, and pull down high salaries. The majority of students at most, if not all, of the county's colleges and universities are women,

Top 25 Baby Names

Santa Clara County		California	
Boys	**Girls**	**Boys**	**Girls**
Michael (232)	Jessica (193)	Daniel (4,384)	Jessica (3,185)
Christopher (200)	Jennifer (148)	Michael (4,252)	Jennifer (2,782)
Daniel (194)	Emily (128)	Jose (4,116)	Ashley (2,608)
David (183)	Samantha(120)	Anthony (3,862)	Emily (2,527)
Jose (181)	Sarah (120)	Christopher (3,690)	Samantha (2,479)
Anthony (177)	Ashley (107)	David (3,674)	Stephanie (2,153)
Andrew (176)	Michelle (104)	Andrew (3,535)	Sarah (2,135)
Kevin (172)	Elizabeth (102)	Jacob (3,218)	Vanessa (1,977)
Alexander (170)	Vanessa (102)	Matthew (3,213)	Elizabeth (1,974)
Jonathan (167)	Stephanie (100)	Jonathan (3,188)	Alexis (1,884)
Matthew (161)	Jasmine (98)	Joshua (3,079)	Maria (1,816)
Brandon (149)	Hannah (92)	Joseph (2,856)	Jasmine (1,794)
Nicholas(149)	Megan (90)	Brandon (2,822)	Alyssa (1,723)
Joshua (146)	Nicole (90)	Nicholas(2,608)	Melissa (1,716)
Justin (143)	Maria (83)	Christian (2,581)	Hannah (1,620)
Jacob (141)	Alyssa (81)	Kevin (2,546)	Kimberly(1,573)
Ryan (132)	Lauren (76)	Luis (2,463)	Victoria (1,442)
Joseph (125)	Alexandra (73)	Ryan (2,351)	Taylor (1,427)
John (110)	Amanda (73)	Juan (2,324)	Amanda (1,400)
Luis (109)	Katherine (73)	Alexander (2,165)	Lauren (1,355)
Eric (108)	Melissa (71)	Justin (2,140)	Natalie (1,342)
Christian (106)	Sabrina (68)	Jesus (2,010)	Madison (1,339)
Kyle (104)	Taylor (68)	Austin (1,940)	Michelle (1,329)
Tyler (99)	Rachel (67)	Tyler (1,863)	Megan (1,321)
Brian (97)	Brianna (66)	John (1,807)	Diana (1,264)

Source: California Department of Health Services, 1997 birth records. Shown in parentheses is the number of children with the given name. Some names would move higher on the list if the state grouped essentially same names with slightly different spellings, for example, Sarah and Sara. But state computer goes by exact spellings.

and women routinely win seats on school boards, city councils and the board of supervisors. Minorities are also showing up more on city councils and government bodies. In 1998 Ron Gonzales was elected mayor of San Jose.

A Little History

Spanish expeditions arrived in 1769 and 1776, intrepid and brave but late. Having ignored California since claiming it in the 1500s, Spain was dismayed to find other countries interested in her province. The Spanish explorers and those who followed were supposed to plant the flag, subdue and convert the Indians and colonize the land. The flag was planted, great ranches carved out, but the colonists were few and the Indians, through disease, hostility and misguided benevolence, were almost exterminated. At a critical time, Spain and Europe were diverted by the Napoleonic wars. On the other side of the continent, the United States secured its independence, bought the Midwest and heard the siren call of California. Over the mountains the Americans came, first for land, then gold. They kicked over the flag (Mexico's, Spain having been ousted) and by purchase, violence, swindles and squatting drove the rancheros into obscurity.

Left behind were city names and a fondness for romanticized Spanish architecture that has influenced the design of banks, churches, colleges and hamburger stands. Also remaining: a mild sense of guilt about seizing the land from the Mexicans, who in the perverse ways of history re-established themselves in Santa Clara County through later immigration.

Era of Rustic Happiness

The new Californians built roads, cities and railroads, cultivated the county into fabled abundance and — in the great American tradition of boosterism and speculation — spent much time and ink trying to lure others to Santa Clara County. Thousands did come but never enough to turn Santa Clara into a metropolis. Well into the 20th century, the county tended the pear, prune and tomato — an era of rustic happiness, fondly recalled in local histories.

On 13 March, 1884, Leland Stanford Jr., age 16, died of typhoid fever. His saddened mom and dad (grocer, railroad tycoon, governor) founded and endowed Stanford University in memory of their only child. Santa Clara County owes much of its prosperity to Stanford U.

The War Boom

On Dec. 7, 1941, the Japanese bombed Pearl Harbor, a blunder that inadvertently did more for real estate in Santa Clara County than 90 years of booster hoopla. War industries blossomed and thousands of servicemen, recalling that pleasant sunshine, returned to the county after the war. The war also made America a superpower, which entailed the support of a military establishment. For decades, defense dollars drove much of the county's economy. Down went the orchards, up went the housing tracts, slowly at first, with some wringing of hands, then rapidly as people poured in. The population, 290,000 people in 1950, doubled, then doubled again.

In 1951, prompted by Fred Terman, vice president of Stanford, the university opened 700 acres for development. Electronics companies, attracted by the proximity of big brains, snapped up parcels. The result: Silicon Valley.

Tinkerers, Entrepreneurs

Actually, it wasn't quite that easy. Santa Clara County has a soft spot for the tinkerers, the Main Street whiz kids who get an idea into their heads, then spend days and weeks in their garages working it into something practical.

Hewlett and Packard, Jobs and Wozniak (Apple) epitomize the romance of the garage. They took their ideas and built industries. Of course, they drew on the work of others. The Apple could not have been built without the microprocessor, a 1971 Silicon Valley invention. The whole technological revolution would have stalled in its tracks without the transistor, developed in Bell Labs, New Jersey, but the co-inventor was William Shockley, Palo Alto native.

How Residents Earn Their Money

City	EX	PF	TC	SA	CL	SV	AG	MF
Campbell	17%	17%	6%	13%	17%	10%	1%	19%
Cupertino	25	27	7	13	12	5	1	10
Gilroy	10	12	4	11	14	12	6	30
Los Altos	29	31	5	13	11	5	1	7
Los Altos Hills	33	32	3	12	9	4	10	6
Los Gatos	23	26	5	16	12	7	1	11
Milpitas	14	16	7	10	17	9	1	27
Monte Sereno	31	31	3	15	9	5	1	6
Morgan Hill	16	16	6	14	15	9	3	21
Mountain View	18	23	8	9	14	10	2	15
Palo Alto	23	36	8	10	10	6	1	6
San Jose	14	15	6	11	17	12	1	25
Santa Clara	16	19	7	10	18	9	1	20
Saratoga	32	26	5	13	12	5	1	7
Stanford	10	41	9	5	21	11	*0	4
Sunnyvale	18	23	8	19	15	8	1	18
Santa Clara County	16	19	6	11	16	10	1	21

Source: 1990 Census. Figures are percent of population, rounded to the nearest whole number. Key: EX (executive and managerial); PF (professional specialty); TC (technicians); SA (sales); CL (clerical and administrative support); SV (service occupations, including household, protective and other services); AG (agricultural, including farming, fishing, forestry); MF (manufacturing, including precision production, craft, repair; also machine operators, assemblers, inspectors, equipment cleaners and handlers, helpers and laborers). *Less than 0.5 percent.

Modern Santa Clara County

Modern Santa Clara County: flourishing, growing, continually arguing over development. San Jose is still building but the days of the fast zonings and marching subdivisions are gone. The city has spent the last two decades putting muscle on its downtown.

With the collapse of the Soviet Union and the end of the Cold War, defense spending was sharply curtailed and this forced painful cutbacks in local industries. The Navy in 1994 quit Moffett Field, its airbase near Mountain View. But so far Santa Clara County seems to be able to shrug off bad news. If one door closes, another opens. Sand Hill Road in Palo Alto has become synonymous with venture capital. Here is where the firms and the people behind them make many of the bets on the ideas that are revolutionizing the globe.

How Government Works

To Sacramento and Washington is where the money goes first these days and that's where much of the power resides. If you want more or less spent on roads, welfare, warfare, schools or pensions, write your congressman, senator or state legislator. Although weakened, local governments are far from penniless and enjoy considerable powers. Major agencies include:

Education Level of Population Age 18 & Older

City or Town	HS	SC	AA	BA	Grad
Campbell	22%	27%	10%	21%	8%
Cupertino	12	24	9	28	20
Gilroy	22	23	8	10	4
Los Altos	12	20	6	32	26
Los Altos Hills	7	20	4	30	35
Los Gatos	15	26	8	29	16
Milpitas	22	25	9	16	7
Monte Sereno	7	20	8	31	30
Morgan Hill	22	25	10	17	8
Mountain View	16	23	8	24	15
Palo Alto	10	17	5	31	31
San Jose	21	24	8	16	7
Santa Clara	22	26	8	20	9
Saratoga	12	21	7	31	24
Stanford	16	35	1	22	26
Sunnyvale	19	24	8	23	11
Santa Clara County	20	24	8	19	11

Source: 1990 Census. Figures are percent of population age 18 and older, rounded to the nearest whole number. Not shown are adults with less than a 9th grade education or with some high school education but no diploma or GED. **Key**: HS (adults with high school diploma or GED only, no college); SC (adults with some college education); AA (adults with an associate degree); BA (adults with a bachelor's degree only); Grad (adults with a master's or higher degree).

Board of Supervisors

Five members are elected countywide, but by districts. (Gilroy, south end of the county, votes for its supervisor, Milpitas, northeast, for its supervisor and so on.) Supervisors are regional and municipal governors. They control spending for courts, animal services, many libraries, social services, public health. In their municipal hats, they build roads, decide zonings and, through the sheriff's department, provide police protection for unincorporated areas and some cities under contractual arrangements. If you live outside the limits of any city, you will be governed from San Jose, seat of county government. This sometimes gets confusing. In some areas, the county governs one side of a street and a city the other side.

City Councils

Generally five members (San Jose has 10 plus an elected mayor, the tie breaker, Palo Alto has nine), one council for each of the county's 15 cities. Councils are responsible for repairing roads, keeping neighborhoods safe, maintaining parks, providing recreation and other municipal chores. Much of their time goes to planning and development.

Special Service Districts

California grew so fast and chaotically that some regional needs, such as sewer and water, were met on an emergency basis by forming taxing districts with their own elected directors.

Santa Clara County Voter Registration

City	Demo	Repub	Clinton	Dole
Campbell	8,604	6,234	7,574	4,332
Cupertino	8,285	8,206	9,123	6,182
Gilroy	7,793	4,407	5,374	3,131
Los Altos	6,901	8,394	7,806	6,654
Los Altos Hills	1,657	2,656	1,760	2,178
Los Gatos	7,000	7,718	7,017	5,563
Milpitas	9,182	6,578	8,658	4,756
Monte Sereno	785	1,157	776	935
Morgan Hill	6,274	5,864	5,094	4,436
Mountain View	15,620	8,583	15,470	6,359
Palo Alto	18,829	9,340	19,223	6,664
San Jose	166,131	105,443	139,040	74,019
Santa Clara	21,296	12,847	19,372	9,479
Saratoga	5,899	9,236	6,250	7,413
Sunnyvale	25,376	18,175	25,107	13,797
Unincorporated	24,246	16,474	19,965	12,393

Source: County registrar of voters,1999. Key: Demo (Democrat), Repub (Republican).

Presidential Voting in Santa Clara County

Year	Democrat	D-Votes	Republican	R-Votes
1948	Truman*	41,905	Dewey	52,982
1952	Stevenson	59,350	Eisenhower*	87,554
1956	Stevenson	72,528	Eisenhower*	105,657
1960	Kennedy*	117,667	Nixon	131,735
1964	Johnson*	161,422	Goldwater	93,448
1968	Humphrey	175,511	Nixon*	163,446
1972	McGovern	208,505	Nixon*	237,329
1976	Carter*	208,023	Ford	219,188
1980	Carter	166,955	Reagan*	229,048
1984	Mondale	229,865	Reagan*	288,638
1988	Dukakis	277,810	Bush*	254,442
1992	Clinton*	276,391	Bush	155,984
1996	Clinton*	297,639	Dole	168,291

Source: California Secretary of State's office. * Election winner nationally.

School Boards

Generally composed of five persons. There are 33 school districts in Santa Clara County, each with an elected school board. A real hodgepodge. Members hire or fire principals and superintendents, negotiate teacher salaries, decide how much should be spent on computers and shop and whether the children should wear uniforms, and more.

Chapter 2 SANTA CLARA COUNTY at the turn of 1900

Famed for its Fruits and Its Good Roads

San Francisco Chronicle, Dec. 31, 1900

"In the first half century of the development of Santa Clara county has made wonderful progress among the counties of the State for the extent and value of her agricultural resources. The change from widely-extending grain and hay fields and stock ranges in the early portion of the half century to small holdings of valuable orchards in all directions brought about a condition that attracted the attention of the National Government to the rural districts of the county, as compared with those of other sections of the country. At Campbell, the notable orchard region, the Post Office authorities at Washington made the first successful experiment in rural mail delivery. The system has spread until now Santa Clara County with her thickly settled and prosperous rural population is like a great city as regards the distribution of the mail of the residents from house to house.

The assessed valuation of property in the county has increased from $4,800,000 in 1850 to nearly $52,000,000 in 1899. In the first thirty years the value of property increased over fivefold, and there has been a doubling of values during the term of service of sixteen years of the present Assessor.

The increase of property values and prosperity in the county is in no doubt due in great measure to the amazing development of her fruit resources. Santa Clara Valley has become famous for the extent and quality of her dried French prune product, which increased in volume from 8,000,000 pounds in 1890 to 70,000,000 in 1898. Of fruit trees Santa Clara valley has nearly 5,000,000, of which over 3,000,000 are prune trees.

The fruit canneries that in season employ many thousands of

continued on next page

men, women and children have now an average annual output of half a million cases, amounting to 30,000,000 pounds. This fruit is shipped to all parts of the world. The product of wine of Santa Clara County, of a fine quality, is about 5,000,000 gallons annually. From grape pomace there is a large output of cream of tartar from a factory in San Jose. One of the largest olive orchards in the world is located near Los Gatos. The average shipment of green, dried and canned fruits from San Jose is over 130,000,000 pounds annually.

The business of seed raising has reached an extent and success in Santa Clara valley, on account of the mild climate allowing winter cultivation, that is scarcely known in any other part of the world. One farm near Santa Clara has an extent of 1,200 acres, of which 150 acres are in seed onions alone.

At Gilroy the dairy interests are immense, annually about 1,300,000 pounds of cheese being manufactured and sent to all part of the world.

The New Almaden quicksilver mine, twelve miles south of San Jose, is surpassed in importance only by the old Almaden mines in Spain. The operations began in 1851, and the value of the product to March 1891, was $14,939,000.

The world-famed Lick Observatory, with its mammoth telescope, is located on Mount Hamilton, thirty miles from San Jose, 4,444 feet above sea level. The country constructed a fine graded road to the observatory at a cost of $100,000.

A magnificent system of public roads that has attracted wide attention and favorable comment is maintained and extended at a cost of $100,000 annually. In San Jose and vicinity there are twenty miles of electric street railway and seven miles of steam-motor road.

The railway company at San Jose has just completed a large brick roundhouse, to replace a wooden structure, and added a great area to its freight yards and warehouse facilities. One of the most important railway improvements for the advancement of the county will be the completion of the road through the Santa Margarita gap, when San Jose will be on a through line to the East.

An important factor in the advancement of the county will be the securing of increased and economical facilities for marketing the product both by sea and land. Alviso harbor, on San Francisco Bay, is only seven miles north of San Jose, and will soon be connected with it by an electric railway line. The Government is about to begin work upon a $48,000 preliminary appropriation for the improvement of the harbor with a view to making it available for the largest sea-going vessels. Undoubtedly, long before the next half century is completed, San Jose will expand over the intervening territory to absorb Alviso, and convert that town into a water front, with a long line of stone docks and warehouses for shipping facilities."

ARTICLES AND ADS FROM THE SAN JOSE HERALD, THE SAN JOSE MERCURY AND OTHER CALIFORNIA NEWSPAPERS

The Bikers Defeat Autos

Secure and Easy Victory and Win Applause Galore from the Crowd

"Pedestrians along First Street yesterday afternoon witnessed an amusing, and for two of the people concerned, a most embarrassing scene.

A handsome automobile, or 'horseless carriage,' came up from the Hotel Vendome at a lively rate, and crossed the railroad track just as 20 paper carriers on bicycles, left the broad gauge depot for the center of town.

Naturally the lads were curious to see the rubber-tired rival of the equine, and waited for it to pass, dropping in behind as it went by. The 'auto' proceeded uptown with the procession of kids receiving new additions at every block, and growing like a society scandal.

The humor of the situation apparently dawned upon the 'autos' when they looked behind and saw behind them fully three dozen 'bikers,' lined up two abreast, the leaders not six feet away. To say that it was embarrassing to have such a horde following through the principal streets would be putting it mildly. The dignified 'autos' tried to remonstrate with the boys but were laughed at. Then they became angry and were jeered. The 'auto' was then sent forward at its best pace but the 'bikers' could not be shaken.... Then as the 'autos' tried to 'look haughty' and proceeded on up the street, the 'bikers' scored an untarnished victory by uttering a vociferous 'toot-toot' every time a rig was passed....With blazing cheeks the two dignified gentleman turned the carriage down the first available side street and it will be a matter of surprise if they are seen in town again for a couple of weeks."

—San Jose Herald, December 29th, 1899

Home for the Homeless

"The ladies of the Home of Benevolence were in session last afternoon. Reports from the managers showed that mumps are prevailing at the home. There have been about 50 cases so far but none serious. It is believed that the epidemic will soon run its course."

—January 3rd, 1900

Halloween Pranks

GATES AND SIGNS WERE CHANGED

Police very busy last night.

"Small boys and boys that were not so small began early to lay and execute their plans last evening for the usual riotous and hilarious observance of Halloween, and the police patrol wagon and entire force were kept on the jump for hours answering calls from anxious property owners, who feared that not only their gates but their fences might be wrecked.

Everything in the way of vehicles that were on wheels and could be gotten at were moved out early and placed in positions on streets in the dark where they were the most likely to cause trouble to the cyclers and others who were out on their usual rounds and were not expecting to run up against any such obstructions.

Shortly after 8 o'clock the chimes of Trinity Church began to ring out very loudly. At first the tunes were such as have often been heard proceeding from that bell tower ... but soon the airs became painfully suggestive of indecorous music that was more fitting for a minstrel hall."

—January 3rd, 1900.

Hints to earthquake victims:

"Stay in bed, you cannot stop the shake by running into the street barefooted and in your night clothes, such doings only help the doctors. Next day don't say the shock lasted 2 minutes, as the real time was 10 seconds. While the universe quakes, hang on tight and repeat these lines:

"No matter what they do or say
The world rolls in the same old way,
And he who would posses his soul
Must hold on tight and let her roll."

—San Diego Union, December 28th, 1899

Will the Earth Be Destroyed Monday

"Professor Rudolph Falb, one of the staff of instructors at the Vienna University and an astronomer whose name is known from one end of the scientific world to the other has settled upon November 13th as the day the world will end.

'On November 13th, our planet is to come in contact with the comet that is known to astronomers as the Comet of 1866 with the result that our planet will be partially if not entirely destroyed,' said the professor."

November 11th, 1899

MAGNETISM AND MASSAGE

Dr. B. Elliott cures female diseases, all nervous, acute or chronic ailments of either sex by vital magnetism and massage.

Diagnosis free • Office 118 South First Street.

Tidbits From the Mercury News

- "LOS GATOS has a very creditable public library of 1,500 volumes, which is supported by a special tax." December 24, 1899
- "WHEN THE TOWN OF CAMPBELL was platted, all deeds contained a clause providing that no saloons should be established. There are, therefore, no saloons within the corporate limits of the town." December 24, 1899
- "THE AVERAGE SALARY PAID to male teachers in the United States is $44.89 per month, and for female teachers, $36.65 per month; while in California the average for male teachers is $80.70 and for female teachers $66.20." December 24, 1899

A RUDE AWAKENING

"It is too late, Madam, your daughter cannot live."

Oh, mothers!

Do not wait for these heartbreaking words regarding those you love. Are your daughters pale, weary, languid? Do they have much headache and backache during their monthly periods? These are Nature's warnings to all sensible mothers, they need a gentle stimulant.

DUFFY'S PURE MALT WHISKEY

It is a specific and safe remedy for these ills peculiar to young women. It acts quickly on the vital organs, stimulating them to healthy action, aids digestion and absorption, thus removing all irregularities and dangers of quick consumption. It will surely give your daughters strength and rosy cheeks, and fit them for their usual sphere in life as healthy, happy wives and mothers.

BEWARE OF IMITATIONS. DRUGGISTS USUALLY SELL IT. IF YOURS DOES NOT A BOTTLE WILL BE SENT TO YOU PRE-PAID FOR 1 DOLLAR, SIX FOR 5 DOLLARS

Dr. Wombat ELIXIR REMEDY

January Clearance Sale Ad Prices

Ladies' kid gloves	89¢
Ladies' gowns	77¢
Skirts	22¢
Black serge dress skirts	$3.95
Children's school hose	14¢
Ladies Cashmere hose	32¢
Pillow cases	9¢ to 50¢
Wool blankets	$3.85 to $6.75
Bedspreads	95¢
Linen towels	$1.75

- DRUNKEN DRIVING. "An incident that occurred on West Santa Clara Street recently suggested to several citizens who beheld it, the idea it would be a great addition to their usefulness if policemen would pay more attention to drunken men who drive around recklessly…. It is observed that often a man who would be considered too drunk to be allowed to walk the street is permitted to drive a lively horse around. The incident in question is that of a man who had the whole street open to him and yet he crashed into every rig that he met within his career on West Santa Clara Street." November 1, 1899
- COLLAR BONE BROKEN. "Dr. E. Wislocki is suffering from a fractured collarbone, received on the morning following the last heavy rain. His horse became fractious over the spattering of mud upon his back from the buggy wheels and kicking out, got one leg fast on the dashboard. In trying to release the animal's leg, the doctor received the kick that did the injury. He is getting along nicely." November 3, 1899
- CARELESS HUNTERS. "There is considerable complaint here in regards to careless hunters. They trespassed recently sowed onion crops, doing considerable damage. On several occasions they have found game to be scarce, and devoted their time and ammunition to killing the cats in the seed fields. Arrests will follow if the trespass continues." December 9, 1899
- TWELFTH STREET COMPLAINT. "After every heavy rain, the street remains for weeks an almost impassable muck hole. The roadway of the muck-hole section has no crown, and consequently there is no drainage to speak of. Why it has been allowed to remain in its disgracefully unimproved condition is a mystery." November 1, 1899

- "DEPUTY SHERIFF MARCEN is doing good work on The Alameda in keeping the disorderly element in check. A man whom whiskey had caused to make a nuisance of himself was landed in the county jail yesterday." November 1, 1899
- LOCAL MAIL CARRIERS WERE PAID $400 per year in 1899 and had to provide their own horse or bicycle.
- CITY OF SANTA CLARA in 1899 had one high school with 170 pupils and 7 teachers.

Tidbits From the San Jose Herald

- THE NEW CENTURY WAS WELCOMED IN A CELEBRATION CALLED THE JUBILEE. It was celebrated with a minstrel show, and music by the Nevada State Band. "Now is the time for every San Josian to turn out and boom his town." December 18, 1899
- SCHOOL PROMOTION, SAN JOSE SUPERINTENDENT RUSSELL
"It is the judgement of your superintendent that above the 2nd grade when a child has spent two terms in the grade and has been over the work twice he should be promoted. The fact that he has not accomplished in two terms what the average child does in one indicates that he has not or never will become a scholar, that he has no interest in the work of that grade and may take more interest in the next, or that he will absorb something at least. The only exception I would make to this would be the 3rd grade, when a child did not know the multiplication table." January 6, 1900

Classified Ads

HELP WANTED:

"Situation for young sober man to take care of horses and garden; private place. Apply 146 West Santa Clara Street." November 1, 1899

SITUATIONS WANTED-FEMALE

"A young lady, daughter of an Episcopalian clergyman, desires position as companion or will do sewing in refined family in return for board and room." November 1, 1899

"Attention!

YOUNG MARRIED PEOPLE

Remember

That Love in the Cottage is Sweeter then in a Boarding House

This is just what you are looking for… modern cottage (San Jose), city water, barn, one block from electric cars, stone sidewalk. Price $1,000."

Opium, Morphine & Cocaine Habits

Perfectly and permanently cured by the India Opium Cure, without pain or loss of time from business.

A perfect home remedy, and yet the most remarkable ever discovered for this purpose, containing the great vital principle lacking in all other cures. Call Dr. Bruce D. Kimmis, 201 Turk St. San Francisco, telephone Folsom 636.

Advertisement — December 10, 1899

SAMPLE OF ADVERTISED SALE PRICES

Women's capes	$4.95 to $14.50
Dresses	$9.95 to $19.75
Skirts	$1.98 to $14.50
Jackets	$1.98 to $9.45
Black ostrich tips	25¢
Natural pelican quills	5¢
Imitation black paradise tails	50¢
Velvet roses	18¢
Girls' hats	$2.25
Men's overcoats	$10
Handkerchiefs	2¢ to 33¢
Children's heavy wool Union Suits	95¢ to $1.25
Men's underwear, shirts or drawers	50¢
Men's cotton hosiery	10¢, 12.5¢, 20¢, 25¢
Boys' top coats	$3.95
Soap, 30 bars	$1.00
Flour, Berst Family, sack	78¢
Table fruits (2.5-pound tins)	25¢
Table claret, per gallon	30¢
Port or sherry wine, per gallon	55¢
Cedar rum whisky, per gallon	$2

Victory Theatre

November 2nd, 1899

ONE NIGHT ONLY

The bright and sparkling farce comedy

"A BREACH OF PROMISE"

New Music, New Dances, New Faces

Up-to-Date Specialties and Pretty Girls

Entire Lower Floor, 75¢

Balcony, 50¢ • Gallery, 25¢

Testimonial from George D. Williams of Michigan.

"My wife had been so helpless for 5 years that she could not turn over in bed alone. After using 2 bottles of Electric Bitters she is wonderfully improved and able to do her own work."

This supreme remedy for female diseases quickly cures nervousness, sleeplessness, melancholy, headache, backache, and fainting and dizzy spells. This miracle-working medicine is a Godsend to weak, sickly, run down people. Every bottle guaranteed. Only 50 cents.

Sold by Bristol & Roley, Druggist.

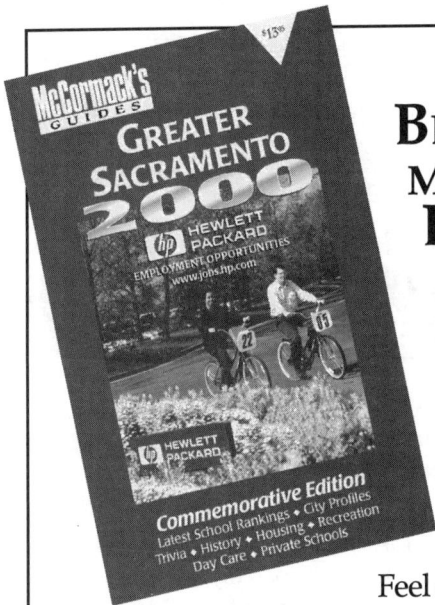

Chapter 3

SANTA CLARA COUNTY

National School Rankings

Here are the results of the 1999 STAR (Stanford) test as administered to almost all public school students by the California Dept. of Education. The test has a major shortcoming that will depress the scores of many California schools.

STAR is based on a national norm. The people who developed the test gave it to students of diverse backgrounds who supposedly represented U.S. students in general. From these results, national standards were drawn up.

The highest score is 99, the lowest is 1. A score of 50 is considered average. A school scoring 75 means that it has done better than about 75 percent of the other schools in the nation. If a school scores 25, it means that about 75 percent of the other schools in the nation have scored higher.

The STAR test became embroiled in arguments over the inclusion of students who spoke little or no English.

Here is the problem. The students tested to come up with the national norm included only 2 percent who spoke limited English.

California schools, in the aggregate, have about 22 percent limited English speaking.

The national sampling, representative of the nation, is not representative of California. If the national sampling were representative of California schools, many of our scores would be higher.

Parents and Realtors should interpret these scores cautiously, especially when a school has enrolled many students with a limited command of English.

For decades, the California Dept. of Education broke out score percentiles that allowed easy comparisons between California schools. The department no longer does this but for ease of comparison, McCormack's Guides continues the practice in Chapter 3B.

See Chapter 4 for a list of school districts and their phone numbers.

Scores range from 1-99, with 50 the average. A school scoring 75 has done better than 75 percent of other public schools in the U.S.
Key: Rd (Reading), Ma (Math), Lg (Language), Sp (Spelling), Sci (Science) and SS (Social Science).

Grade	Rd	Ma	Lg	Sp	Sci	SS
Santa Clara County						
2	56	61	58	56		
3	52	61	58	55		
4	55	57	58	54		
5	54	59	59	54		
6	56	66	60	56		
7	54	61	63	54		
8	55	61	59	47		
9	44	65	59		52	52
10	39	60	47		53	48
11	42	60	53		52	63
Alum Rock Union Elem. School Dist.						
2	30	35	29	31		
3	23	31	27	30		
4	24	28	30	22		
5	27	32	32	30		
6	29	39	35	30		
7	27	35	36	30		
8	32	36	35	28		
Arbuckle Elem.						
2	24	20	23	32		
3	31	29	26	27		
4	15	16	19	15		
5	24	38	31	27		
Cassell Elem.						
2	45	54	39	47		
3	35	47	39	52		
4	40	43	42	38		
5	31	40	35	35		
Chavez Elem.						
2	14	24	13	15		
3	19	27	20	16		
4	24	31	26	15		
5	18	26	29	21		
Cureton Elem.						
2	43	46	50	43		
3	29	30	33	36		
4	31	35	42	30		
5	27	27	34	31		
Dorsa Elem.						
2	19	30	17	21		
3	15	23	18	20		
4	16	16	20	13		
5	19	27	24	18		
Fischer Middle						
6	25	27	29	22		
7	26	35	31	24		
8	35	37	37	26		
George Middle						
6	37	56	39	35		
7	39	51	46	44		
8	38	39	38	34		
Goss Elem.						
2	38	41	33	37		
3	22	16	20	21		
4	16	19	21	17		
5	22	22	25	24		

Grade	Rd	Ma	Lg	Sp	Sci	SS
Hubbard Elem.						
2	21	22	21	20		
3	12	22	19	21		
4	19	22	23	14		
5	20	20	21	21		
Linda Vista Elem.						
2	41	40	38	39		
3	40	40	43	36		
4	38	33	49	34		
5	43	42	40	39		
Lyndale Elem.						
2	33	36	34	27		
3	23	36	25	30		
4	25	29	27	26		
5	31	44	32	32		
Mathson Middle						
6	19	29	27	21		
7	19	24	26	19		
8	25	32	27	20		
McCollam Elem.						
2	41	43	52	47		
3	21	28	30	36		
4	37	44	44	35		
5	37	31	36	36		
Meyer Elem.						
2	30	34	28	29		
3	19	28	24	26		
4	24	21	28	17		
5	29	27	34	29		
Miller Elem.						
2	31	36	31	31		
3	20	26	27	27		
4	14	23	23	14		
5	23	29	26	28		
Ocala Middle						
6	39	54	46	40		
7	27	38	42	31		
8	32	39	39	30		
Painter Elem.						
2	32	42	26	32		
3	31	40	31	43		
4	31	40	33	36		
5	33	37	29	47		
Pala Middle						
6	25	32	33	28		
7	24	30	35	30		
8	30	31	35	27		
Rogers Elem.						
2	40	44	43	47		
3	32	46	39	47		
4	29	37	37	33		
5	41	55	56	56		
Ryan Elem.						
2	26	37	26	28		
3	23	42	31	27		
4	23	24	27	16		
5	22	26	27	23		

Scores range from 1-99, with 50 the average. A school scoring 75 has done better than 75 percent of other public schools in the U.S.
Key: Rd (Reading), Ma (Math), Lg (Language), Sp (Spelling), Sci (Science) and SS (Social Science).

ALUM ROCK DIST. (Continued)

Grade	Rd	Ma	Lg	Sp	Sci	SS
San Antonio Elem.						
2	24	27	22	26		
3	17	21	21	22		
4	19	21	29	20		
5	20	28	30	23		
Sheppard Middle						
6	33	40	41	41		
7	29	35	38	37		
8	34	37	36	31		
Shields Elem.						
2	35	37	30	39		
3	24	36	31	32		
4	18	27	29	21		
5	23	26	30	24		
Slonaker Elem.						
2	19	31	18	20		
3	16	25	19	20		
4	18	24	30	19		
5	24	33	39	24		

Berryessa Union Elem. School Dist.

Grade	Rd	Ma	Lg	Sp	Sci	SS
2	53	59	55	59		
3	49	59	57	63		
4	52	54	56	57		
5	49	53	53	58		
6	54	64	57	58		
7	50	60	59	57		
8	52	59	57	48		
Brooktree Elem.						
2	67	65	65	66		
3	44	53	47	56		
4	54	54	57	62		
5	56	61	66	65		
Cherrywood Elem.						
2	42	36	39	48		
3	44	54	55	59		
4	40	47	51	54		
5	43	45	45	55		
Laneview Elem.						
2	57	60	52	67		
3	48	58	54	63		
4	49	52	55	55		
5	46	47	42	56		
Majestic Way Elem.						
2	45	53	49	54		
3	47	61	58	61		
4	47	44	48	53		
5	42	47	42	45		
Morrill Middle						
6	51	60	55	56		
7	42	50	48	50		
8	45	56	50	45		
Noble Elem.						
2	63	74	70	60		
3	58	58	60	64		
4	50	57	57	48		
5	50	52	52	53		
Northwood Elem.						
2	48	58	55	53		
3	48	56	53	62		
4	55	44	61	61		
5	59	68	66	65		
Piedmont Middle						
6	49	64	52	54		
7	49	64	61	56		
8	50	57	51	43		
Ruskin Elem.						
2	72	83	76	73		
3	64	79	77	76		
4	77	81	75	82		
5	64	68	67	66		
Sierramont Middle						
6	60	69	63	64		
7	61	66	70	67		
8	63	68	71	57		
Summerdale Elem.						
2	45	47	44	53		
3	43	44	44	54		
4	47	47	47	46		
5	43	44	47	59		
Toyon Elem.						
2	48	61	55	58		
3	49	65	59	63		
4	47	47	46	43		
5	44	45	48	50		
Vinci Park Elem.						
2	39	46	42	56		
3	43	51	51	63		
4	53	54	58	59		
5	49	55	57	63		

Cambrian Elem. School Dist.

Grade	Rd	Ma	Lg	Sp	Sci	SS
2	71	75	74	68		
3	63	71	69	63		
4	65	61	69	66		
5	70	72	76	69		
6	68	77	74	66		
7	67	73	75	62		
8	72	67	73	55		
Bagby Elem.						
2	72	75	80	69		
3	69	74	74	68		
4	71	65	73	73		
5	67	70	72	70		
Fammatre Elem.						
2	73	74	71	60		
3	69	76	70	65		
4	65	60	66	67		
5	69	76	74	59		
Farnham Elem.						
2	65	73	72	68		
3	56	67	65	60		
4	56	60	61	56		
5	79	70	80	80		
Ida Price Middle						
6	68	77	74	66		
7	67	70	75	62		
8	72	67	73	55		

Scores range from 1-99, with 50 the average. A school scoring 75 has done better than 75 percent of other public schools in the U.S.
Key: Rd (Reading), Ma (Math), Lg (Language), Sp (Spelling), Sci (Science) and SS (Social Science).

CAMBRIAN DIST. (Continued)

Sartorette Elem.

Grade	Rd	Ma	Lg	Sp	Sci	SS
2	72	77	71	74		
3	53	58	61	57		
4	65	61	72	62		
5	63	71	76	61		

Campbell Union Elem. School Dist.

Grade	Rd	Ma	Lg	Sp	Sci	SS
2	53	64	58	50		
3	53	66	59	52		
4	54	59	57	49		
5	51	54	56	46		
6	57	62	62	54		
7	51	55	61	47		
8	52	52	60	43		

Blackford Elem.

Grade	Rd	Ma	Lg	Sp	Sci	SS
2	43	56	47	42		
3	47	63	55	47		
4	53	59	58	47		
5	49	51	54	48		

Campbell Middle

Grade	Rd	Ma	Lg	Sp	Sci	SS
5	36	40	48	38		
6	49	51	57	45		
7	46	43	57	41		
8	44	44	55	36		

Capri Elem.

Grade	Rd	Ma	Lg	Sp	Sci	SS
2	62	76	68	62		
3	64	82	71	66		
4	62	65	65	54		
5	66	66	70	50		

Castlemont Elem.

Grade	Rd	Ma	Lg	Sp	Sci	SS
2	64	75	69	61		
3	62	71	66	58		
4	64	62	63	58		
5	61	70	64	49		

Forest Hill Elem.

Grade	Rd	Ma	Lg	Sp	Sci	SS
2	74	81	86	67		
3	67	81	71	60		
4	75	82	77	68		
5	74	80	74	63		

Hazelwood Elem.

Grade	Rd	Ma	Lg	Sp	Sci	SS
2	48	66	52	43		
3	55	72	59	51		
4	53	54	53	50		
5	45	36	38	33		

Lynhaven Elem.

Grade	Rd	Ma	Lg	Sp	Sci	SS
2	40	39	40	39		
3	51	50	54	50		
4	51	57	58	44		
5	44	41	47	38		

Marshall Lane Elem.

Grade	Rd	Ma	Lg	Sp	Sci	SS
2	85	87	86	82		
3	71	80	78	68		
4	65	71	67	66		
5	78	81	83	65		

Monroe Middle

Grade	Rd	Ma	Lg	Sp	Sci	SS
5	42	44	47	42		
6	56	63	63	54		
7	46	57	58	44		
8	46	46	52	38		

Rolling Hills Middle

Grade	Rd	Ma	Lg	Sp	Sci	SS
5	57	62	59	48		
6	64	68	64	59		
7	60	61	66	54		
8	63	64	69	52		

Rosemary Elem.

Grade	Rd	Ma	Lg	Sp	Sci	SS
2	28	35	35	27		
3	28	41	34	32		
4	22	31	33	24		

Sherman Oaks Elem.

Grade	Rd	Ma	Lg	Sp	Sci	SS
2	23	60	24	29		
3	25	51	30	31		
4	28	38	32	27		

Campbell Union High School Dist.

Grade	Rd	Ma	Lg	Sp	Sci	SS
9	42	62	57		49	48
10	39	53	47		51	46
11	33	49	45		47	56

Blackford High (Cont.)

Grade	Rd	Ma	Lg	Sp	Sci	SS
10	17	25	21		35	21
11	20	25	28		29	32

Del Mar High

Grade	Rd	Ma	Lg	Sp	Sci	SS
9	35	54	47		41	43
10	29	45	37		38	40
11	25	43	35		34	46

Leigh High

Grade	Rd	Ma	Lg	Sp	Sci	SS
9	50	66	63		57	54
10	50	59	57		61	57
11	47	59	58		63	70

Prospect High

Grade	Rd	Ma	Lg	Sp	Sci	SS
9	38	64	54		47	44
10	35	55	45		50	43
11	27	48	40		44	51

Westmont High

Grade	Rd	Ma	Lg	Sp	Sci	SS
9	42	63	61		51	47
10	41	54	49		56	43
11	38	51	53		51	59

Cupertino Union Elem. School Dist.

Grade	Rd	Ma	Lg	Sp	Sci	SS
2	76	84	81	79		
3	75	83	82	78		
4	79	84	80	81		
5	76	84	80	75		
6	77	89	81	78		
7	76	86	84	76		
8	74	84	79	68		

Blue Hills Elem.

Grade	Rd	Ma	Lg	Sp	Sci	SS
2	84	92	86	86		
3	82	86	88	81		
4	85	93	86	90		
5	80	91	89	81		
6	82	91	81	85		

Collins Elem.

Grade	Rd	Ma	Lg	Sp	Sci	SS
2	76	83	79	80		
3	75	87	84	84		
4	72	83	80	75		
5	64	80	71	65		
6	73	85	81	75		

Scores range from 1-99, with 50 the average. A school scoring 75 has done better than 75 percent of other public schools in the U.S.
Key: Rd (Reading) ,Ma (Math), Lg (Language), Sp (Spelling), Sci (Science) and SS (Social Science).

Grade	Rd	Ma	Lg	Sp	Sci	SS
Cupertino Int.						
6	90	96	90	87		
7	74	81	84	69		
8	75	81	79	65		
De Vargas Elem.						
2	50	66	59	54		
3	47	63	57	56		
4	62	72	65	70		
5	56	67	58	59		
6	51	75	62	46		
Dilworth Elem.						
2	77	88	84	82		
3	82	92	89	84		
4	79	85	80	85		
5	80	87	85	80		
6	75	87	75	75		
Eaton Elem.						
2	76	86	81	81		
3	80	87	85	81		
4	81	86	83	85		
5	83	86	80	80		
Eisenhower Elem.						
2	69	75	78	66		
3	69	73	71	73		
4	77	83	76	76		
5	70	73	74	62		
6	78	86	82	80		
Faria Elem.						
2	87	95	89	93		
3	87	96	93	94		
4	91	94	89	93		
5	88	96	94	93		
6	78	94	86	86		
Garden Gate Elem.						
2	68	85	76	76		
3	78	90	87	80		
4	78	87	83	80		
5	76	82	74	69		
6	75	88	81	78		
Hyde Int.						
6	94	98	95	96		
7	63	77	75	65		
8	59	72	66	53		
Kennedy Int.						
6	89	96	90	90		
7	81	91	87	81		
8	80	88	84	74		
Lincoln Elem.						
2	76	77	76	80		
3	77	85	83	82		
4	82	85	79	82		
5	80	89	85	83		
6	79	91	85	80		
McAuliffe Elem.						
2	80	81	70	67		
3	85	78	85	72		
4	84	79	74	73		
5	81	77	75	72		
6	87	85	78	71		

Grade	Rd	Ma	Lg	Sp	Sci	SS
Meyerholz Elem.						
2	80	90	88	85		
3	76	84	82	78		
4	67	62	65	66		
5	72	79	74	70		
6	59	80	69	58		
Miller Int.						
6	89	97	92	93		
7	83	91	87	83		
8	81	92	84	78		
Montclaire Elem.						
2	90	91	91	85		
3	84	87	88	84		
4	87	87	88	88		
5	88	90	92	83		
6	84	91	86	84		
Muir Elem.						
2	65	78	67	72		
3	61	83	72	71		
4	71	82	74	74		
5	65	81	73	65		
6	52	85	66	53		
Nimitz Elem.						
2	56	68	71	52		
3	46	61	59	52		
4	54	67	64	50		
5	43	65	59	46		
6	56	73	68	56		
Portal Elem.						
2	81	89	87	89		
3	86	90	91	88		
4	90	91	89	93		
5	82	87	89	83		
6	84	93	92	89		
Regnart Elem.						
2	83	86	86	86		
3	77	86	87	86		
4	88	92	89	91		
5	84	93	89	86		
6	76	91	84	82		
Sedgwick Elem.						
2	73	72	77	71		
3	66	65	66	69		
4	61	69	65	67		
5	66	71	73	65		
6	64	56	68	65		
Stevens Creek Elem.						
2	78	80	84	82		
3	82	86	86	77		
4	84	85	82	84		
5	80	85	81	78		
6	74	84	80	71		
Stocklmeir Elem.						
2	75	83	81	74		
3	75	76	80	71		
4	79	85	79	78		
5	76	82	80	76		
6	77	87	77	72		

Scores range from 1-99, with 50 the average. A school scoring 75 has done better than 75 percent of other public schools in the U.S.
Key: Rd (Reading) ,Ma (Math), Lg (Language), Sp (Spelling), Sci (Science) and SS (Social Science).

CUPERTINO DIST. (Continued)

West Valley Elem.

Grade	Rd	Ma	Lg	Sp	Sci	SS
2	86	91	89	82		
3	78	85	84	73		
4	80	85	80	81		
5	83	87	83	81		
6	76	88	76	75		

East Side Union High School Dist.

Grade	Rd	Ma	Lg	Sp	Sci	SS
9	34	55	52		45	42
10	30	56	38		44	38
11	32	53	44		44	52

Apollo High (Cont.)

Grade	Rd	Ma	Lg	Sp	Sci	SS
11	18	23	21		23	27

Foothill High (Cont.)

Grade	Rd	Ma	Lg	Sp	Sci	SS
9	14	15	22		25	23
10	12	19	13		22	19
11	16	23	22		22	33

Genesis High (Cont.)

Grade	Rd	Ma	Lg	Sp	Sci	SS
11	18	20	23		20	26

Hill High

Grade	Rd	Ma	Lg	Sp	Sci	SS
9	28	48	41		37	38
10	23	48	27		33	32
11	26	44	35		35	51

Independence High

Grade	Rd	Ma	Lg	Sp	Sci	SS
9	31	54	49		42	40
10	28	56	38		42	38
11	33	56	46		42	53

Lick High

Grade	Rd	Ma	Lg	Sp	Sci	SS
9	25	43	45		34	33
10	20	44	30		33	25
11	27	37	39		32	41

Mt. Pleasant High

Grade	Rd	Ma	Lg	Sp	Sci	SS
9	36	62	55		52	46
10	34	62	39		50	42
11	30	52	43		47	52

Oak Grove High

Grade	Rd	Ma	Lg	Sp	Sci	SS
9	39	56	57		48	45
10	37	58	44		54	47
11	38	57	53		52	62

Overfelt High

Grade	Rd	Ma	Lg	Sp	Sci	SS
9	25	49	46		34	31
10	20	48	28		30	26
11	22	46	35		31	36

Pegasus High (Cont.)

Grade	Rd	Ma	Lg	Sp	Sci	SS
11	13	23	17		21	22

Phoenix High (Cont.)

Grade	Rd	Ma	Lg	Sp	Sci	SS
11	19	22	24		31	39

Piedmont Hills High

Grade	Rd	Ma	Lg	Sp	Sci	SS
9	46	66	64		53	47
10	47	70	54		60	49
11	50	71	57		59	68

Santa Teresa High

Grade	Rd	Ma	Lg	Sp	Sci	SS
9	55	65	64		61	55
10	46	64	53		63	50
11	49	63	59		61	64

Silver Creek High

Grade	Rd	Ma	Lg	Sp	Sci	SS
9	39	60	57		48	48
10	34	58	41		42	43
11	34	55	48		44	59

Yerba Buena High

Grade	Rd	Ma	Lg	Sp	Sci	SS
9	22	47	43		41	35
10	19	47	24		35	28
11	21	52	33		37	41

Evergreen Elem. School Dist.

Grade	Rd	Ma	Lg	Sp	Sci	SS
2	62	71	66	65		
3	56	74	69	68		
4	55	65	63	60		
5	54	65	62	61		
6	56	69	65	58		
7	50	61	63	61		
8	50	61	59	52		

Cadwallader Elem.

Grade	Rd	Ma	Lg	Sp	Sci	SS
2	46	47	43	47		
3	50	57	55	58		
4	47	53	57	57		
5	41	41	43	45		
6	49	59	55	54		

Cedar Grove Elem.

Grade	Rd	Ma	Lg	Sp	Sci	SS
2	52	63	60	53		
3	53	73	68	65		
4	58	73	70	61		
5	53	68	68	59		
6	51	63	56	49		

Chaboya Middle

Grade	Rd	Ma	Lg	Sp	Sci	SS
6	28	33	28	30		
7	53	60	63	61		
8	53	64	60	52		

Dove Hill Elem.

Grade	Rd	Ma	Lg	Sp	Sci	SS
2	52	66	53	51		
3	48	75	60	62		
4	45	57	59	45		
5	43	61	57	56		
6	47	61	59	46		

Evergreen Elem.

Grade	Rd	Ma	Lg	Sp	Sci	SS
2	75	80	78	79		
3	72	83	79	78		
4	76	83	79	77		
5	53	67	62	57		
6	65	82	73	67		

Holly Oak Elem.

Grade	Rd	Ma	Lg	Sp	Sci	SS
2	58	62	56	60		
3	54	68	75	70		
4	45	57	57	49		
5	47	66	61	57		
6	72	71	90	69		

Laurelwood Elem.

Grade	Rd	Ma	Lg	Sp	Sci	SS
2	56	60	67	52		
3	58	70	66	52		
4	68	75	77	63		
5	63	65	65	57		
6	61	68	65	56		

Leyva Int.

Grade	Rd	Ma	Lg	Sp	Sci	SS
6	43	59	52	44		
7	46	59	59	55		
8	46	56	56	48		

Scores range from 1-99, with 50 the average. A school scoring 75 has done better than 75 percent of other public schools in the U.S.
Key: Rd (Reading), Ma (Math), Lg (Language), Sp (Spelling), Sci (Science) and SS (Social Science).

EVERGREEN DIST. (Continued)

Matsumoto Elem.

Grade	Rd	Ma	Lg	Sp	Sci	SS
2	74	80	80	77		
3	70	87	76	76		
4	55	58	61	66		
5	74	79	82	77		
6	72	87	79	74		

Millbrook Elem.

Grade	Rd	Ma	Lg	Sp	Sci	SS
2	70	83	77	69		
3	47	62	54	59		
4	46	56	54	52		
5	59	72	66	66		
6	65	80	73	67		

Montgomery Elem.

Grade	Rd	Ma	Lg	Sp	Sci	SS
2	68	78	70	66		
3	58	78	73	67		
4	52	58	58	56		
5	50	58	55	54		
6	49	55	60	50		

Norwood Creek Elem.

Grade	Rd	Ma	Lg	Sp	Sci	SS
2	69	71	77	76		
3	72	84	86	81		
4	61	70	67	70		
5	64	73	65	70		

Quimby Oak Int.

Grade	Rd	Ma	Lg	Sp	Sci	SS
6	57	79	65	68		
7	51	64	68	66		
8	51	61	61	54		

Silver Oak Elem.

Grade	Rd	Ma	Lg	Sp	Sci	SS
2	76	85	84	78		
3	79	88	83	79		
4	77	80	81	82		
5	74	82	78	79		
6	81	86	88	84		

Smith Elem.

Grade	Rd	Ma	Lg	Sp	Sci	SS
2	55	64	53	64		
3	36	61	55	63		
4	44	57	50	49		
5	37	52	49	50		

Whaley Elem.

Grade	Rd	Ma	Lg	Sp	Sci	SS
2	58	66	52	62		
3	44	69	59	66		
4	43	63	54	52		
5	40	52	53	55		

Franklin-McKinley Elem. School Dist.

Grade	Rd	Ma	Lg	Sp	Sci	SS
2	32	44	34	39		
3	26	39	32	38		
4	26	32	37	30		
5	24	32	35	33		
6	33	43	41	33		
7	28	35	34	30		
8	31	39	34	28		

Fair Jr. High

Grade	Rd	Ma	Lg	Sp	Sci	SS
7	24	34	30	29		
8	26	35	29	24		

Franklin Elem.

Grade	Rd	Ma	Lg	Sp	Sci	SS
2	36	51	37	41		
3	23	28	28	34		
4	26	27	37	32		
5	21	22	31	29		
6	31	44	41	35		

Hellyer Elem.

Grade	Rd	Ma	Lg	Sp	Sci	SS
2	43	63	46	53		
3	40	62	51	59		
4	34	42	47	39		
5	33	45	46	46		

Hillsdale Elem.

Grade	Rd	Ma	Lg	Sp	Sci	SS
2	26	39	34	42		
3	22	29	28	24		
4	23	26	30	24		
5	22	27	31	28		

Kennedy Elem.

Grade	Rd	Ma	Lg	Sp	Sci	SS
2	37	44	41	46		
3	28	44	36	45		
4	27	40	41	39		
5	30	38	38	37		
6	34	56	44	36		

Los Arboles Elem.

Grade	Rd	Ma	Lg	Sp	Sci	SS
2	29	48	26	32		
3	19	36	24	33		
4	27	47	35	31		
5	26	34	33	31		
6	31	48	40	32		

McKinley Elem.

Grade	Rd	Ma	Lg	Sp	Sci	SS
2	17	18	18	21		
3	13	24	16	20		
4	17	26	22	13		
5	13	18	21	18		
6	23	31	34	21		

Meadows Elem.

Grade	Rd	Ma	Lg	Sp	Sci	SS
2	36	39	36	49		
3	28	36	35	45		
4	23	27	38	37		
5	28	35	44	39		
6	33	37	41	37		

Santee Elem.

Grade	Rd	Ma	Lg	Sp	Sci	SS
2	18	41	18	23		
3	16	22	18	24		
4	17	18	28	18		
5	15	23	23	22		
6	18	25	24	17		

Seven Trees Elem.

Grade	Rd	Ma	Lg	Sp	Sci	SS
2	30	42	32	31		
3	21	39	32	30		
4	20	22	29	20		
5	21	26	30	28		
6	38	43	40	34		

Stonegate Elem.

Grade	Rd	Ma	Lg	Sp	Sci	SS
2	41	46	40	43		
3	39	52	48	52		
4	37	36	49	40		
5	28	40	49	48		
6	52	60	64	56		
7	45	67	63	54		
8	53	62	54	55		

Sylvandale Junior High

Grade	Rd	Ma	Lg	Sp	Sci	SS
6	33	40	39	33		
7	29	32	35	28		
8	33	40	39	29		

Scores range from 1-99, with 50 the average. A school scoring 75 has done better than 75 percent of other public schools in the U.S.
Key: Rd (Reading) ,Ma (Math), Lg (Language), Sp (Spelling), Sci (Science) and SS (Social Science).

Grade	Rd	Ma	Lg	Sp	Sci	SS
Windmill Springs Elem.						
2	42	57	45	45		
3	36	56	43	56		
4	33	44	50	46		
5	25	32	35	34		
6	33	46	41	35		
7	29	35	36	27		
8	41	53	46	37		
Fremont Union High School Dist.						
9	59	81	71		65	65
10	55	78	65		69	63
11	59	81	70		69	77
Cupertino High						
9	55	82	67		65	63
10	44	68	54		60	52
11	53	80	66		68	75
Fremont High						
9	36	56	50		42	44
10	36	57	46		47	44
11	36	54	46		42	57
Homestead High						
9	57	74	70		61	60
10	50	75	61		66	58
11	57	77	67		63	74
Lynbrook High						
9	73	92	83		77	77
10	68	89	78		82	78
11	75	92	82		85	87
Monta Vista High						
9	70	89	81		76	76
10	66	88	76		80	72
11	70	91	82		81	87
Gilroy Unified School Dist.						
2	43	40	39	38		
3	36	35	38	35		
4	37	37	40	33		
5	44	41	46	40		
6	47	50	50	44		
7	43	38	49	40		
8	42	40	45	34		
9	35	46	47		37	42
10	33	42	39		44	40
11	30	40	40		39	52
Aprea Fundamental Elem.						
2	78	79	80	77		
3	63	71	68	68		
4	76	80	76	74		
5	75	76	69	70		
6	68	76	68	74		
Brownell Acad. Of Hum. & Fine Arts Jr.						
7	48	40	54	43		
8	43	41	47	35		
El Roble Elem.						
2	39	39	31	34		
3	44	29	32	28		
4	30	30	31	21		
5	37	34	33	40		
6	40	45	40	34		

Grade	Rd	Ma	Lg	Sp	Sci	SS
Eliot Elem.						
2	45	41	49	37		
3	39	36	43	36		
4	37	38	46	32		
5	35	31	43	30		
6	35	35	51	36		
Gilroy High						
9	35	47	48		37	42
10	34	43	41		46	42
11	34	44	44		42	57
Glen View Elem.						
2	35	25	30	33		
3	28	30	25	26		
4	23	25	29	20		
5	35	40	44	37		
6	33	48	41	36		
Jordan Elem.						
2	44	44	35	32		
3	21	18	24	25		
4	24	25	27	30		
5	31	24	33	28		
6	49	47	52	39		
Kelley Rod Elem.						
2	50	54	41	36		
3	39	50	41	40		
4	51	45	53	42		
5	56	57	51	50		
6	52	46	52	39		
Las Animas Elem.						
2	20	15	15	20		
3	16	15	25	22		
4	38	39	35	32		
5	41	36	43	32		
6	37	47	40	48		
Mt. Madonna High (Cont.)						
10	11	17	13		17	20
11	16	18	22		22	32
Rucker Elem.						
2	34	46	32	28		
3	44	37	42	38		
4	43	30	45	35		
5	66	54	56	49		
6	53	51	54	48		
San Ysidro Elem.						
2	38	30	38	40		
3	29	30	38	33		
4	38	36	30	30		
5	26	20	34	29		
6	48	56	54	42		
So. Valley School Of Science & Global Studies						
6	51	54	54	47		
7	38	36	44	38		
8	42	39	43	33		
Lakeside Joint Elem. School Dist.						
Lakeside Elem.						
2	71	86	85	44		
3	83	82	72	44		
4	79	83	69	76		
5	80	86	81	69		
6	77	80	81	80		

Scores range from 1-99, with 50 the average. A school scoring 75 has done better than 75 percent of other public schools in the U.S.
Key: Rd (Reading), Ma (Math), Lg (Language), Sp (Spelling), Sci (Science) and SS (Social Science).

Loma Prieta Union Elem. School Dist.

English Middle

Grade	Rd	Ma	Lg	Sp	Sci	SS
6	70	75	68	63		
7	77	76	79	73		
8	72	63	73	59		

Loma Prieta Elem.

Grade	Rd	Ma	Lg	Sp	Sci	SS
2	78	79	83	69		
3	80	73	76	66		
4	81	77	73	74		
5	80	77	75	63		

Los Altos Elem. School Dist.

Grade	Rd	Ma	Lg	Sp	Sci	SS
2	84	87	88	83		
3	87	90	91	85		
4	90	88	88	88		
5	87	91	89	87		
6	89	93	89	88		
7	86	93	92	85		
8	87	92	90	82		

Almond Elem.

Grade	Rd	Ma	Lg	Sp	Sci	SS
2	83	82	83	84		
3	86	89	90	87		
4	91	86	88	86		
5	87	95	92	91		
6	87	94	91	86		

Blach Int.

Grade	Rd	Ma	Lg	Sp	Sci	SS
7	87	93	92	84		
8	88	94	92	85		

Bullis-Purissima Elem.

Grade	Rd	Ma	Lg	Sp	Sci	SS
2	82	87	88	83		
3	87	91	88	81		
4	88	88	83	85		
5	87	93	90	88		
6	91	95	89	88		

Egan Int.

Grade	Rd	Ma	Lg	Sp	Sci	SS
7	85	92	92	85		
8	85	90	89	79		

Loyola Elem.

Grade	Rd	Ma	Lg	Sp	Sci	SS
2	83	88	91	84		
3	84	90	90	82		
4	93	89	87	89		
5	87	90	88	86		
6	91	94	91	91		

Oak Ave. Elem.

Grade	Rd	Ma	Lg	Sp	Sci	SS
2	87	87	89	84		
3	89	87	90	83		
4	91	90	91	91		
5	87	93	90	84		
6	91	94	89	91		

Santa Rita Elem.

Grade	Rd	Ma	Lg	Sp	Sci	SS
2	86	94	89	83		
3	89	95	93	88		
4	88	84	84	84		
5	90	91	90	89		
6	87	89	83	81		

Springer Elem.

Grade	Rd	Ma	Lg	Sp	Sci	SS
2	83	83	85	82		
3	86	88	93	85		
4	90	92	93	92		
5	86	85	84	82		
6	86	93	89	91		

Los Gatos Union Elem. School Dist.

Grade	Rd	Ma	Lg	Sp	Sci	SS
2	70	74	78	65		
3	79	83	81	67		
4	83	79	80	72		
5	78	82	80	71		
6	72	81	71	69		
7	77	82	82	74		
8	74	81	77	61		

Blossom Hill Elem.

Grade	Rd	Ma	Lg	Sp	Sci	SS
2	79	77	81	73		
3	80	85	80	67		
4	85	82	82	78		
5	79	84	82	77		

Daves Ave. Elem.

Grade	Rd	Ma	Lg	Sp	Sci	SS
2	69	71	77	65		
3	83	83	84	68		
4	83	77	82	69		
5	78	82	79	69		

Fisher Middle

Grade	Rd	Ma	Lg	Sp	Sci	SS
6	72	81	71	69		
7	77	82	82	74		
8	74	81	77	61		

Lexington Elem.

Grade	Rd	Ma	Lg	Sp	Sci	SS
2	68	58	75	61		
3	73	85	75	64		
4	77	72	73	55		
5	79	84	77	68		

Louise Van Meter Elem.

Grade	Rd	Ma	Lg	Sp	Sci	SS
2	62	80	77	57		
3	74	81	81	67		
4	82	81	76	73		
5	77	79	79	66		

Los Gatos-Saratoga High School Dist.

Grade	Rd	Ma	Lg	Sp	Sci	SS
9	72	84	79		73	76
10	71	78	74		76	74
11	67	83	78		76	83

Los Gatos High

Grade	Rd	Ma	Lg	Sp	Sci	SS
9	70	82	77		73	74
10	64	74	69		73	70
11	63	76	71		74	80

Saratoga High

Grade	Rd	Ma	Lg	Sp	Sci	SS
9	74	87	81		73	77
10	78	82	80		79	79
11	72	89	85		77	86

Luther Burbank Elem. School Dist.

Luther Burbank Elem.

Grade	Rd	Ma	Lg	Sp	Sci	SS
2	33	28	25	34		
3	31	35	29	32		
4	35	30	37	33		
5	26	20	31	31		
6	19	26	21	19		
7	26	37	36	25		
8	38	50	38	32		

Scores range from 1-99, with 50 the average. A school scoring 75 has done better than 75 percent of other public schools in the U.S.
Key: Rd (Reading) ,Ma (Math), Lg (Language), Sp (Spelling), Sci (Science) and SS (Social Science).

Milpitas Unified School Dist.

Grade	Rd	Ma	Lg	Sp	Sci	SS
2	59	63	58	63		
3	51	59	55	61		
4	54	55	54	57		
5	52	57	58	54		
6	57	66	59	62		
7	57	66	64	61		
8	57	61	60	53		
9	42	64	60		50	53
10	36	52	46		46	45
11	40	57	54		49	61

Burnett Elem.

Grade	Rd	Ma	Lg	Sp	Sci	SS
2	61	59	60	59		
3	51	56	53	57		
4	54	63	56	54		
5	44	50	54	49		
6	38	40	41	44		

Calaveras Hills (Cont.)

Grade	Rd	Ma	Lg	Sp	Sci	SS
9	12	22	24		22	19
10	19	33	27		34	35

Curtner Elem.

Grade	Rd	Ma	Lg	Sp	Sci	SS
2	65	67	61	70		
3	57	73	66	67		
4	68	72	63	74		
5	64	67	66	66		
6	66	80	69	74		

Milpitas High

Grade	Rd	Ma	Lg	Sp	Sci	SS
9	43	65	61		51	54
10	37	52	47		46	45
11	41	58	55		49	62

Pomeroy Elem.

Grade	Rd	Ma	Lg	Sp	Sci	SS
2	66	69	65	73		
3	55	64	62	61		
4	58	62	62	63		
5	65	76	72	66		
6	70	80	73	74		

Rancho Milpitas Jr. High

Grade	Rd	Ma	Lg	Sp	Sci	SS
7	51	57	57	52		
8	55	61	58	49		

Randall Elem.

Grade	Rd	Ma	Lg	Sp	Sci	SS
2	46	57	53	52		
3	41	54	43	51		
4	41	46	41	46		
5	30	40	42	45		
6	41	43	46	49		

Rose Elem.

Grade	Rd	Ma	Lg	Sp	Sci	SS
2	54	51	44	51		
3	45	54	47	55		
4	41	34	47	40		
5	47	46	57	49		
6	45	50	54	48		

Russell Jr. High

Grade	Rd	Ma	Lg	Sp	Sci	SS
7	62	74	70	69		
8	59	60	63	57		

Sinnott Elem.

Grade	Rd	Ma	Lg	Sp	Sci	SS
2	71	83	72	73		
3	62	70	68	78		
4	66	71	66	65		
5	61	73	66	65		
6	69	83	66	69		

Spangler Elem.

Grade	Rd	Ma	Lg	Sp	Sci	SS
2	46	48	54	56		
3	41	42	45	48		
4	39	37	40	36		
5	46	43	47	40		
6	39	48	39	34		

Weller Elem.

Grade	Rd	Ma	Lg	Sp	Sci	SS
2	51	65	51	59		
3	43	45	48	53		
4	59	55	58	70		
5	46	40	53	48		
6	69	65	64	73		

Zanker Elem.

Grade	Rd	Ma	Lg	Sp	Sci	SS
2	56	55	56	63		
3	57	71	59	75		
4	52	38	50	50		
5	59	61	52	54		
6	63	76	70	75		

Moreland Elem. School Dist.

Grade	Rd	Ma	Lg	Sp	Sci	SS
2	66	68	70	64		
3	63	69	69	62		
4	62	61	62	61		
5	60	62	65	55		
6	61	72	63	59		
7	62	71	69	60		
8	61	69	64	49		

Anderson Elem.

Grade	Rd	Ma	Lg	Sp	Sci	SS
2	36	31	37	38		
3	29	36	39	39		
4	34	42	38	32		
5	29	39	35	27		

Baker Elem.

Grade	Rd	Ma	Lg	Sp	Sci	SS
2	73	77	80	72		
3	64	71	72	64		
4	51	51	54	50		
5	63	74	67	63		

Castro Middle

Grade	Rd	Ma	Lg	Sp	Sci	SS
6	67	78	71	67		
7	67	76	74	65		
8	64	68	66	50		

Country Lane Elem.

Grade	Rd	Ma	Lg	Sp	Sci	SS
2	78	82	82	79		
3	80	84	83	76		
4	80	75	79	79		
5	77	71	80	72		

Easterbrook Elem.

Grade	Rd	Ma	Lg	Sp	Sci	SS
2	65	72	73	56		
3	51	55	60	53		
4	63	60	63	56		
5	43	42	44	37		

Latimer Elem.

Grade	Rd	Ma	Lg	Sp	Sci	SS
2	59	52	59	59		
3	64	73	71	65		
4	59	64	60	67		
5	63	69	67	54		

Moreland Discovery Elem.

Grade	Rd	Ma	Lg	Sp	Sci	SS
2	71	75	77	66		
3	79	77	73	59		
4	77	77	74	72		

Scores range from 1-99, with 50 the average. A school scoring 75 has done better than 75 percent of other public schools in the U.S.
Key: Rd (Reading), Ma (Math), Lg (Language), Sp (Spelling), Sci (Science) and SS (Social Science).

MORELAND DIST. (Continued)

Grade	Rd	Ma	Lg	Sp	Sci	SS
Payne Elem.						
2	75	80	80	74		
3	64	72	72	66		
4	64	58	63	67		
5	69	70	80	68		
Rogers Middle						
6	56	66	56	52		
7	58	66	64	54		
8	58	69	63	49		

Morgan Hill Unified School Dist.

Grade	Rd	Ma	Lg	Sp	Sci	SS
2	59	58	57	54		
3	58	63	60	54		
4	58	55	58	52		
5	56	59	60	50		
6	57	62	56	51		
7	57	57	61	50		
8	58	60	59	43		
9	52	70	62		60	59
10	41	56	45		55	50
11	42	59	48		55	65
Britton Middle						
7	59	57	63	49		
8	57	58	55	41		
9	53	71	61		60	60
Burnett Elem.						
2	55	49	52	48		
3	36	42	41	37		
4	53	42	52	39		
5	44	46	51	39		
6	38	42	42	34		
Central High (Cont.)						
10	8	14	11		15	12
11	12	21	22		27	38
El Toro Elem.						
2	61	74	64	62		
3	61	77	62	55		
4	66	55	58	53		
5	49	46	51	42		
6	51	61	52	46		
Encinal Elem.						
4	57	60	62	57		
5	66	74	71	65		
6	53	60	54	49		
Jackson Elem.						
2	52	45	50	52		
3	51	59	56	49		
4	56	56	54	44		
5	60	70	59	53		
6	59	64	54	50		
Live Oak High						
10	44	59	47		58	53
11	43	60	49		56	66
Los Paseos Elem.						
2	68	71	58	59		
3	64	77	71	67		
Murphy Middle						
7	54	57	59	50		
8	59	63	62	46		
9	51	70	62		60	59
Nordstrom Elem.						
2	73	77	76	66		
3	66	65	70	61		
4	69	74	74	70		
5	62	70	65	54		
6	75	85	75	75		
Paradise Valley/Machado Elem.						
2	52	53	58	45		
3	79	67	71	57		
4	57	50	55	50		
5	62	65	71	57		
6	77	78	73	64		
San Martin/Gwinn Elem.						
2	51	46	47	48		
3	48	47	50	53		
4	46	45	47	43		
5	48	53	55	45		
6	41	39	44	39		
Walsh Elem.						
2	57	44	48	51		
3	42	49	39	42		
4	52	51	48	42		
5	52	47	52	46		
6	54	52	48	48		

Mountain View Elem. School Dist.

Grade	Rd	Ma	Lg	Sp	Sci	SS
2	61	64	64	60		
3	59	67	60	57		
4	65	64	64	60		
5	57	60	63	56		
6	49	50	54	47		
7	52	50	60	45		
8	55	58	61	46		
Bubb Elem.						
2	74	74	85	78		
3	58	55	60	51		
4	73	74	76	67		
5	76	71	79	66		
Castro Elem.						
2	19	35	17	19		
3	25	43	28	29		
4	23	34	30	22		
5	21	24	26	22		
Graham Middle						
6	49	50	54	47		
7	52	50	60	45		
8	55	58	61	46		
Huff Elem.						
2	83	81	84	79		
3	86	90	83	79		
4	87	77	80	85		
5	77	86	78	70		
Landels Elem.						
2	70	65	75	63		
3	64	74	63	65		
4	69	69	63	63		
5	70	77	77	71		

Scores range from 1-99, with 50 the average. A school scoring 75 has done better than 75 percent of other public schools in the U.S.
Key: Rd (Reading) ,Ma (Math), Lg (Language), Sp (Spelling), Sci (Science) and SS (Social Science).

Grade	Rd	Ma	Lg	Sp	Sci	SS
Slater Elem.						
2	74	70	72	80		
3	69	71	74	66		
4	80	71	75	78		
5	58	54	65	66		

Mt. View-Los Altos Union HS Dist.

Grade	Rd	Ma	Lg	Sp	Sci	SS
9	57	74	68		62	67
10	50	68	59		66	60
11	54	66	60		63	71
Alta Vista High (Cont.)						
10	20	20	10		20	21
11	19	17	17		19	30
Los Altos High						
9	54	73	69		63	65
10	47	70	59		67	59
11	58	74	67		67	76
Moffett High (Alt.)						
11	37	26	55		41	45
Mountain View High						
9	59	76	68		62	68
10	56	71	64		69	64
11	61	72	65		71	76

Mt. Pleasant Elem. School Dist.

Grade	Rd	Ma	Lg	Sp	Sci	SS
2	47	48	49	47		
3	34	42	41	43		
4	35	42	50	37		
5	41	47	61	45		
6	43	49	57	48		
7	43	47	50	46		
8	37	40	46	38		
Boeger Jr. High						
7	43	37	50	46		
8	37	40	46	38		
Foothill Int.						
4	37	45	50	41		
5	41	47	61	45		
6	43	49	57	48		
Mt. Pleasant Elem.						
2	29	28	32	30		
3	27	28	33	30		
4	30	32	47	24		
Sanders Elem.						
2	42	51	42	46		
3	30	34	34	45		
Valle Vista Elem.						
2	64	59	69	62		
3	44	62	54	51		

Oak Grove Elem. School Dist.

Grade	Rd	Ma	Lg	Sp	Sci	SS
2	56	69	56	56		
3	51	68	56	51		
4	52	62	53	49		
5	51	61	56	50		
6	55	70	57	53		
7	55	65	65	57		
8	56	69	57	46		

Grade	Rd	Ma	Lg	Sp	Sci	SS
Anderson Elem.						
2	49	62	40	49		
3	53	81	57	46		
4	55	60	53	44		
5	54	60	53	45		
6	63	77	69	66		
Baldwin Elem.						
2	63	83	65	67		
3	59	81	64	61		
4	53	62	51	51		
5	54	68	58	59		
6	48	66	54	52		
Bernal Int.						
7	61	72	70	63		
8	62	76	63	52		
Blossom Valley Elem.						
2	72	73	65	75		
3	58	84	68	63		
4	64	72	64	70		
5	59	69	69	66		
6	70	82	76	77		
Christopher Elem.						
2	35	39	33	36		
3	29	51	35	33		
4	30	41	31	28		
5	40	47	35	38		
6	43	59	43	37		
Davis Elem.						
7	44	53	50	46		
8	50	54	50	42		
Del Roble Elem.						
2	64	84	73	61		
3	57	76	65	48		
4	55	69	59	51		
5	51	63	56	55		
6	53	64	51	53		
Edenvale Elem.						
2	30	50	33	33		
3	33	42	39	34		
4	32	54	37	30		
5	32	45	47	33		
6	39	63	58	47		
Frost Elem.						
2	65	78	72	69		
3	52	63	58	50		
4	60	70	63	62		
5	45	54	45	42		
6	54	72	54	47		
Glider Elem.						
2	63	66	66	65		
3	57	75	69	65		
4	58	68	65	66		
5	57	75	70	64		
6	66	80	67	65		
Hayes Elem.						
2	65	80	65	66		
3	65	75	65	61		
4	58	73	59	54		
5	67	78	67	60		
6	55	66	50	57		

Scores range from 1-99, with 50 the average. A school scoring 75 has done better than 75 percent of other public schools in the U.S.
Key: Rd (Reading), Ma (Math), Lg (Language), Sp (Spelling), Sci (Science) and SS (Social Science).

OAK GROVE DIST. (Continued)

Grade	Rd	Ma	Lg	Sp	Sci	SS
Herman Int.						
7	60	69	73	61		
8	55	74	58	44		
Miner Elem.						
2	47	56	47	45		
3	34	47	32	35		
4	41	42	42	35		
5	44	51	54	49		
6	47	69	52	40		
Oak Ridge Elem.						
2	57	69	62	62		
3	52	59	55	50		
4	69	70	64	59		
5	59	71	60	48		
6	62	73	60	54		
Parkview Elem.						
2	65	79	62	70		
3	47	66	54	58		
4	54	63	57	59		
5	55	60	65	59		
6	63	69	61	64		
Sakamoto Elem.						
2	66	60	60	59		
3	68	82	70	68		
4	62	62	55	56		
5	66	66	63	59		
6	56	64	52	50		
San Anselmo Elem.						
2	62	77	63	56		
3	55	61	53	47		
4	51	63	52	47		
5	48	53	55	52		
6	56	73	55	47		
Santa Teresa Elem.						
2	65	79	64	60		
3	63	82	73	63		
4	45	69	53	47		
5	55	63	61	55		
6	58	72	55	50		
Stipe Elem.						
2	29	57	34	34		
3	28	51	31	30		
4	31	49	40	30		
5	30	45	36	32		
6	43	66	53	40		
Taylor Elem.						
2	67	77	66	57		
3	65	77	71	70		
4	66	77	67	63		
5	72	76	70	59		
6	66	78	63	55		

Orchard Elem. School Dist.

Grade	Rd	Ma	Lg	Sp	Sci	SS
Orchard Elem.						
2	31	26	32	39		
3	38	55	47	45		
4	34	38	37	34		
5	45	40	49	47		
6	27	40	39	24		
7	40	44	47	41		
8	36	43	40	25		

Palo Alto Unified School Dist.

Grade	Rd	Ma	Lg	Sp	Sci	SS
2	81	86	84	77		
3	83	86	85	78		
4	86	82	80	82		
5	85	87	86	78		
6	85	91	81	80		
7	83	86	88	78		
8	82	87	86	72		
9	77	90	83		77	80
10	72	87	75		82	80
11	75	88	80		82	88
Addison Elem.						
2	83	82	84	77		
3	87	90	88	80		
4	92	83	82	85		
5	88	87	87	76		
Barron Park Elem.						
2	71	65	79	55		
3	82	75	76	77		
4	84	76	78	76		
5	80	81	87	74		
Briones Elem.						
2	73	78	76	66		
3	65	65	67	49		
4	68	61	65	60		
5	81	85	79	61		
Duveneck Elem.						
2	85	88	91	84		
3	86	89	87	82		
4	88	83	80	85		
5	90	94	90	83		
El Carmelo Elem.						
2	77	85	80	70		
3	84	82	81	74		
4	84	82	78	82		
5	78	83	76	77		
Escondido Elem.						
2	67	80	74	60		
3	80	82	82	75		
4	82	74	73	71		
5	83	83	89	78		
Fairmeadow Elem.						
2	82	90	90	84		
3	79	84	84	75		
4	85	79	75	76		
5	75	80	80	72		
Gunn High						
9	76	92	85		80	79
10	77	90	79		86	82
11	74	88	78		83	87
Hays Elem.						
2	89	93	89	83		
3	91	94	92	88		
4	93	93	88	93		
5	90	93	91	88		
Hoover Elem.						
2	84	91	86	91		
3	88	95	91	89		
4	90	93	91	92		
5	87	94	86	86		

Scores range from 1-99, with 50 the average. A school scoring 75 has done better than 75 percent of other public schools in the U.S.
Key: Rd (Reading) ,Ma (Math), Lg (Language), Sp (Spelling), Sci (Science) and SS (Social Science).

Grade	Rd	Ma	Lg	Sp	Sci	SS
Jordan Middle						
6	87	92	82	84		
7	81	87	86	77		
8	83	87	86	73		
Nixon Elem.						
2	79	80	80	74		
3	85	88	87	78		
4	88	86	82	82		
5	83	87	87	77		
Ohlone Elem.						
2	84	85	81	77		
3	84	81	83	72		
4	84	71	73	75		
5	87	86	85	73		
Palo Alto High						
9	77	88	82		74	80
10	67	82	70		78	79
11	77	89	81		82	89
Palo Verde Elem.						
2	82	87	90	82		
3	80	87	83	83		
4	81	74	76	84		
5	86	84	86	80		
Stanford Middle						
6	83	90	79	78		
7	85	86	89	79		
8	81	87	86	70		

San Jose Unified School Dist.

Grade	Rd	Ma	Lg	Sp	Sci	SS
2	43	50	46	41		
3	41	47	45	42		
4	46	43	48	41		
5	46	47	50	41		
6	46	51	50	43		
7	44	51	54	44		
8	47	52	52	40		
9	42	63	57		48	52
10	37	53	44		47	45
11	45	61	56		52	65
Allen Elem.						
2	49	62	46	50		
3	56	58	53	59		
4	33	40	42	40		
5	45	56	45	54		
Almaden Elem.						
2	61	79	51	39		
3	34	42	36	30		
4	29	34	37	26		
5	28	26	33	25		
Bachrodt Elem.						
2	20	22	19	21		
3	27	37	35	26		
4	28	28	31	22		
5	30	29	34	31		
Booksin Elem.						
2	66	70	72	60		
3	71	69	75	62		
4	71	72	67	66		
5	66	69	71	58		

Grade	Rd	Ma	Lg	Sp	Sci	SS
Broadway High (Cont.)						
9	12	21	21		19	24
10	13	21	12		21	20
11	12	25	17		22	36
Burnett Middle						
6	19	24	23	17		
7	17	23	19	21		
8	22	26	23	19		
Carson Elem.						
2	45	41	52	46		
3	45	58	48	57		
4	56	54	57	47		
5	49	52	57	42		
Castillero Middle						
6	58	63	60	54		
7	52	58	59	48		
8	58	61	63	47		
Cory Elem.						
2	39	41	41	39		
Darling Elem.						
2	15	39	19	18		
3	21	36	21	24		
4	22	24	28	17		
5	23	24	30	20		
Empire Gardens Elem.						
2	19	18	19	25		
3	19	23	25	26		
4	28	22	29	20		
5	32	34	36	31		
Erikson Elem.						
2	27	32	23	26		
3	29	29	31	28		
4	37	33	44	33		
5	32	33	35	28		
Gardner Elem.						
2	24	25	20	24		
3	19	32	21	19		
4	17	21	26	15		
5	22	24	23	22		
Grant Elem.						
2	23	36	25	23		
3	22	26	26	26		
4	25	22	30	18		
5	29	31	37	27		
Graystone Elem.						
2	75	78	82	78		
3	75	76	75	75		
4	80	82	75	84		
5	78	88	78	80		
Gunderson High						
9	37	55	48		39	33
10	32	49	38		41	37
11	34	53	48		41	48
Gunderson Plus (Cont.)						
11	21	19	26		31	25
Hacienda Sci./Envir. Elem.						
2	69	65	77	56		
3	54	46	55	45		
4	64	57	59	55		
5	63	62	62	52		

Scores range from 1-99, with 50 the average. A school scoring 75 has done better than 75 percent of other public schools in the U.S.
Key: Rd (Reading), Ma (Math), Lg (Language), Sp (Spelling), Sci (Science) and SS (Social Science).

SAN JOSE DIST. (Continued)

Grade	Rd	Ma	Lg	Sp	Sci	SS
Hammer Elem. (Alt.)						
2	49	41	41	47		
3	41	34	43	52		
Harte Middle						
6	74	83	79	73		
7	73	80	81	72		
8	72	80	77	63		
Hester Elem.						
2	29	36	25	35		
3	24	32	29	30		
4	27	24	38	26		
5	30	32	31	30		
Hoover Middle						
6	35	39	37	30		
7	30	34	37	32		
8	37	38	37	32		
Leland High						
9	64	84	76		68	70
10	61	80	69		73	68
11	68	86	77		76	82
Leland Plus (Cont.)						
11	21	26	27		39	46
Liberty High (Alt.)						
9	24	32	32		21	
10	24	30	20		25	26
11	27	25	28		30	48
Lincoln High						
9	39	59	55		45	51
10	49	55	55		51	53
11	52	60	63		54	71
Los Alamitos Elem.						
2	70	72	77	70		
3	67	67	74	61		
4	73	62	71	72		
5	69	64	73	60		
Lowell Elem.						
2	21	32	15	20		
3	18	24	22	30		
4	23	30	28	19		
5	29	30	31	31		
Mann Elem.						
2	22	19	28	25		
3	14	16	20	18		
4	27	19	28	18		
5	24	18	23	17		
Markham Middle						
6	44	44	47	38		
7	44	52	56	48		
8	45	42	49	39		
Muir Middle						
6	36	39	44	39		
7	35	40	47	36		
8	40	45	45	30		
Olinder Elem.						
2	21	41	33	28		
3	20	22	25	24		
4	20	16	24	19		
5	22	19	26	19		

Grade	Rd	Ma	Lg	Sp	Sci	SS
Pioneer High						
9	45	69	58		54	60
10	40	62	48		54	49
11	45	63	54		50	65
Pioneer Plus (Cont.)						
11	19	19	30		21	30
Randol Elem.						
2	50	51	54	47		
3	47	60	52	46		
4	62	64	60	64		
5	66	62	65	45		
Reed Elem.						
2	60	57	68	56		
3	62	61	62	53		
4	70	68	70	66		
5	63	66	67	55		
River Glen Elem.						
2	38	52	42	25		
3	49	58	49	35		
4	55	59	56	48		
5	59	60	69	38		
6	36	43	45	35		
7	59	79	74	53		
8	59	74	62	37		
San Jose High Acad.						
9	29	50	46		37	44
10	22	41	30		36	33
11	30	49	42		38	57
Schallenberger Elem.						
2	47	52	49	47		
3	44	53	47	40		
4	46	42	56	40		
5	46	42	53	36		
Simonds Elem.						
2	79	82	85	69		
3	71	76	74	69		
4	68	63	63	68		
5	59	54	62	61		
Steinbeck Middle						
6	35	43	39	35		
7	32	41	44	31		
8	33	45	41	34		
Tamien Elem.						
2	13	17	12	14		
3	17	21	21	24		
Terrell Elem.						
2	46	47	48	43		
3	53	53	55	47		
4	54	46	56	45		
5	58	53	57	45		
Trace Elem.						
3	36	46	41	41		
4	40	37	44	32		
5	40	48	50	42		
Washington Elem.						
2	17	34	18	20		
3	13	22	16	19		
4	19	19	26	17		
5	30	26	27	23		

Scores range from 1-99, with 50 the average. A school scoring 75 has done better than 75 percent of other public schools in the U.S.
Key: Rd (Reading) ,Ma (Math), Lg (Language), Sp (Spelling), Sci (Science) and SS (Social Science).

Grade	Rd	Ma	Lg	Sp	Sci	SS
	Williams Elem.					
2	82	90	87	79		
3	84	91	89	81		
4	83	81	83	82		
5	83	91	88	84		
	Willow Glen Elem.					
2	50	58	59	48		
3	36	37	39	42		
4	41	37	47	39		
5	39	38	41	36		
	Willow Glen High					
9	33	46	48		41	45
10	30	38	38		39	40
11	38	47	47		40	61
	Willow Glen Plus (Cont.)					
11	16	24	30		24	34

Santa Clara COE

Grade	Rd	Ma	Lg	Sp	Sci	SS
	County Community					
7	11	12	11	17		
8	18	19	15	16		
9	12	18	17		20	20
10	12	19	11		21	17
11	15	18	17		17	24
	Juvenile Hall					
7	21	15	21	31		
8	14	13	16	17		
9	16	21	21		23	22
10	10	21	12		22	17
11	10	19	13		18	21

Santa Clara Unified School Dist.

Grade	Rd	Ma	Lg	Sp	Sci	SS
2	51	54	54	54		
3	49	51	54	53		
4	54	51	58	51		
5	52	51	56	50		
6	55	58	57	53		
7	51	54	54	46		
8	52	53	54	43		
9	37	55	52		48	43
10	33	49	42		47	40
11	35	53	46		49	58
	Bowers Elem.					
2	41	49	52	49		
3	55	57	60	59		
4	50	50	59	52		
5	52	53	58	51		
	Bracher Elem.					
2	66	71	68	64		
3	58	60	63	61		
4	57	49	59	52		
5	41	42	42	40		
	Braly Elem.					
2	58	64	53	67		
3	45	43	48	50		
4	61	53	53	61		
5	62	47	65	52		
	Briarwood Elem.					
2	44	46	48	45		
3	45	40	49	49		
4	48	57	50	47		
5	50	58	52	48		

Grade	Rd	Ma	Lg	Sp	Sci	SS
	Buchser Middle					
6	48	52	53	47		
7	49	49	52	44		
8	53	51	54	43		
	Cabrillo Middle					
6	49	51	48	50		
7	46	47	53	46		
8	44	44	47	39		
	Haman Elem.					
2	35	26	26	29		
3	36	27	34	39		
4	39	32	37	28		
5	41	33	33	44		
	Hughes Elem.					
2	43	39	40	54		
3	42	52	59	54		
4	58	56	66	64		
5	49	46	58	58		
	Laurelwood Elem.					
2	74	73	76	68		
3	59	63	68	64		
4	72	69	76	74		
5	67	73	74	66		
	Mayne Elem.					
2	23	31	20	22		
3	30	33	37	31		
4	29	19	35	24		
5	35	35	40	26		
	Millikin Elem.					
2	83	87	85	83		
3	79	82	88	81		
4	88	81	81	78		
5	78	88	88	77		
	Montague Elem.					
2	48	47	65	65		
3	48	41	50	62		
4	42	53	61	54		
5	46	49	56	51		
	New Valley Cont. High					
10	13	23	9		23	22
11	14	18	25		25	30
	Peterson Middle					
6	63	67	65	58		
7	55	62	57	48		
8	58	63	61	46		
	Pomeroy Elem.					
2	54	63	59	58		
3	50	51	52	57		
4	41	51	50	40		
5	40	40	41	41		
	Ponderosa Elem.					
2	62	57	63	67		
3	58	59	60	62		
4	70	62	70	64		
5	66	63	71	57		
	Santa Clara High					
9	35	53	50		49	41
10	32	48	38		49	40
11	34	56	43		55	60

Scores range from 1-99, with 50 the average. A school scoring 75 has done better than 75 percent of other public schools in the U.S.
Key: Rd (Reading), Ma (Math), Lg (Language), Sp (Spelling), Sci (Science) and SS (Social Science).

SANTA CLARA DIST. (Continued)

Scott Lane Elem.

Grade	Rd	Ma	Lg	Sp	Sci	SS
2	30	29	30	37		
3	24	28	31	39		
4	25	25	37	25		
5	27	28	32	32		

Sutter Elem.

Grade	Rd	Ma	Lg	Sp	Sci	SS
2	50	52	65	48		
3	67	79	69	60		
4	49	44	53	41		
5	60	56	60	54		

Washington Elem.

Grade	Rd	Ma	Lg	Sp	Sci	SS
2	73	79	65	65		
3	58	61	57	45		
4	78	76	70	68		
5	71	63	64	53		

Westwood Elem.

Grade	Rd	Ma	Lg	Sp	Sci	SS
2	58	63	64	60		
3	43	40	41	43		
4	51	32	58	47		
5	58	52	64	56		

Wilcox High

Grade	Rd	Ma	Lg	Sp	Sci	SS
9	41	61	58		50	47
10	37	54	49		50	43
11	39	57	52		47	61

Wilson Alt.

Grade	Rd	Ma	Lg	Sp	Sci	SS
7	41	38	43	46		
8	28	17	19	20		
9	24	34	37		32	32
10	27	30	31		35	31
11	33	36	39		41	49

Saratoga Union Elem. School Dist.

Grade	Rd	Ma	Lg	Sp	Sci	SS
2	87	91	89	83		
3	84	89	86	82		
4	88	87	83	88		
5	85	91	88	84		
6	85	94	89	89		
7	86	93	91	85		
8	84	91	90	81		

Argonaut Elem.

Grade	Rd	Ma	Lg	Sp	Sci	SS
2	86	91	87	86		
3	84	88	87	88		
4	87	88	83	91		
5	88	92	91	90		

Foothill Elem.

Grade	Rd	Ma	Lg	Sp	Sci	SS
2	90	93	90	83		
3	83	90	88	79		
4	89	85	84	89		
5	82	90	87	81		

Redwood Middle

Grade	Rd	Ma	Lg	Sp	Sci	SS
6	85	94	89	89		
7	86	93	91	85		
8	84	91	90	81		

Saratoga Elem.

Grade	Rd	Ma	Lg	Sp	Sci	SS
2	85	88	89	79		
3	86	88	82	76		
4	88	86	82	83		
5	82	89	85	77		

Sunnyvale Elem. School Dist.

Grade	Rd	Ma	Lg	Sp	Sci	SS
2	62	67	67	64		
3	56	67	61	63		
4	60	67	66	61		
5	53	61	62	57		
6	59	70	65	62		
7	52	64	62	57		
8	51	59	54	46		

Bishop Elem.

Grade	Rd	Ma	Lg	Sp	Sci	SS
2	59	57	64	62		
3	49	69	61	63		
4	59	64	68	53		
5	48	48	55	52		

Cherry Chase Elem.

Grade	Rd	Ma	Lg	Sp	Sci	SS
2	76	76	76	74		
3	82	85	79	73		
4	70	69	64	64		
5	70	73	74	66		

Columbia Middle

Grade	Rd	Ma	Lg	Sp	Sci	SS
6	49	57	52	56		
7	45	56	52	51		
8	43	44	46	41		

Cumberland Elem.

Grade	Rd	Ma	Lg	Sp	Sci	SS
2	66	75	70	62		
3	70	80	69	62		
4	74	83	81	72		
5	66	66	75	67		

Ellis Elem.

Grade	Rd	Ma	Lg	Sp	Sci	SS
2	63	66	65	63		
3	54	70	60	62		
4	65	72	65	74		
5	50	80	59	58		

Fairwood Elem.

Grade	Rd	Ma	Lg	Sp	Sci	SS
2	73	90	81	79		
3	38	54	48	53		
4	41	59	55	57		
5	50	59	62	55		

Lakewood Elem.

Grade	Rd	Ma	Lg	Sp	Sci	SS
2	47	50	59	54		
3	39	49	45	59		
4	46	53	56	48		
5	43	53	50	51		

San Miguel Elem.

Grade	Rd	Ma	Lg	Sp	Sci	SS
2	65	64	71	70		
3	55	63	61	68		
4	66	77	75	73		
5	54	65	70	55		

Sunnyvale Middle

Grade	Rd	Ma	Lg	Sp	Sci	SS
6	69	80	78	68		
7	58	71	71	63		
8	59	73	61	52		

Vargas Elem.

Grade	Rd	Ma	Lg	Sp	Sci	SS
2	59	68	60	59		
3	60	64	67	62		
4	50	50	53	46		
5	51	47	61	53		

Scores range from 1-99, with 50 the average. A school scoring 75 has done better than 75 percent of other public schools in the U.S.
Key: Rd (Reading) ,Ma (Math), Lg (Language), Sp (Spelling), Sci (Science) and SS (Social Science).

Grade	Rd	Ma	Lg	Sp	Sci	SS
Union Elem. School Dist.						
2	67	71	73	67		
3	71	72	73	64		
4	72	67	73	70		
5	65	62	70	59		
6	70	76	76	68		
7	68	84	78	64		
8	65	71	72	53		
Alta Vista Elem.						
2	76	83	83	81		
3	77	78	79	67		
4	78	69	82	75		
5	75	74	81	68		
Athenour Elem.						
2	67	75	75	63		
3	71	67	72	68		
4	71	69	77	67		
5	59	57	64	57		
Carlton Elem.						
2	67	64	72	62		
3	68	78	68	63		
4	78	72	76	74		
5	63	64	61	55		
Dartmouth Middle						
6	71	74	77	71		
7	71	77	77	65		
8	66	65	70	53		
Guadalupe Elem.						
2	73	76	76	72		
3	77	79	84	71		
4	75	70	75	74		
5	73	76	81	71		
Lietz Elem.						
2	59	61	62	63		
3	57	55	61	56		
4	63	58	57	65		
5	58	46	58	48		
Lone Hill Elem.						
2	62	64	68	66		
3	77	74	77	70		
4	73	69	71	75		
5	67	66	78	63		

Grade	Rd	Ma	Lg	Sp	Sci	SS
Noddin Elem.						
2	66	76	75	66		
3	75	78	78	65		
4	72	71	72	69		
5	63	65	70	58		
Oster Elem.						
2	65	61	71	64		
3	63	61	62	57		
4	70	59	71	64		
5	63	51	61	49		
Union Middle						
6	69	78	75	65		
7	64	70	79	62		
8	64	76	73	53		
Whisman Elem. School Dist.						
2	57	56	57	57		
3	52	53	57	53		
4	58	51	60	60		
5	51	48	51	45		
6	48	52	44	49		
7	50	49	57	52		
8	57	51	57	47		
Crittenden Middle						
5	51	48	51	45		
6	48	52	44	49		
7	50	49	57	52		
8	57	51	57	47		
Monta Loma Elem.						
2	61	68	58	59		
3	57	55	59	55		
4	57	51	62	52		
Theuerkauf Elem.						
2	54	36	50	54		
3	46	51	53	53		
4	58	56	62	67		
Whisman Elem.						
2	60	75	71	62		
3	55	53	60	50		
4	57	46	57	57		

Chapter 3b

SANTA CLARA COUNTY

State School Rankings

• What do these numbers mean?

These percentile rankings, drawn from the scores on the 1999 STAR test, compare California schools and grades, one against the other.

If a school scores in the 91st percentile, it has done better than 91 percent of the other public schools in the state. If it scores in the 51st percentile, it has done better than 51 percent of the others; the 40th rank, better than 40 percent of the others. If a school scores in the first percentile, 99 percent of the other schools have scored higher.

High school rankings are correct within several points. Where data was suspect, McCormack's Guides deleted some high school scores, slightly affecting the overall rankings.

• How do these numbers differ from the rankings in Chapter 3.

The results broken out in Chapter 3 are based on a comparison against a national norm or standard where the national average is 50.

Although the results in Chapter 3B are based on the same data as the results in the Chapter 3, the Chapter 3B approach presents the results in a different way. Chapter 3B isolates California schools and simply ranks them one against the other, without regard to a national standard. These scores have no "average." Readers should interpret the Chapter 3B scores as a rough measure of how California schools compare against one another.

Note: Chapter 3 ranks school districts and schools. Chapter 3B is limited just to schools.

• Do the numbers in this chapter tell whether California education is improving?

No. Ranking systems don't recognize overall gains or losses. If every school in California raised raw scores 20 percent, some schools would still be ranked at the bottom, a few at the top. The same if every raw score dropped. A ranking system shows how one school did against all other schools.

Alum Rock Union Elem. Sch. Dist.

Arbuckle Elem.

2	14	4	15	25
3	34	15	18	16
4	6	3	3	6
5	20	39	24	22

Cassell Elem.

2	50	57	39	56
3	40	47	40	67
4	46	48	42	47
5	32	42	31	39

Chavez Elem.

2	2	7	2	2
3	13	13	7	2
4	21	28	13	6
5	9	17	20	12

Cureton Elem.

2	47	44	56	47
3	30	17	30	33
4	32	35	42	33
5	25	19	29	31

Dorsa Elem.

2	7	16	6	7
3	6	7	5	5
4	8	3	4	4
5	11	19	12	7

Fischer Middle

6	12	7	11	10
7	19	27	17	14
8	28	32	29	22

George Middle

6	32	53	28	32
7	41	58	41	52
8	34	35	30	41

Goss Elem.

2	38	35	29	35
3	19	2	7	6
4	8	6	5	10
5	17	10	14	17

Hubbard Elem.

2	10	5	12	5
3	2	6	6	6
4	12	11	8	5
5	13	7	7	12

Linda Vista Elem.

2	43	32	37	39
3	48	35	47	33
4	42	32	55	40
5	50	45	39	46

Lyndale Elem.

2	29	26	31	16
3	20	28	16	21
4	23	24	15	26
5	32	48	25	33

Mathson Middle

6	5	9	9	8
7	10	10	11	7
8	14	22	14	10

Scores range from 1-99. A school scoring 75 has done better than 75 percent of other public schools in California.
Key: Rd (Reading), Ma (Math), Lg (Language), Sp (Spelling), Sci (Science) and SS (Social Science).

ALUM ROCK DIST. (Continued)

Grade	Rd	Ma	Lg	Sp	Sci	SS
McCollam Elem.						
2	43	38	58	56		
3	17	14	25	33		
4	41	50	45	42		
5	41	27	33	40		
Meyer Elem.						
2	24	22	22	20		
3	13	14	14	14		
4	21	9	17	10		
5	29	19	29	26		
Miller Elem.						
2	26	26	26	23		
3	14	11	20	16		
4	4	13	8	5		
5	19	23	15	24		
Ocala Middle						
6	35	50	41	41		
7	21	33	35	25		
8	24	35	32	31		
Painter Elem.						
2	27	36	19	25		
3	34	35	27	49		
4	32	44	26	44		
5	35	37	20	62		
Pala Middle						
6	12	13	18	19		
7	16	19	22	23		
8	21	20	25	24		
Rogers Elem.						
2	42	40	45	56		
3	35	45	41	57		
4	29	39	33	39		
5	47	66	66	77		
Ryan Elem.						
2	18	28	19	18		
3	20	38	27	16		
4	20	15	15	8		
5	17	17	17	15		
San Antonio Elem.						
2	14	11	13	14		
3	9	5	9	7		
4	12	9	19	15		
5	13	21	22	15		
Sheppard Middle						
6	25	25	32	43		
7	24	27	28	37		
8	27	32	27	33		
Shields Elem.						
2	33	28	25	39		
3	22	28	27	25		
4	11	21	19	17		
5	19	17	22	17		
Slonaker Elem.						
2	7	17	8	5		
3	8	10	6	5		
4	11	15	21	13		
5	20	30	38	17		

Berryessa Union Elem. Sch. Dist.

Grade	Rd	Ma	Lg	Sp	Sci	SS
Brooktree Elem.						
2	84	73	76	86		
3	54	56	54	74		
4	66	66	69	82		
5	70	74	81	89		
Cherrywood Elem.						
2	45	26	39	58		
3	54	58	66	79		
4	46	55	59	72		
5	50	50	48	76		
Laneview Elem.						
2	70	66	58	87		
3	60	64	64	85		
4	59	63	65	74		
5	55	54	42	77		
Majestic Way Elem.						
2	50	55	54	69		
3	59	69	70	83		
4	56	50	53	71		
5	49	54	43	58		
Morrill Middle						
6	56	60	59	72		
7	46	56	45	66		
8	47	68	54	71		
Noble Elem.						
2	79	84	82	78		
3	74	64	73	86		
4	60	71	68	63		
5	61	62	59	72		
Northwood Elem.						
2	56	63	63	67		
3	60	61	63	84		
4	67	50	75	81		
5	75	82	81	89		
Piedmont Middle						
6	52	67	53	69		
7	58	80	68	78		
8	57	70	56	66		
Ruskin Elem.						
2	90	94	89	94		
3	82	92	93	97		
4	93	96	93	98		
5	82	82	82	90		
Sierramont Middle						
6	72	75	74	84		
7	79	82	83	92		
8	81	85	88	90		
Summerdale Elem.						
2	50	45	46	67		
3	53	42	49	71		
4	56	56	51	60		
5	50	48	51	81		
Toyon Elem.						
2	56	68	63	76		
3	61	74	72	85		
4	56	55	49	55		
5	52	50	52	67		

Scores range from 1-99. A school scoring 75 has done better than 75 percent of other public schools in California.
Key: Rd (Reading), Ma (Math), Lg (Language), Sp (Spelling), Sci (Science) and SS (Social Science).

Grade	Rd	Ma	Lg	Sp	Sci	SS
Vinci Park Elem.						
2	40	44	43	73		
3	53	53	60	85		
4	64	66	70	79		
5	59	66	68	87		

Cambrian Elem. School Dist.

Grade	Rd	Ma	Lg	Sp	Sci	SS
Bagby Elem.						
2	90	86	93	90		
3	88	85	90	92		
4	88	81	91	93		
5	85	85	88	93		
Fammatre Elem.						
2	91	85	83	78		
3	88	88	86	88		
4	80	75	83	88		
5	87	91	90	81		
Farnham Elem.						
2	81	83	84	89		
3	71	76	79	81		
4	68	75	75	75		
5	96	85	95	98		
Ida Price Middle						
6	84	85	89	86		
7	88	86	90	87		
8	94	84	90	88		
Sartorette Elem.						
2	90	88	83	94		
3	67	64	74	76		
4	80	76	90	82		
5	81	86	92	84		

Campbell Union Elem. School Dist.

Grade	Rd	Ma	Lg	Sp	Sci	SS
Blackford Elem.						
2	47	60	51	45		
3	59	72	66	57		
4	64	73	70	62		
5	59	61	63	63		
Campbell Middle						
5	39	42	52	44		
6	52	44	63	52		
7	52	43	61	46		
8	45	45	63	48		
Capri Elem.						
2	77	87	79	81		
3	82	94	87	89		
4	77	81	81	72		
5	84	80	86	67		
Castlemont Elem.						
2	80	86	81	80		
3	79	82	81	78		
4	79	77	78	78		
5	78	85	78	65		
Forest Hill Elem.						
2	92	93	98	87		
3	86	93	87	81		
4	91	97	94	89		
5	92	94	90	87		

Grade	Rd	Ma	Lg	Sp	Sci	SS
Hazelwood Elem.						
2	56	75	58	47		
3	70	83	72	65		
4	64	66	62	67		
5	53	35	36	35		
Lynhaven Elem.						
2	42	31	40	39		
3	64	51	64	64		
4	62	71	70	57		
5	52	44	51	44		
Marshall Lane Elem.						
2	99	97	98	98		
3	90	93	94	92		
4	80	87	84	87		
5	95	94	97	89		
Monroe Middle						
5	49	48	51	52		
6	64	66	74	69		
7	52	69	62	52		
8	49	49	58	53		
Rolling Hills Middle						
5	72	75	71	63		
6	78	74	75	77		
7	77	76	76	74		
8	81	81	86	84		
Rosemary Elem.						
2	21	24	33	16		
3	29	36	32	25		
4	18	28	26	22		
Sherman Oaks Elem.						
2	13	66	16	20		
3	24	53	25	23		
4	28	41	24	28		

Campbell Union High School Dist.

Grade	Rd	Ma	Lg	Sp	Sci	SS
Blackford High (Cont.)						
10	29	30	35		43	26
11	28	30	32		32	22
Del Mar High						
9	59	69	58		54	61
10	57	66	63		49	66
11	39	58	44		42	46
Leigh High						
9	84	85	87		86	82
10	89	87	90		88	91
11	80	83	86		89	88
Prospect High						
9	64	82	71		66	63
10	68	82	76		73	72
11	43	67	54		61	56
Westmont High						
9	72	81	83		74	69
10	78	81	82		82	72
11	66	71	77		72	70

Scores range from 1-99. A school scoring 75 has done better than 75 percent of other public schools in California.
Key: Rd (Reading), Ma (Math), Lg (Language), Sp (Spelling), Sci (Science) and SS (Social Science).

Cupertino Union Elem. Sch. Dist.

Blue Hills Elem.

Grade	Rd	Ma	Lg	Sp	Sci	SS
2	99	99	98	99		
3	98	97	99	99		
4	98	99	99	99		
5	97	99	99	99		
6	97	98	96	99		

Collins Elem.

Grade	Rd	Ma	Lg	Sp	Sci	SS
2	94	94	92	98		
3	93	98	98	99		
4	89	97	96	95		
5	82	94	87	89		
6	90	94	96	94		

Cupertino Int.

Grade	Rd	Ma	Lg	Sp	Sci	SS
6	99	99	99	99		
7	95	95	97	94		
8	95	96	95	97		

De Vargas Elem.

Grade	Rd	Ma	Lg	Sp	Sci	SS
2	59	75	68	69		
3	59	72	69	74		
4	77	88	81	91		
5	70	81	69	81		
6	56	83	72	53		

Dilworth Elem.

Grade	Rd	Ma	Lg	Sp	Sci	SS
2	95	98	96	98		
3	98	99	99	99		
4	95	98	96	99		
5	97	98	98	98		
6	92	96	90	94		

Eaton Elem.

Grade	Rd	Ma	Lg	Sp	Sci	SS
2	94	97	94	98		
3	97	98	98	98		
4	96	98	98	99		
5	98	97	95	98		

Eisenhower Elem.

Grade	Rd	Ma	Lg	Sp	Sci	SS
2	86	86	91	86		
3	88	84	87	95		
4	93	97	94	95		
5	88	88	90	86		
6	95	95	96	97		

Faria Elem.

Grade	Rd	Ma	Lg	Sp	Sci	SS
2	99	99	99	99		
3	99	99	99	99		
4	99	99	99	99		
5	99	100	100	99		
6	95	99	98	99		

Garden Gate Elem.

Grade	Rd	Ma	Lg	Sp	Sci	SS
2	85	96	89	96		
3	96	99	99	98		
4	94	99	98	97		
5	94	95	90	92		
6	92	97	96	96		

Hyde Int.

Grade	Rd	Ma	Lg	Sp	Sci	SS
6	99	100	100	99		
7	83	93	90	90		
8	73	90	82	85		

Kennedy Int.

Grade	Rd	Ma	Lg	Sp	Sci	SS
6	99	99	99	99		
7	98	99	98	99		
8	98	99	98	99		

Lincoln Elem.

Grade	Rd	Ma	Lg	Sp	Sci	SS
2	94	88	89	98		
3	95	96	97	99		
4	97	98	96	98		
5	96	99	98	99		
6	95	98	98	97		

McAuliffe Elem.

Grade	Rd	Ma	Lg	Sp	Sci	SS
2	97	93	82	87		
3	99	90	98	95		
4	98	95	92	93		
5	97	92	91	95		
6	99	94	93	91		

Meyerholz Elem.

Grade	Rd	Ma	Lg	Sp	Sci	SS
2	97	99	99	99		
3	94	96	96	98		
4	83	77	81	87		
5	90	93	90	93		
6	70	89	83	75		

Miller Int.

Grade	Rd	Ma	Lg	Sp	Sci	SS
6	99	99	99	99		
7	99	99	98	99		
8	98	99	98	99		

Montclaire Elem.

Grade	Rd	Ma	Lg	Sp	Sci	SS
2	99	99	99	99		
3	98	98	99	99		
4	99	99	99	99		
5	99	99	99	99		
6	98	98	98	98		

Muir Elem.

Grade	Rd	Ma	Lg	Sp	Sci	SS
2	81	89	78	93		
3	78	95	88	94		
4	88	97	92	94		
5	83	94	89	89		
6	57	94	79	67		

Nimitz Elem.

Grade	Rd	Ma	Lg	Sp	Sci	SS
2	68	77	83	66		
3	57	69	72	67		
4	66	83	80	67		
5	50	79	71	60		
6	64	81	81	72		

Portal Elem.

Grade	Rd	Ma	Lg	Sp	Sci	SS
2	97	98	98	99		
3	99	99	99	99		
4	99	99	99	99		
5	97	98	99	99		
6	98	99	99	99		

Regnart Elem.

Grade	Rd	Ma	Lg	Sp	Sci	SS
2	98	97	98	99		
3	95	97	99	99		
4	99	99	99	99		
5	98	99	99	99		
6	93	98	98	98		

Sedgwick Elem.

Grade	Rd	Ma	Lg	Sp	Sci	SS
2	91	82	90	92		
3	85	74	81	93		
4	75	85	81	88		
5	84	86	89	89		
6	78	53	81	85		

Scores range from 1-99. A school scoring 75 has done better than 75 percent of other public schools in California.
Key: Rd (Reading), Ma (Math), Lg (Language), Sp (Spelling), Sci (Science) and SS (Social Science).

Grade	Rd	Ma	Lg	Sp	Sci	SS
Stevens Creek Elem.						
2	96	92	96	99		
3	98	97	98	97		
4	98	98	98	98		
5	97	97	96	98		
6	91	93	95	91		
Stocklmeir Elem.						
2	93	94	94	94		
3	93	88	95	94		
4	95	98	96	96		
5	94	95	95	97		
6	94	96	92	92		
West Valley Elem.						
2	99	99	99	99		
3	96	96	98	96		
4	96	98	96	97		
5	98	98	97	99		
6	93	97	92	94		

East Side Union High School Dist.

Grade	Rd	Ma	Lg	Sp	Sci	SS
Apollo High (Cont.)						
11	24	26	21		19	13
Foothill High (Cont.)						
9	12	3	14		16	13
10	15	15	18		15	20
11	18	26	23		18	23
Genesis High (Cont.)						
11	23	19	25		13	12
Hill High						
9	45	57	47		45	49
10	45	71	46		39	52
11	41	59	44		45	56
Independence High						
9	50	69	62		56	54
10	56	83	64		58	63
11	56	79	66		57	60
Lick High						
9	38	48	54		37	37
10	37	64	51		39	35
11	43	49	52		38	37
Mt. Pleasant High						
9	61	80	73		76	68
10	66	90	66		73	70
11	49	72	60		67	58
Oak Grove High						
9	66	71	76		68	65
10	71	86	75		79	79
11	66	80	77		74	75
Overfelt High						
9	38	59	56		37	32
10	37	72	47		33	38
11	32	63	44		37	28
Pegasus High (Cont.)						
11	12	26	13		16	7
Phoenix High (Cont.)						
11	25	24	26		37	34
Piedmont Hills High						
9	78	86	88		78	69
10	85	95	87		87	82
11	84	94	84		85	85
Santa Teresa High						
9	91	84	88		91	84
10	84	91	86		90	84
11	82	86	88		87	79
Silver Creek High						
9	66	77	77		68	71
10	66	86	70		58	72
11	58	77	69		61	70
Yerba Buena High						
9	31	56	50		54	42
10	34	70	41		44	42
11	30	72	41		49	37

Evergreen Elem. School Dist.

Grade	Rd	Ma	Lg	Sp	Sci	SS
Cadwallader Elem.						
2	52	45	45	56		
3	63	63	66	78		
4	56	65	69	76		
5	47	44	44	58		
6	52	59	59	69		
Cedar Grove Elem.						
2	62	71	69	67		
3	67	84	83	88		
4	71	89	88	81		
5	66	82	83	82		
6	56	66	61	59		
Chaboya Middle						
6	16	15	10	23		
7	65	74	72	85		
8	62	81	72	84		
Dove Hill Elem.						
2	62	75	60	64		
3	60	87	73	84		
4	53	71	72	58		
5	50	74	68	77		
6	49	62	67	53		
Evergreen Elem.						
2	93	92	91	97		
3	91	95	95	98		
4	92	97	96	96		
5	66	81	75	79		
6	80	91	88	87		
Holly Oak Elem.						
2	72	69	64	78		
3	69	77	91	93		
4	53	71	69	65		
5	57	80	73	79		
6	89	78	99	89		
Laurelwood Elem.						
2	68	67	78	66		
3	74	80	81	67		
4	84	91	94	83		
5	81	79	79	79		
6	73	74	77	72		
Leyva Int.						
6	41	59	53	49		
7	52	72	64	75		
8	49	68	65	77		

Scores range from 1-99. A school scoring 75 has done better than 75 percent of other public schools in California.
Key: Rd (Reading), Ma (Math), Lg (Language), Sp (Spelling), Sci (Science) and SS (Social Science).

EVERGREEN DIST. (Continued)

Grade	Rd	Ma	Lg	Sp	Sci	SS
Matsumoto Elem.						
2	92	92	93	97		
3	89	98	92	97		
4	67	72	75	87		
5	92	93	97	98		
6	89	96	94	93		
Millbrook Elem.						
2	88	95	90	90		
3	59	70	64	79		
4	55	69	63	70		
5	75	87	81	90		
6	80	89	88	87		
Montgomery Elem.						
2	85	89	82	86		
3	74	90	89	91		
4	63	72	70	75		
5	61	70	64	74		
6	52	51	68	61		
Norwood Creek Elem.						
2	86	81	90	96		
3	91	96	98	99		
4	75	86	84	91		
5	82	88	79	93		
Quimby Oak Int.						
6	66	88	77	88		
7	62	80	80	91		
8	58	77	74	87		
Silver Oak Elem.						
2	94	96	96	97		
3	97	98	97	98		
4	93	95	97	98		
5	92	95	94	98		
6	97	95	99	98		
Smith Elem.						
2	66	72	60	84		
3	42	69	66	85		
4	52	71	57	65		
5	41	62	54	67		
Whaley Elem.						
2	72	75	58	81		
3	54	79	72	89		
4	50	79	63	70		
5	45	62	61	76		

Franklin-McKinley Elem. Sch. Dist.

Grade	Rd	Ma	Lg	Sp	Sci	SS
Fair Jr. High						
7	16	25	16	21		
8	15	28	16	18		
Franklin Elem.						
2	35	52	36	43		
3	20	14	22	29		
4	24	21	33	37		
5	15	10	24	26		
6	22	32	32	32		
Hellyer Elem.						
2	47	71	49	67		
3	48	70	60	79		
4	36	47	51	49		
5	35	50	49	60		
Hillsdale Elem.						
2	18	31	31	45		
3	19	15	22	10		
4	20	18	21	22		
5	17	19	24	24		
Kennedy Elem.						
2	37	40	42	54		
3	29	42	35	53		
4	26	44	40	49		
5	30	39	36	42		
6	27	53	37	34		
Los Arboles Elem.						
2	22	47	19	25		
3	13	28	14	27		
4	26	56	30	35		
5	24	32	27	31		
6	22	38	29	26		
McKinley Elem.						
2	5	2	8	7		
3	3	8	3	5		
4	9	18	7	4		
5	3	5	8	7		
6	9	12	20	8		
Meadows Elem.						
2	35	31	34	60		
3	29	28	34	53		
4	20	21	35	46		
5	27	34	46	46		
6	25	21	32	36		
Santee Elem.						
2	6	35	8	9		
3	8	6	5	10		
4	9	5	17	11		
5	5	12	11	14		
6	3	5	6	4		
Seven Trees Elem.						
2	24	36	28	23		
3	17	33	29	21		
4	14	11	19	15		
5	15	17	22	24		
6	33	30	29	30		
Stonegate Elem.						
2	43	44	40	47		
3	47	55	55	67		
4	41	37	55	50		
5	27	42	54	63		
6	57	60	75	72		
7	50	84	72	74		
8	62	78	61	88		
Sylvandale Jr. High						
6	25	25	28	28		
7	24	22	22	20		
8	25	37	32	28		
Windmill Springs Elem.						
2	45	62	48	52		
3	42	61	47	74		
4	35	50	57	60		
5	22	28	31	37		
6	25	35	32	32		
7	24	27	24	18		
8	39	64	46	51		

Scores range from 1-99. A school scoring 75 has done better than 75 percent of other public schools in California.
Key: Rd (Reading), Ma (Math), Lg (Language), Sp (Spelling), Sci (Science) and SS (Social Science).

Fremont Union High School Dist.

Cupertino High

Grade	Rd	Ma	Lg	Sp	Sci	SS
9	91	98	91		95	93
10	82	94	87		87	86
11	87	97	93		94	94

Fremont High

Grade	Rd	Ma	Lg	Sp	Sci	SS
9	61	71	63		56	63
10	69	84	77		67	74
11	61	76	66		57	65

Homestead High

Grade	Rd	Ma	Lg	Sp	Sci	SS
9	92	93	94		91	89
10	89	97	94		93	92
11	92	96	95		89	93

Lynbrook High

Grade	Rd	Ma	Lg	Sp	Sci	SS
9	99	99	99		99	99
10	98	99	99		99	99
11	99	99	99		99	99

Monta Vista High

Grade	Rd	Ma	Lg	Sp	Sci	SS
9	98	99	99		99	99
10	98	99	98		99	98
11	98	99	99		99	99

Gilroy Unified School Dist.

Aprea Fundamental Elem.

Grade	Rd	Ma	Lg	Sp	Sci	SS
2	96	90	93	97		
3	81	82	83	92		
4	92	95	94	94		
5	93	91	84	93		
6	84	84	81	93		

Brownell Acad.-Humanities Jr.

Grade	Rd	Ma	Lg	Sp	Sci	SS
7	56	37	55	50		
8	42	39	48	44		

El Roble Elem.

Grade	Rd	Ma	Lg	Sp	Sci	SS
2	40	31	26	29		
3	54	15	29	17		
4	31	26	23	17		
5	41	32	27	48		
6	37	34	29	30		

Eliot Elem.

Grade	Rd	Ma	Lg	Sp	Sci	SS
2	50	35	54	35		
3	47	28	47	33		
4	41	41	49	37		
5	38	27	44	29		
6	28	18	50	34		

Gilroy High

Grade	Rd	Ma	Lg	Sp	Sci	SS
9	59	56	60		45	59
10	66	63	70		65	70
11	58	60	63		57	65

Glen View Elem.

Grade	Rd	Ma	Lg	Sp	Sci	SS
2	33	9	25	27		
3	29	17	16	14		
4	20	16	19	15		
5	38	42	46	42		
6	25	38	32	34		

Jordan Elem.

Grade	Rd	Ma	Lg	Sp	Sci	SS
2	49	40	33	25		
3	17	3	14	12		
4	21	16	15	33		
5	32	14	27	24		
6	52	37	53	39		

Kelley Rod Elem.

Grade	Rd	Ma	Lg	Sp	Sci	SS
2	59	57	42	33		
3	47	51	44	42		
4	62	52	62	53		
5	70	69	57	67		
6	57	35	53	39		

Las Animas Elem.

Grade	Rd	Ma	Lg	Sp	Sci	SS
2	8	1	4	5		
3	8	1	16	7		
4	42	43	30	37		
5	47	35	44	33		
6	32	37	30	58		

Mt. Madonna High (Cont.)

Grade	Rd	Ma	Lg	Sp	Sci	SS
10	13	10	18		5	23
11	18	14	23		18	22

Rucker Elem.

Grade	Rd	Ma	Lg	Sp	Sci	SS
2	31	44	28	18		
3	54	29	45	37		
4	50	26	47	42		
5	84	65	66	65		
6	59	44	57	58		

San Ysidro Elem.

Grade	Rd	Ma	Lg	Sp	Sci	SS
2	38	16	37	41		
3	30	17	39	27		
4	42	37	21	44		
5	24	7	29	26		
6	51	53	57	45		

So. Valley Sch. Of Sci. & Global Stdy.

Grade	Rd	Ma	Lg	Sp	Sci	SS
6	56	50	57	56		
7	39	29	38	40		
8	41	35	40	39		

Lakeside Joint Elem. School Dist.

Lakeside Elem.

Grade	Rd	Ma	Lg	Sp	Sci	SS
2	89	97	97	50		
3	98	94	88	51		
4	95	97	87	95		
5	97	97	96	92		
6	94	89	96	97		

Loma Prieta Union Elem. Sch. Dist.

English Middle

Grade	Rd	Ma	Lg	Sp	Sci	SS
6	87	83	81	82		
7	96	92	93	96		
8	94	79	90	92		

Loma Prieta Elem.

Grade	Rd	Ma	Lg	Sp	Sci	SS
2	96	90	95	90		
3	97	84	92	89		
4	96	93	91	94		
5	97	92	91	87		

Scores range from 1-99. A school scoring 75 has done better than 75 percent of other public schools in California.
Key: Rd (Reading), Ma (Math), Lg (Language), Sp (Spelling), Sci (Science) and SS (Social Science).

Los Altos Elem. School Dist.

Almond Elem.

Grade	Rd	Ma	Lg	Sp	Sci	SS
2	98	94	95	99		
3	99	99	99	99		
4	99	98	99	99		
5	99	99	99	99		
6	99	99	99	99		

Blach Int.

Grade	Rd	Ma	Lg	Sp	Sci	SS
7	99	99	99	99		
8	99	99	99	99		

Bullis-Purissima Elem.

Grade	Rd	Ma	Lg	Sp	Sci	SS
2	98	97	99	99		
3	99	99	99	99		
4	99	99	98	99		
5	99	99	99	99		
6	99	99	99	99		

Egan Int.

Grade	Rd	Ma	Lg	Sp	Sci	SS
7	99	99	99	99		
8	99	99	99	99		

Loyola Elem.

Grade	Rd	Ma	Lg	Sp	Sci	SS
2	98	98	99	99		
3	99	99	99	99		
4	99	99	99	99		
5	99	99	99	99		
6	99	99	99	99		

Oak Ave. Elem.

Grade	Rd	Ma	Lg	Sp	Sci	SS
2	99	97	99	99		
3	99	98	99	99		
4	99	99	99	99		
5	99	99	99	99		
6	99	99	99	99		

Santa Rita Elem.

Grade	Rd	Ma	Lg	Sp	Sci	SS
2	99	99	99	99		
3	99	99	99	99		
4	99	98	99	98		
5	99	99	99	99		
6	99	97	97	98		

Springer Elem.

Grade	Rd	Ma	Lg	Sp	Sci	SS
2	98	95	97	99		
3	99	98	99	99		
4	99	99	99	99		
5	99	97	98	99		
6	98	99	99	99		

Los Gatos Union Elem. Sch. Dist.

Blossom Hill Elem.

Grade	Rd	Ma	Lg	Sp	Sci	SS
2	96	88	94	94		
3	97	96	95	91		
4	98	97	98	96		
5	96	96	97	98		

Daves Ave. Elem.

Grade	Rd	Ma	Lg	Sp	Sci	SS
2	86	81	90	85		
3	98	95	98	92		
4	97	93	98	90		
5	95	95	95	92		

Fisher Middle

Grade	Rd	Ma	Lg	Sp	Sci	SS
6	89	91	86	89		
7	96	96	96	97		
8	95	96	94	94		

Lexington Elem.

Grade	Rd	Ma	Lg	Sp	Sci	SS
2	85	63	87	80		
3	92	96	91	86		
4	93	88	91	74		
5	96	96	93	92		

Louise Van Meter Elem.

Grade	Rd	Ma	Lg	Sp	Sci	SS
2	77	92	90	74		
3	93	93	96	91		
4	97	96	94	93		
5	95	93	95	90		

Los Gatos-Saratoga Union HS Dist.

Los Gatos High

Grade	Rd	Ma	Lg	Sp	Sci	SS
9	98	98	97		98	98
10	97	97	97		98	98
11	96	96	97		97	97

Saratoga High

Grade	Rd	Ma	Lg	Sp	Sci	SS
9	99	99	99		98	99
10	99	98	99		99	99
11	98	99	99		98	99

Luther Burbank Elem. School Dist.

Luther Burbank Elem.

Grade	Rd	Ma	Lg	Sp	Sci	SS
2	29	13	17	29		
3	34	26	23	25		
4	38	26	33	39		
5	24	7	24	31		
6	5	6	3	6		
7	19	31	24	16		
8	34	58	30	36		

Milpitas Unified School Dist.

Burnett Elem.

Grade	Rd	Ma	Lg	Sp	Sci	SS
2	76	65	69	77		
3	64	61	63	76		
4	66	79	67	72		
5	52	59	63	65		
6	33	25	32	49		

Calaveras Hills Cont. High

Grade	Rd	Ma	Lg	Sp	Sci	SS
9	8	14	17		11	5
10	34	45	46		42	58

Curtner Elem.

Grade	Rd	Ma	Lg	Sp	Sci	SS
2	82	76	71	91		
3	73	84	81	91		
4	84	88	78	94		
5	82	81	81	90		
6	82	90	83	93		

Milpitas High

Grade	Rd	Ma	Lg	Sp	Sci	SS
9	73	84	84		74	82
10	71	78	79		66	77
11	70	81	81		69	75

Pomeroy Elem.

Grade	Rd	Ma	Lg	Sp	Sci	SS
2	83	78	76	94		
3	70	73	76	83		
4	71	77	76	83		
5	83	91	88	90		
6	87	90	88	93		

Scores range from 1-99. A school scoring 75 has done better than 75 percent of other public schools in California.
Key: Rd (Reading), Ma (Math), Lg (Language), Sp (Spelling), Sci (Science) and SS (Social Science).

Rancho Milpitas Jr. High

Grade	Rd	Ma	Lg	Sp	Sci	SS
7	62	69	61	69		
8	66	77	69	79		

Randall Elem.

Grade	Rd	Ma	Lg	Sp	Sci	SS
2	52	62	60	66		
3	50	58	47	65		
4	47	54	40	60		
5	30	42	43	58		
6	38	30	41	60		

Rose Elem.

Grade	Rd	Ma	Lg	Sp	Sci	SS
2	65	52	46	64		
3	56	58	54	73		
4	47	34	51	50		
5	57	52	68	65		
6	45	42	57	58		

Russell Jr. High

Grade	Rd	Ma	Lg	Sp	Sci	SS
7	80	91	84	94		
8	73	75	77	90		

Sinnott Elem.

Grade	Rd	Ma	Lg	Sp	Sci	SS
2	89	95	84	94		
3	79	80	83	98		
4	82	87	83	86		
5	78	88	81	89		
6	86	92	79	90		

Spangler Elem.

Grade	Rd	Ma	Lg	Sp	Sci	SS
2	52	47	61	73		
3	50	38	50	59		
4	44	39	38	44		
5	55	47	51	48		
6	35	38	28	30		

Weller Elem.

Grade	Rd	Ma	Lg	Sp	Sci	SS
2	61	73	57	77		
3	53	43	55	69		
4	73	68	70	91		
5	55	42	61	63		
6	86	69	75	93		

Zanker Elem.

Grade	Rd	Ma	Lg	Sp	Sci	SS
2	68	59	64	83		
3	73	82	72	97		
4	63	41	57	67		
5	75	74	59	74		
6	77	84	84	94		

Moreland Elem. School Dist.

Anderson Elem.

Grade	Rd	Ma	Lg	Sp	Sci	SS
2	35	17	36	37		
3	30	28	41	40		
4	36	47	35	37		
5	29	41	31	22		

Baker Elem.

Grade	Rd	Ma	Lg	Sp	Sci	SS
2	91	88	93	93		
3	82	82	88	86		
4	62	62	63	67		
5	81	89	82	87		

Castro Middle

Grade	Rd	Ma	Lg	Sp	Sci	SS
6	83	87	86	87		
7	88	92	89	90		
8	82	85	82	81		

Country Lane Elem.

Grade	Rd	Ma	Lg	Sp	Sci	SS
2	96	94	95	97		
3	97	96	97	97		
4	96	91	96	97		
5	95	86	95	95		

Easterbrook Elem.

Grade	Rd	Ma	Lg	Sp	Sci	SS
2	81	82	85	73		
3	64	60	73	69		
4	78	75	78	75		
5	50	45	46	42		

Latimer Elem.

Grade	Rd	Ma	Lg	Sp	Sci	SS
2	73	54	68	77		
3	82	84	87	88		
4	73	80	73	88		
5	81	84	82	74		

Moreland Discovery

Grade	Rd	Ma	Lg	Sp	Sci	SS
2	89	86	90	86		
3	97	89	89	79		
4	93	93	92	92		

Payne Elem.

Grade	Rd	Ma	Lg	Sp	Sci	SS
2	93	92	93	95		
3	82	83	88	89		
4	79	72	78	88		
5	87	85	95	92		

Rogers Middle

Grade	Rd	Ma	Lg	Sp	Sci	SS
6	64	71	61	65		
7	74	82	73	74		
8	71	86	77	78		

Morgan Hill Unified School Dist.

Britton Middle

Grade	Rd	Ma	Lg	Sp	Sci	SS
7	75	69	72	64		
8	69	72	63	61		
9	88	91	84		90	89

Burnett Elem.

Grade	Rd	Ma	Lg	Sp	Sci	SS
2	66	49	58	58		
3	42	38	44	35		
4	64	47	61	49		
5	52	52	57	46		
6	33	29	34	30		

Central High (Cont.)

Grade	Rd	Ma	Lg	Sp	Sci	SS
10	5	3	12		3	3
11	10	22	23		29	32

El Toro Elem.

Grade	Rd	Ma	Lg	Sp	Sci	SS
2	76	85	74	81		
3	78	89	76	73		
4	82	68	70	71		
5	59	52	57	53		
6	56	62	53	53		

Encinal Elem.

Grade	Rd	Ma	Lg	Sp	Sci	SS
4	70	75	76	76		
5	84	89	87	89		
6	59	60	57	59		

Jackson Elem.

Grade	Rd	Ma	Lg	Sp	Sci	SS
2	62	42	56	66		
3	64	66	67	62		
4	68	69	64	57		
5	77	85	71	72		
6	70	67	57	61		

Scores range from 1-99. A school scoring 75 has done better than 75 percent of other public schools in California.
Key: Rd (Reading), Ma (Math), Lg (Language), Sp (Spelling), Sci (Science) and SS (Social Science).

MORGAN HILL DIST. (Continued)

Grade	Rd	Ma	Lg	Sp	Sci	SS
Live Oak High						
10	82	87	79		85	87
11	74	84	71		80	82
Los Paseos Elem.						
2	85	81	67	77		
3	82	89	87	91		
Murphy Middle						
7	67	69	64	66		
8	73	79	75	73		
9	85	90	85		90	88
Nordstrom Elem.						
2	91	88	89	86		
3	85	74	86	83		
4	85	90	92	91		
5	79	85	79	74		
6	92	94	90	94		
Paradise Valley/Machado Elem.						
2	62	55	67	52		
3	97	76	87	76		
4	70	60	65	67		
5	79	79	87	79		
6	94	87	88	84		
San Martin/Gwinn Elem.						
2	61	44	51	58		
3	60	47	58	69		
4	55	52	51	55		
5	58	64	64	58		
6	38	24	37	39		
Walsh Elem.						
2	70	40	52	64		
3	51	49	41	47		
4	63	62	53	53		
5	64	54	59	60		
6	61	46	45	58		

Mountain View Elem. School Dist.

Grade	Rd	Ma	Lg	Sp	Sci	SS
Bubb Elem.						
2	92	85	97	97		
3	74	60	73	65		
4	90	90	94	88		
5	94	86	95	90		
Castro Elem.						
2	7	24	6	4		
3	24	40	22	19		
4	20	33	21	19		
5	15	14	15	14		
Graham Middle						
6	52	42	57	56		
7	63	56	66	54		
8	66	72	74	73		
Huff Elem.						
2	98	93	96	97		
3	99	99	97	98		
4	99	93	97	99		
5	95	97	94	93		
Landels Elem.						
2	88	73	87	83		
3	82	85	77	88		
4	85	85	78	83		
5	88	92	93	94		
Slater Elem.						
2	92	79	84	98		
3	88	82	90	89		
4	96	87	93	96		
5	73	65	80	90		

Mt. View-Los Altos Union HS Dist.

Grade	Rd	Ma	Lg	Sp	Sci	SS
Alta Vista High (Cont.)						
10	37	18	10		11	26
11	26	11	13		11	18
Los Altos High						
9	89	92	93		93	94
10	85	95	92		94	93
11	93	95	95		93	95
Moffett High (Alt.)						
11	64	33	81		55	44
Mountain View High						
9	93	95	92		92	96
10	94	96	95		95	96
11	95	95	92		96	95

Mt. Pleasant Elem. School Dist.

Grade	Rd	Ma	Lg	Sp	Sci	SS
Boeger Jr. High						
7	47	31	48	56		
8	32	37	46	53		
Foothill Int.						
4	41	52	57	52		
5	47	54	73	58		
6	41	40	63	58		
Mt. Pleasant Elem.						
2	22	13	28	21		
3	27	14	30	21		
4	31	29	51	22		
Sanders Elem.						
2	45	52	43	54		
3	32	24	32	53		
Valle Vista Elem.						
2	80	65	81	81		
3	54	70	64	65		

Oak Grove Elem. School Dist.

Grade	Rd	Ma	Lg	Sp	Sci	SS
Anderson Elem.						
2	57	69	40	60		
3	67	93	69	55		
4	67	75	62	57		
5	67	73	61	58		
6	76	86	83	86		
Baldwin Elem.						
2	79	95	76	88		
3	76	93	78	83		
4	64	77	59	68		
5	67	82	69	82		
6	51	71	57	65		
Bernal Int.						
7	79	89	84	88		
8	78	93	77	84		

Scores range from 1-99. A school scoring 75 has done better than 75 percent of other public schools in California.
Key: Rd (Reading), Ma (Math), Lg (Language), Sp (Spelling), Sci (Science) and SS (Social Science).

Grade	Rd	Ma	Lg	Sp	Sci	SS
Blossom Valley Elem.						
2	90	83	76	95		
3	75	96	83	85		
4	79	88	80	91		
5	75	84	84	90		
6	87	92	92	95		
Christopher Elem.						
2	33	31	29	33		
3	30	53	34	27		
4	31	46	23	29		
5	45	54	31	44		
6	41	59	35	36		
Davis Elem.						
7	49	62	48	56		
8	57	65	54	64		
Del Roble Elem.						
2	80	95	85	80		
3	73	88	79	59		
4	67	85	72	68		
5	63	77	66	76		
6	59	67	51	67		
Edenvale Elem.						
2	24	50	29	27		
3	37	38	41	29		
4	33	66	33	33		
5	33	50	51	35		
6	35	66	65	56		
Frost Elem.						
2	81	89	84	90		
3	66	72	70	64		
4	74	86	78	82		
5	53	65	48	53		
6	61	79	57	56		
Glider Elem.						
2	79	75	77	85		
3	73	87	85	88		
4	71	84	81	87		
5	72	90	86	88		
6	82	89	80	85		
Hayes Elem.						
2	81	92	76	86		
3	83	87	79	83		
4	71	89	72	72		
5	85	92	82	83		
6	63	71	49	74		
Herman Int.						
7	77	85	87	85		
8	66	92	69	69		
Miner Elem.						
2	54	60	51	52		
3	38	47	29	31		
4	47	47	42	42		
5	52	61	63	65		
6	49	75	53	41		
Oak Ridge Elem.						
2	70	78	72	81		
3	66	66	66	64		
4	85	86	80	79		
5	75	86	72	63		
6	75	81	68	69		

Grade	Rd	Ma	Lg	Sp	Sci	SS
Parkview Elem.						
2	81	90	72	91		
3	59	75	64	78		
4	66	79	69	79		
5	69	73	80	82		
6	76	75	70	84		
Sakamoto Elem.						
2	83	67	69	77		
3	87	94	86	92		
4	77	77	65	75		
5	84	80	76	82		
6	64	67	53	62		
San Anselmo Elem.						
2	77	88	73	73		
3	70	69	63	57		
4	62	79	61	62		
5	58	64	64	70		
6	64	81	59	56		
Santa Teresa Elem.						
2	81	90	74	78		
3	81	94	89	85		
4	53	85	62	62		
5	69	77	73	76		
6	68	80	59	62		
Stipe Elem.						
2	22	62	31	29		
3	29	53	27	21		
4	32	59	38	33		
5	30	50	33	33		
6	41	71	55	41		
Taylor Elem.						
2	84	88	77	75		
3	83	89	87	93		
4	82	93	84	83		
5	90	91	86	82		
6	82	87	74	71		

Orchard Elem. School Dist.

Grade	Rd	Ma	Lg	Sp	Sci	SS
Orchard Elem.						
2	26	10	28	39		
3	45	60	54	53		
4	36	41	33	40		
5	53	42	54	62		
6	15	25	28	13		
7	43	45	43	46		
8	30	43	34	19		

Palo Alto Unified School Dist.

Grade	Rd	Ma	Lg	Sp	Sci	SS
Addison Elem.						
2	98	94	96	97		
3	99	99	99	98		
4	99	97	98	99		
5	99	98	99	97		
Barron Park Elem.						
2	89	73	92	71		
3	98	87	92	97		
4	98	92	95	95		
5	97	94	99	96		

Scores range from 1-99. A school scoring 75 has done better than 75 percent of other public schools in California.
Key: Rd (Reading), Ma (Math), Lg (Language), Sp (Spelling), Sci (Science) and SS (Social Science).

PALO ALTO DIST. (Continued)

Grade	Rd	Ma	Lg	Sp	Sci	SS
Briones Elem.						
2	91	89	89	86		
3	83	74	82	62		
4	84	76	81	80		
5	97	97	95	84		
Duveneck Elem.						
2	99	98	99	99		
3	99	99	99	99		
4	99	97	97	99		
5	99	99	99	99		
El Carmelo Elem.						
2	95	96	93	91		
3	99	94	96	96		
4	98	97	95	98		
5	95	96	92	98		
Escondido Elem.						
2	84	92	86	78		
3	97	94	96	97		
4	97	90	91	92		
5	98	96	99	98		
Fairmeadow Elem.						
2	98	99	99	99		
3	97	96	98	97		
4	98	95	93	95		
5	93	94	95	95		
Gunn High						
9	99	99	99		99	99
10	99	99	99		99	99
11	99	99	98		99	99
Hays Elem.						
2	99	99	99	99		
3	99	99	99	99		
4	100	99	99	99		
5	99	99	99	99		
Hoover Elem.						
2	99	99	98	99		
3	99	99	99	99		
4	99	99	99	99		
5	99	99	98	99		
Jordan Middle						
6	99	98	96	98		
7	98	98	98	98		
8	99	98	98	99		
Nixon Elem.						
2	96	92	93	95		
3	99	98	99	98		
4	99	98	98	98		
5	98	98	99	98		
Ohlone Elem.						
2	99	96	94	97		
3	99	93	97	95		
4	98	87	91	95		
5	99	97	98	95		
Palo Alto High						
9	99	99	99		99	99
10	98	98	97		99	99
11	99	99	99		99	99
Palo Verde Elem.						
2	98	97	99	99		
3	97	98	97	99		
4	96	90	94	98		
5	99	96	98	98		
Stanford Middle						
6	98	98	94	96		
7	99	98	99	99		
8	98	98	98	98		

San Jose Unified School Dist.

Grade	Rd	Ma	Lg	Sp	Sci	SS
Allen Elem.						
2	57	69	49	62		
3	71	64	63	79		
4	35	44	42	50		
5	53	68	48	74		
Almaden Elem.						
2	76	90	57	39		
3	38	38	35	21		
4	29	33	33	26		
5	27	17	27	19		
Bachrodt Elem.						
2	8	5	9	7		
3	27	30	34	14		
4	28	22	23	19		
5	30	23	29	31		
Booksin Elem.						
2	83	79	84	78		
3	90	79	91	84		
4	88	88	84	87		
5	84	84	87	80		
Broadway High (Cont.)						
9	8	12	12		5	15
10	18	21	15		13	23
11	10	30	13		18	28
Burnett Middle						
6	5	5	5	4		
7	7	9	5	9		
8	10	12	8	9		
Carson Elem.						
2	50	35	58	54		
3	56	64	55	76		
4	68	66	69	62		
5	60	62	68	53		
Castillero Middle						
6	68	66	68	69		
7	63	71	64	61		
8	71	77	77	75		
Cory Elem.						
2	40	35	42	39		
Darling Elem.						
2	3	31	9	3		
3	17	28	9	10		
4	18	15	17	10		
5	19	14	22	10		
Empire Gardens Elem.						
2	7	2	9	12		
3	13	7	16	14		
4	28	11	19	15		
5	33	32	33	31		

Scores range from 1-99. A school scoring 75 has done better than 75 percent of other public schools in California.
Key: Rd (Reading), Ma (Math), Lg (Language), Sp (Spelling), Sci (Science) and SS (Social Science).

Grade	Rd	Ma	Lg	Sp	Sci	SS
Erikson Elem.						
2	19	19	15	14		
3	30	16	27	17		
4	41	32	45	39		
5	33	30	31	24		
Gardner Elem.						
2	14	9	10	11		
3	13	20	9	4		
4	9	9	13	6		
5	17	14	11	14		
Grant Elem.						
2	13	26	17	9		
3	19	11	18	14		
4	23	11	21	11		
5	29	27	34	22		
Graystone Elem.						
2	93	89	95	97		
3	93	88	91	97		
4	96	97	93	98		
5	95	98	94	98		
Gunderson High						
9	63	70	60		50	38
10	62	74	65		57	61
11	58	74	69		55	50
Gunderson Plus (Cont.)						
11	30	16	29		37	10
Hacienda Sci./Env. Elem.						
2	86	73	90	73		
3	69	45	66	53		
4	79	71	72	74		
5	81	75	75	70		
Hammer Elem. (Alt.)						
2	57	35	42	56		
3	50	24	47	67		
Harte Middle						
6	91	92	94	93		
7	94	95	95	96		
8	94	95	94	96		
Hester Elem.						
2	22	26	17	32		
3	22	20	23	21		
4	26	15	35	26		
5	30	28	24	29		
Hoover Middle						
6	28	24	25	23		
7	26	25	26	27		
8	32	33	29	36		
Leland High						
9	96	98	97		97	97
10	97	98	97		98	97
11	98	99	98		98	98
Leland Plus (Cont.)						
11	30	33	31		52	46
Liberty High (Alt.)						
9	36	28	29		9	
10	47	40	33		21	38
11	43	30	32		35	50
Lincoln High						
9	66	76	73		63	78
10	88	82	88		74	87
11	86	84	91		77	90

Grade	Rd	Ma	Lg	Sp	Sci	SS
Los Alamitos Elem.						
2	88	82	90	91		
3	86	76	90	83		
4	90	77	89	92		
5	87	77	89	83		
Lowell Elem.						
2	10	19	4	5		
3	11	8	11	21		
4	20	26	17	13		
5	29	25	24	31		
Mann Elem.						
2	11	3	22	12		
3	5	2	8	3		
4	26	6	17	11		
5	20	5	11	5		
Markham Middle						
6	43	32	43	37		
7	49	60	59	61		
8	47	41	52	56		
Muir Middle						
6	30	24	37	39		
7	34	37	43	35		
8	37	48	44	31		
Olinder Elem.						
2	10	35	29	18		
3	14	6	16	10		
4	14	4	9	13		
5	17	6	15	8		
Pioneer High						
9	76	89	79		81	89
10	75	90	80		79	82
11	77	87	79		71	80
Pioneer Plus (Cont.)						
11	26	16	36		16	18
Randol Elem.						
2	59	52	61	56		
3	59	67	61	55		
4	77	80	73	84		
5	85	75	80	58		
Reed Elem.						
2	75	62	79	73		
3	79	69	76	69		
4	86	84	88	87		
5	81	80	82	76		
River Glen Elem.						
2	38	54	43	12		
3	61	64	57	31		
4	67	73	67	63		
5	75	73	85	44		
6	30	30	39	32		
7	75	94	89	71		
8	73	92	75	51		
San Jose High Acad.						
9	46	61	56		45	63
10	42	59	51		45	54
11	50	68	58		51	65
Schallenberger Elem.						
2	54	54	54	56		
3	54	56	54	42		
4	55	47	67	50		
5	55	45	61	40		

Scores range from 1-99. A school scoring 75 has done better than 75 percent of other public schools in California.
Key: Rd (Reading), Ma (Math), Lg (Language), Sp (Spelling), Sci (Science) and SS (Social Science).

SAN JOSE DIST. (Continued)

Grade	Rd	Ma	Lg	Sp	Sci	SS
Simonds Elem.						
2	96	94	97	90		
3	90	88	90	93		
4	84	79	78	89		
5	75	65	75	84		
Steinbeck Middle						
6	28	30	28	32		
7	28	39	38	25		
8	25	48	35	41		
Tamien Elem.						
2	2	2	2	1		
3	9	5	9	10		
Terrell Elem.						
2	52	46	52	47		
3	67	56	66	58		
4	66	54	67	58		
5	73	64	68	58		
Trace Elem.						
3	42	45	44	45		
4	46	39	46	37		
5	45	55	56	53		
Washington Elem.						
2	5	23	8	5		
3	3	6	3	4		
4	12	6	13	10		
5	30	17	17	15		
Williams Elem.						
2	98	99	98	97		
3	99	99	99	99		
4	97	96	98	98		
5	98	99	99	99		
Willow Glen Elem.						
2	59	63	68	58		
3	42	30	41	47		
4	47	39	51	49		
5	44	39	41	40		
Willow Glen High						
9	55	53	60		54	65
10	59	53	65		52	67
11	66	65	68		54	73
Willow Glen Plus (Cont.)						
11	18	28	36		22	25

Santa Clara COE

Grade	Rd	Ma	Lg	Sp	Sci	SS
County Community						
7	2	1	2	5		
8	5	5	3	5		
9	8	6	6		7	6
10	15	15	12		13	15
11	16	14	13		7	9
Juvenile Hall						
7	12	2	6	25		
8	2	2	4	6		
9	16	12	12		13	10
10	10	21	15		15	15
11	5	16	6		8	6

Santa Clara Unified School Dist.

Grade	Rd	Ma	Lg	Sp	Sci	SS
Bowers Elem.						
2	43	49	58	60		
3	70	63	73	79		
4	60	60	72	70		
5	64	64	69	69		
Bracher Elem.						
2	83	81	79	84		
3	75	67	77	83		
4	70	59	72	70		
5	47	45	43	48		
Braly Elem.						
2	72	72	60	88		
3	56	40	55	64		
4	75	65	62	81		
5	79	54	80	70		
Briarwood Elem.						
2	49	44	52	52		
3	56	35	57	62		
4	57	71	57	62		
5	61	70	59	63		
Buchser Middle						
6	51	46	55	56		
7	58	54	52	52		
8	62	60	61	66		
Cabrillo Middle						
6	52	44	45	62		
7	52	51	53	56		
8	45	45	48	56		
Haman Elem.						
2	33	10	19	20		
3	42	13	32	40		
4	44	29	33	29		
5	47	30	27	56		
Hughes Elem.						
2	47	31	40	69		
3	51	55	72	71		
4	71	69	83	84		
5	60	52	69	80		
Laurelwood Elem.						
2	92	83	89	89		
3	76	72	83	86		
4	89	85	94	94		
5	85	88	90	90		
Mayne Elem.						
2	13	17	10	8		
3	32	22	37	23		
4	29	6	30	22		
5	38	34	39	21		
Millikin Elem.						
2	98	98	97	99		
3	97	94	99	99		
4	99	96	97	96		
5	95	99	99	98		
Montague Elem.						
2	56	46	76	85		
3	60	36	58	84		
4	49	65	75	72		
5	55	57	66	69		

Scores range from 1-99. A school scoring 75 has done better than 75 percent of other public schools in California.
Key: Rd (Reading), Ma (Math), Lg (Language), Sp (Spelling), Sci (Science) and SS (Social Science).

Grade	Rd	Ma	Lg	Sp	Sci	SS
New Valley Cont. High						
10	18	27	8		16	28
11	13	14	27		24	18
Peterson Middle						
6	77	72	77	75		
7	69	77	61	62		
8	71	79	74	73		
Pomeroy Elem.						
2	65	71	68	76		
3	63	53	61	76		
4	47	62	57	50		
5	45	42	41	51		
Ponderosa Elem.						
2	77	62	73	88		
3	75	66	73	84		
4	86	77	88	84		
5	85	77	87	79		
Santa Clara High						
9	59	67	63		69	57
10	63	72	65		71	67
11	58	79	60		79	71
Scott Lane Elem.						
2	24	14	25	35		
3	22	14	27	40		
4	23	16	34	24		
5	25	21	25	33		
Sutter Elem.						
2	59	54	76	58		
3	86	92	85	81		
4	59	50	62	52		
5	77	68	72	74		
Washington Elem.						
2	91	90	76	85		
3	75	69	69	53		
4	94	92	88	89		
5	90	77	78	72		
Westwood Elem.						
2	72	71	74	78		
3	53	35	44	49		
4	62	29	70	62		
5	73	62	78	77		
Wilcox High						
9	69	79	79		72	69
10	71	81	82		73	72
11	67	80	76		67	73
Wilson Altern.						
7	44	33	36	56		
8	18	4	5	10		
9	36	33	37		32	35
10	53	40	53		44	49
11	56	47	52		55	51

Saratoga Union Elem. School Dist.

Grade	Rd	Ma	Lg	Sp	Sci	SS
Argonaut Elem.						
2	99	99	98	99		
3	99	98	99	99		
4	99	99	98	99		
5	99	99	99	99		
Foothill Elem.						
2	99	99	99	99		
3	98	99	99	98		
4	99	98	99	99		
5	98	99	99	99		
Redwood Middle						
6	98	99	99	99		
7	99	99	99	99		
8	99	99	99	99		
Saratoga Elem.						
2	99	98	99	97		
3	99	98	96	97		
4	99	98	98	98		
5	98	99	98	98		

Sunnyvale Elem. School Dist.

Grade	Rd	Ma	Lg	Sp	Sci	SS
Bishop Elem.						
2	73	62	74	81		
3	61	79	74	85		
4	73	80	85	71		
5	58	55	64	70		
Cherry Chase Elem.						
2	94	87	89	95		
3	98	96	95	96		
4	86	85	80	84		
5	88	88	90	90		
Columbia Middle						
6	52	55	53	72		
7	50	67	52	68		
8	43	45	46	61		
Cumberland Elem.						
2	83	86	82	81		
3	89	93	85	84		
4	91	97	97	93		
5	85	80	91	91		
Ellis Elem.						
2	79	75	76	83		
3	69	80	73	84		
4	80	88	81	94		
5	61	94	71	80		
Fairwood Elem.						
2	91	99	94	98		
3	45	58	55	69		
4	47	73	65	76		
5	61	72	75	76		
Lakewood Elem.						
2	54	50	68	69		
3	47	49	50	79		
4	55	65	67	63		
5	50	64	56	69		
San Miguel Elem.						
2	81	72	83	91		
3	70	72	74	92		
4	82	93	93	93		
5	67	79	86	76		
Sunnyvale Middle						
6	86	90	93	88		
7	74	87	85	88		
8	73	91	74	84		

Scores range from 1-99. A school scoring 75 has done better than 75 percent of other public schools in California.
Key: Rd (Reading), Ma (Math), Lg (Language), Sp (Spelling), Sci (Science) and SS (Social Science).

SUNNYVALE DIST. (Continued)

Vargas Elem.

Grade	Rd	Ma	Lg	Sp	Sci	SS
2	73	77	69	77		
3	77	73	82	84		
4	60	60	62	60		
5	63	54	73	72		

Union Elem. School Dist.

Alta Vista Elem.

Grade	Rd	Ma	Lg	Sp	Sci	SS
2	94	95	95	98		
3	95	90	95	91		
4	94	85	98	95		
5	93	89	96	92		

Athenour Elem.

Grade	Rd	Ma	Lg	Sp	Sci	SS
2	84	86	87	83		
3	90	76	88	92		
4	88	85	94	88		
5	75	69	78	79		

Carlton Elem.

Grade	Rd	Ma	Lg	Sp	Sci	SS
2	84	72	84	81		
3	87	91	83	85		
4	94	88	94	94		
5	81	77	73	76		

Dartmouth Middle

Grade	Rd	Ma	Lg	Sp	Sci	SS
6	88	82	92	91		
7	92	93	92	90		
8	85	82	87	85		

Guadalupe Elem.

Grade	Rd	Ma	Lg	Sp	Sci	SS
2	91	87	89	93		
3	95	92	98	94		
4	91	86	93	94		
5	91	91	96	94		

Lietz Elem.

Grade	Rd	Ma	Lg	Sp	Sci	SS
2	73	68	72	83		
3	73	60	74	74		
4	78	72	69	85		
5	73	52	69	63		

Lone Hill Elem.

Grade	Rd	Ma	Lg	Sp	Sci	SS
2	77	72	79	86		
3	95	85	93	93		
4	90	85	89	95		
5	85	80	94	87		

Noddin Elem.

Grade	Rd	Ma	Lg	Sp	Sci	SS
2	83	87	87	86		
3	93	91	94	88		
4	89	87	90	90		
5	81	79	86	80		

Oster Elem.

Grade	Rd	Ma	Lg	Sp	Sci	SS
2	82	68	83	84		
3	81	69	76	76		
4	86	73	89	84		
5	81	61	73	65		

Union Middle

Grade	Rd	Ma	Lg	Sp	Sci	SS
6	86	87	90	85		
7	84	86	93	87		
8	82	94	90	85		

Whisman Elem. School Dist.

Crittenden Middle

Grade	Rd	Ma	Lg	Sp	Sci	SS
5	63	55	57	58		
6	51	46	37	59		
7	60	54	61	69		
8	69	60	67	75		

Monta Loma Elem.

Grade	Rd	Ma	Lg	Sp	Sci	SS
2	76	77	67	77		
3	73	60	72	73		
4	70	62	76	70		

Theuerkauf Elem.

Grade	Rd	Ma	Lg	Sp	Sci	SS
2	65	26	56	69		
3	57	53	63	69		
4	71	69	76	88		

Whisman Elem.

Grade	Rd	Ma	Lg	Sp	Sci	SS
2	75	86	83	81		
3	70	56	73	64		
4	70	54	69	77		

Chapter 4

SANTA CLARA COUNTY

How Public Schools Work

SCORES MEASURE ACADEMIC success but they have their shortcomings. Some students know the material but are not adept at taking tests and some tests are so poorly designed that they fail to assess what has been taught. The rankings in the previous chapter do not break out students as individuals. A basic exam tests the least the children should know, not the most. Scores cannot assess goodness, kindness or wisdom or predict how helpful students will be to society.

There are other legitimate criticisms of probably every test given to California school children. Nonetheless, the tests have their value and except for a few cases probably give an accurate picture of how the schools are doing academically. Students who do well in elementary school generally do well in high school and score high on the SAT and go on to succeed in college. With rare exceptions, the scores correlate with teacher assessments, and so on. The exceptions cannot be ignored. A student who does poorly in one educational arrangement may thrive in another.

When your children attend a school with high test scores, they are not assured of success. These schools have their failures. Neither can you be certain that your children will get the best teachers or the right programs. Other schools with lower scores might do better on these points. What you can be certain of is that your children are entering a setting that has proven successful for many students.

The main problem with making sense out of scores concerns what is called socioeconomics, a theory educators love, hate and widely believe.

Socioeconomics

In its crudest form, socioeconomics means rich kids score high, middle-class kids score about the middle and poor kids score low. Not all the time, not predictably by individual. Many children from poor and middle-class homes succeed in school and attend the best colleges. But as a general rule socioeconomics enjoys much statistical support.

Compare the rankings in the preceding chapter with income by cities. Los

Scholastic Aptitude Test (SAT) Scores

High School	*Enrollment	% Tested	Verbal	Math
Cupertino	250	51	521	584
Del Mar	227	34	528	542
Fremont	302	28	496	530
Gilroy	421	34	500	497
Gunderson	212	29	450	501
Gunn	333	86	587	627
Hill	325	44	417	462
Homestead	352	63	539	596
Independence	711	46	457	495
Leigh	326	42	536	560
Leland	405	77	539	580
Lick	206	32	444	450
Lincoln	280	47	531	512
Live Oak	552	33	528	540
Los Altos	299	68	560	595
Los Gatos	323	77	572	588
Lynbrook	343	79	573	638
Milpitas	493	49	474	511
Monta Vista	445	80	568	646
Mt. Pleasant	337	39	456	478
Mountain View	251	74	563	589
Oak Grove	423	39	485	516
Overfelt	NA	NA	NA	NA
Palo Alto	282	82	601	617
Piedmont Hills	336	52	482	531
Pioneer	234	42	506	521
Prospect	282	39	518	531
San Jose	175	33	529	535
Santa Clara	278	46	470	520
Santa Teresa	427	42	494	518
Saratoga	263	88	594	634
Silver Creek	350	41	457	489
Westmont	270	40	505	542
Wilcox	359	50	480	528
Willow Glen	184	27	468	483
Yerba Buena	304	36	445	493

Source: California Dept. of Education, 1998-99 tests. SAT scores are greatly influenced by who and how many take the test. The state education department has been pushing schools to have more students take the SAT. A school that has more marginal students taking the test will, by one line of reasoning, be doing a good job, but the scores are likely to be lower. NA Data not available. *Senior class.

Altos Hills and Los Gatos, rich or well-to-do, high scores; Alum Rock Elementary School District (East San Jose), low income or poor, low scores; Morgan Hill and Milpitas, middle-class towns, middling scores. The SAT scores reflect the basic test scores.

The same pattern shows up in Alameda County. The schools in the poorer neighborhoods of Oakland score low; well-to-do Piedmont scores high. And the pattern shows up around the Bay Area, the country and in other countries.

Top SAT Math Scores-1997-1998

22 public high schools in California scoring over 600 in math

High School	County	City	Math
Albany	Alameda	Albany	603
Mission San Jose	Alameda	Fremont	616
Piedmont	Alameda	Piedmont	613
Acalanes	Contra Costa	Lafayette	600
Campolindo	Contra Costa	Moraga	610
Miramonte	Contra Costa	Orinda	610
Cerritos	Los Angeles	Cerritos	604
Whitney	Los Angeles	Cerritos	680
Arcadia	Los Angeles	Arcadia	619
La Cañada	Los Angeles	La Cañada	619
Palos Verdes	Los Angeles	Rolling Hills Est.	618
San Marino	Los Angeles	San Marino	626
South Pasadena	Los Angeles	South Pasadena	601
Sunny Hills	Orange	Fullerton	613
University	Orange	Irvine	637
Mira Loma	Sacramento	Sacramento	603
Lynbrook	Santa Clara	San Jose	636
Monta Vista	Santa Clara	Cupertino	652
Saratoga	Santa Clara	Saratoga	636
Gunn	Santa Clara	Palo Alto	641
Palo Alto	Santa Clara	Palo Alto	629
Lowell	San Francisco	San Francisco	620

Source: Calif. Dept. of Education, 1997-98 tests. The charts on pages 74 and 76 contain the SAT scores from the most recent academic year, 1998-1999.

The federal study, "Japanese Education Today," notes a "solid correlation between poverty and poor school performance ...."

Family and Culture

In its refined form, socioeconomics moves away from the buck and toward culture and family influence.

Note the chart on Page 20. The towns with the highest number of college educated are generally also the towns with the highest scores. If your mom or dad attended college, chances are you will attend college or do well at school because in a thousand ways while you were growing up they and their milieu pushed you in this direction. Emphasis on "chances are." Nothing is certain when dealing with human beings.

What if mom and dad never got beyond the third grade? Or can't even speak English? Historically, many poor and immigrant children have succeeded at school because their parents badgered, bullied and encouraged them every step of the way and made sacrifices so they would succeed. Asian kids are the latest example of poor kids succeeding but we can also point to the children of peasant Europeans and Africans brought to this country as slaves.

Does it make a difference if the child is English proficient? Immigrant children unfamiliar with English will have more difficulties with literature and language-proficient courses than native-born children. They will need extra or special help in schools.

National Scholastic Aptitude Test (SAT) Scores

State	*Tested (%)	Verbal	Math
Alabama	9	561	555
Alaska	50	516	514
Arizona	34	524	525
Arkansas	6	563	556
California	**49**	**497**	**514**
Colorado	32	536	540
Connecticut	80	510	509
Delaware	67	503	497
Dist. of Columbia	77	494	478
Florida	53	499	498
Georgia	63	487	482
Hawaii	52	482	513
Idaho	16	542	540
Illinois	12	569	585
Indiana	60	496	498
Iowa	5	594	598
Kansas	9	578	576
Kentucky	12	547	547
Louisiana	8	561	558
Maine	68	507	503
Maryland	65	507	507
Massachusetts	78	511	511
Michigan	11	557	565
Minnesota	9	586	598
Mississippi	4	563	548
Missouri	8	572	572
Montana	21	545	546
Nebraska	8	568	571
Nevada	34	512	517
New Hampshire	72	520	518
New Jersey	80	498	510
New Mexico	12	549	542
New York	76	495	502
North Carolina	61	493	493
North Dakota	5	594	605
Ohio	25	534	538
Oklahoma	8	567	560
Oregon	53	525	525
Pennsylvania	70	498	495
Rhode Island	70	504	499
South Carolina	61	479	475
South Dakota	4	585	588
Tennessee	13	559	553
Texas	50	494	499
Utah	5	570	568
Vermont	70	514	506
Virginia	65	508	499
Washington	52	525	526
West Virginia	18	527	512
Wisconsin	7	584	595
Wyoming	10	546	551
Nationwide	**43**	**505**	**511**

Source: California Dept. of Education, 1999 tests. *Percentage of class taking the test.

Nonetheless, the home-school correlation retains much validity: The stronger the educational support the child receives at home, the better he or she will do at school.

Role of Schools

If you carry the logic of socioeconomics too far, you come to the conclusion that schools and teachers and teaching methods don't matter: Students succeed or fail according to their family or societal backgrounds.

Just not the case. No matter how dedicated or well-intentioned the parent, if the teacher is grossly inept the child probably will learn little. If material or textbooks are out-of-date or inaccurate, what the student learns will be useless or damaging. Conversely, if the teacher is dedicated and knowledgeable, if the material is well-presented and appropriate, what the child comes away with will be helpful and, to society, more likely to be beneficial. Almost every one of us can recall a favorite teacher who worked with us and influenced our lives.

The late Albert Shanker, president of the American Federation of Teachers, argued that U.S. students would improve remarkably if schools refused to tolerate disruptive behavior, if national or state academic standards were adopted, if external agencies (not the schools themselves) tested students and if colleges and employers, in admissions and hiring, rewarded academic achievement and penalized failure. These four reforms do little or nothing to address socioeconomics but many educators believe they have merit.

Admittedly, however, this is a contentious area. Theories abound as to what is wrong with our schools and what should be done to fix them.

Where the Confusion Enters

It's very difficult, if not impossible, to separate the influence of home and schools.

When scores go up, often principals or superintendents credit this or that instructional program, or extra efforts by teachers.

But the scores may have risen because mom and dad cracked down on excessive TV. Or a city with old and faded low-income housing (low scores) approves a high-end development. The new residents are more middle class, more demographically inclined to push their kids academically.

One last joker-in-the deck, mobility. Johnny is doing great at his school, which has low to middling scores, but programs that seem to be working. And his family is doing better. Mom has a job, Dad a promotion. What does the family do? It moves. Happens all the time in the U.S.A. and this also makes precise interpretation of scores difficult.

Back to Scores

If a school's scores are middling, it may still be capable of doing an excellent job, if it has dedicated teachers and sound programs. The middling scores may reflect socioeconomics, not instructional quality.

Don't judge us by our overall scores, many schools say. Judge us by our ability to deliver for your son or daughter.

This gets tricky because children do influence one another and high-income parents often interact differently with schools than low-income parents. To some extent, the school must structure its programs to the abilities of the students. But schools with middling and middling-plus grades can point to many successes.

Basic Instruction-Ability Grouping

California and American schools attempt to meet the needs of students by providing a good basic education and by addressing individual and subgroup needs by special classes and ability grouping.

In the first six years in an average school, children receive some special help according to ability but for the most part they share the same class experiences and get the same instruction.

About the seventh grade, until recently, students were divided into classes for low achievers, middling students and high achievers, or low-middle and advanced — tracking. Texts, homework and expectations were different for each group. The high achievers were on the college track, the low, the vocational.

Pressured by the state, schools are curtailing this practice, but many schools retain accelerated English and math classes for advanced seventh and eighth graders. Parents can always request a transfer from one group to another (whether they can get it is another matter). The reality often is, however, that remedial and middle children can't keep pace with the high achievers.

In the last 30 years or so schools introduced into the early grades special programs aimed at low achievers or children with learning difficulties. Although they vary greatly, these programs typically pull the children out of class for instruction in small groups then return them to the regular class.

Many schools also pull out gifted (high I.Q.) students and a few cluster them in their own classes.

College Influence

So many local students attend the University of California and California State University schools that public and private high schools must of necessity teach the classes demanded by these institutions.

So the typical high school will have a prep program that meets University of California requirements. The school also will offer general education classes in math and English but these will not be as tough as the prep courses and will not be recognized by the state universities. And usually the school will teach some trades so those inclined can secure jobs upon graduation.

California College Admissions of Public School Graduates

High School	UC	CSU	Com	Total
Cupertino	49	19	104	172
Del Mar	15	33	97	145
Fremont	20	30	119	184
Gilroy	6	23	222	251
Gunderson	8	18	79	105
Gunn	105	16	56	177
Hill	23	52	56	131
Homestead	75	46	111	232
Independence	46	129	1,445	1,620
Leigh	22	43	7	72
Leland	100	53	147	300
Lick	4	33	62	99
Lincoln	13	36	105	154
Live Oak	41	47	264	352
Los Altos	62	32	81	175
Los Gatos	54	48	128	230
Lynbrook	117	19	70	206
Milpitas	46	62	224	332
Monta Vista	144	25	113	182
Mt. Pleasant	13	59	91	163
Mtn. View	54	21	80	155
Oak Grove	27	53	201	281
Overfelt	10	44	73	127
Palo Alto	74	22	62	158
Piedmont Hills	36	50	109	195
Pioneer	10	25	109	144
Prospect	21	26	172	219
San Jose	14	27	42	81
Santa Clara	14	35	136	185
Santa Teresa	38	57	187	282
Saratoga	72	26	61	159
Silver Creek	29	62	120	211
Westmont	24	18	145	187
Wilcox	28	43	149	220
Willow Glen	6	17	60	83
Yerba Buena	13	43	92	148

Source: California Department of Education. The chart lists the local public high schools and shows how many students they advanced in 1998 into California public colleges and universities. The state does not track graduates enrolling in private or out-of-state colleges. Continuation schools not included in list. Key: UC (University of California system); CSU (Cal State system); Com (Community Colleges); Total (total number of graduates attending California colleges).

Can a school with mediocre or even low basic scores field a successful college prep program? With comprehensive programs, the answer is yes.

How Middling Schools Succeed — College Admissions

Freshmen attending a California State University, a public community college or a University of California (Berkeley, Los Angeles, San Diego, Davis, etc.) are asked to identify their high schools. In this way and others, the state finds out how many students individual high schools are advancing to college.

The chart on the previous page breaks out the high schools in Santa Clara County (data collected fall 1998) and shows how many students from each school went on to the public colleges. For an idea of the size of the graduating class, see the SAT chart on Page 74.

The UCs generally restrict themselves to the top 13 percent in the state. The Cal States take the top third.

Every school on the chart is graduating kids into college but obviously some are more successful at it than others. Does this mean that the 'lesser" schools have awful teachers or misguided programs? We have no idea. It simply may be demographics at work.

Parents with college ambitions for their children should find out as much as possible about prospective schools and their programs and make sure that their kids get into the college-track classes.

Where does the chart mislead? For starters, the Cal States and UCs run on academics, the community colleges run on academics and vocational classes. Just because a student attends a community college does not mean he or she is pursuing a bachelor's degree.

Secondly, students who qualify for a Cal State or even a UC often take their freshman and sophomore years at a community college. It's cheaper and closer to home. The chart suggests that middle- and low-income communities send more kids proportionally to community colleges than high-income towns.

To attract minority students, the universities, in some instances, have modified their admission policies, a practice that has critics and supporters. The numbers mentioned previously and listed in the accompanying chart may not consist of the top students. This policy, because of a recently passed state initiative, is being changed but the new policy, under a different name, might accomplish what the old one did.

The chart does not track private colleges. It doesn't tell us how many local students went to Mills College or the University of San Francisco or Stanford or Harvard. Or public colleges out of the state.

Many college students drop out. These numbers are not included.

The chart does confirm the influence of socioeconomics: the rich towns, the educated towns or neighborhoods, send more kids to the UCs than the poorer ones.

But socioeconomics does not sweep the field. Not every student from a high-scoring school goes on to college. Many students from low- and middle-income towns come through.

Assessing High Schools

The California Department of Education recently put together a new assessment package for public high schools. The chart on the opposite page presents the new assessment tools. All the numbers are in percentile rankings, comparing California high schools against one another. The highest ranking is 99, the lowest 1.

- **A-F.** High schools teach a variety of academic courses but not all count toward meeting the admission requirements of the University of California or California State universities. Those that do are termed "A - F." A high number indicates that as a percentage of school enrollment, many students are enrolled in college-prep courses.
- **National Average.** Based on scores from Scholastic Assessment Test (SAT) and American College Testing, tests designed to measure ability to do college work. This assessment breaks out scores above the national average, then ranks the numbers from each California public school. A high number suggests that students are scoring high on these tests (compared to other California students).
- **AP.** Top-notch high school students often take Advanced Placement (AP) or International Baccalaureate exams. A high number in these rankings suggests that the school offers many tough courses and has many top students (as compared to other high schools).

Contradictions: A school with high National Average figures and high Advanced Placement figures but middling college-bound figures (see other charts in this chapter) may be sending many students to out-of-state colleges or private institutions. The highest-scoring schools usually are located in the high-income towns; parents would have the means to send the kids out of state or to USC, Stanford, etc. The state has sparse data on students who attend private or out-of-state colleges. For a more rounded picture of an individual school, see the rankings in the previous chapters.

Dissatisfaction

If high schools can deliver on college education and train students for vocations, why are so many people dissatisfied with public schools? These schools can cite other accomplishments: Textbooks and curriculums have been improved, the dropout rate has been decreased and proficiency tests have been adopted to force high school students to meet minimum academic standards.

Yet almost every year or so, some group releases a study showing many California children are scoring below expectations or doing poorly as com-

High School Assessments

High School	A-F	Nat. Avg.	AP
Cupertino	62	85	81
Del Mar	38	57	67
Fremont	81	63	31
Gilroy	18	39	35
Gunderson	43	34	62
Gunn	94	99	99
Hill	20	22	64
Homestead	93	94	88
Independence	44	39	62
Leigh	52	72	81
Leland	91	96	96
Lick	28	19	41
Lincoln	40	52	87
Live Oak	55	62	37
Los Altos	84	95	97
Los Gatos	93	97	97
Lynbrook	94	98	96
Milpitas	38	70	59
Monta Vista	91	98	96
Mt. Pleasant	51	28	49
Mtn. View	73	94	96
Oak Grove	93	46	57
Overfelt	35	21	49
Palo Alto	95	98	98
Piedmont Hills	62	54	54
Pioneer	54	68	71
Prospect	51	53	73
San Jose	29	34	80
Santa Clara	77	60	66
Santa Teresa	71	68	65
Saratoga	96	99	99
Silver Creek	19	33	59
Westmont	63	61	70
Wilcox	37	69	69
Willow Glen	44	46	76
Yerba Buena	89	30	17

Source: California Department of Education, High School Performance Report, 1996-97.

pared to Japanese or European children.

Employers report that many high school grads are unable to understand instructions or write competently. Colleges complain that honor high school students often need remedial math and English.

The California system is expensive, over $33 billion annually for just the kindergarten-through-twelfth schools.

Comparisons between countries are tricky. If Japanese or European high

UCs Chosen by Public School Graduates

School	Berk	Davis	Irv	UCLA	River	SD	SB	SC	Total
Cupertino	12	12	0	3	2	3	12	5	49
Del Mar	4	4	0	1	0	1	2	3	15
Fremont	7	1	1	1	0	5	3	2	20
Gilroy	0	1	0	1	0	1	0	3	6
Gunderson	0	0	1	3	0	1	3	0	8
Gunn	28	14	2	10	3	15	17	16	105
Hill	4	9	0	4	1	2	0	3	23
Homestead	14	16	4	11	2	10	14	4	75
Independence	3	19	3	4	5	5	2	5	46
Leigh	6	3	0	2	2	2	1	5	*21
Leland	25	16	3	15	2	25	8	6	100
Lick	1	1	0	1	0	1	0	0	4
Lincoln	1	2	0	4	0	1	1	4	13
Live Oak	5	10	0	3	1	4	10	8	41
Los Altos	14	10	1	15	2	2	14	4	62
Los Gatos	8	8	4	6	0	10	14	4	54
Lynbrook	32	16	8	17	4	21	13	6	117
Milpitas	5	19	4	2	3	5	3	5	46
Monta Vista	38	21	6	15	5	29	18	12	144
Mt. Pleasant	2	5	0	4	0	1	0	1	13
Mtn. View	7	9	2	4	1	11	14	6	54
Oak Grove	7	10	0	1	0	1	6	2	27
Overfelt	1	4	2	1	0	1	1	0	10
Palo Alto	17	14	2	8	0	17	5	11	74
Piedmont Hills	8	13	1	4	2	3	2	3	36
Pioneer	2	1	1	1	0	1	2	2	10
Prospect	3	7	0	3	1	0	6	1	21
San Jose	6	3	0	1	0	2	0	2	14
Santa Clara	2	2	1	2	0	0	3	4	14
Santa Teresa	7	5	2	3	5	4	6	6	38
Saratoga	20	10	6	5	1	14	10	6	72
Silver Creek	6	7	4	0	0	5	2	5	29
Westmont	2	10	3	4	0	1	2	2	24
Wilcox	6	10	0	3	1	3	3	2	28
Willow Glen	0	3	0	1	0	1	0	1	6
Yerba Buena	1	9	0	0	1	0	1	1	13

Source: California Dept. of Education. The chart shows the University of California choices of 1998 local public high school graduates. The state does not track graduates enrolling in private colleges or out-of-state colleges. **Key**: Berk (Berkeley), Irv (Irvine), SD (San Diego), SB (Santa Barbara), River (Riverside), SC (Santa Cruz). * Dept. of Education showed 22 UC students for Leigh High, the school itself showed 21.

school students fail or do poorly on their tests, they are often denied admission to college. Those who do well, however, are marked not only for college but the higher-paying jobs. Our system gives second and third chances and allows easy admission to colleges, but bears down on students during college and after they graduate. Then they have to prove themselves at work to get ahead, and this forces many to return to college or get training. Their system pressures teenagers; ours pressures young adults. Some studies suggest that by age 30 the differences even out.

As intriguing as this theory is, many parents and teachers would feel much better if the learning curve showed a sharper rise for the high-school scholars and, of course, our top universities — Cal, Stanford, Harvard — demand top scores for admission.

Registering For School

To get into kindergarten, your child must turn five before Dec. 3 of the year he or she enters the grade.

For first grade, your child must be six before Dec. 3. If he is six on Dec. 4, if she is a mature Jan. 6 birthday girl, speak to the school. There may be some wiggle room.

For registration, you are required to show proof of immunization for polio, diphtheria, hepatitus B, tetanus, pertussis (whooping cough), measles, rubella and mumps. If the kid is seven or older, you can skip mumps and whooping cough. New law: continuing students entering the seventh grade must show proof of being immunized against hepatitus B.

Register Early

Just because you enroll your child first does not necessarily mean that you will get your first choice of schools or teachers.

But in some school districts first-come does mean first-served. Enrollment and transfer policies change from year to year in some districts, depending on the number of children enrolled and the space available. When new schools are opened, attendance boundaries are often changed.

Even if the school district says, "There's plenty of time to register," do it as soon as possible. If a dispute arises over attendance — the school might get an unexpected influx of students — early registration might give you a leg up in any negotiations. Persistence sometimes helps in trying for transfers.

Choosing the "Right" School

Almost all public schools have attendance zones, usually the immediate neighborhood. The school comes with the neighborhood; often you have no choice. Your address determines your school.

Always call the school district to find out what school your children will be attending. Sometimes school districts change attendance boundaries and do not inform local Realtors. Sometimes crowding forces kids out of their neighborhood schools. It's always good to go to the first source.

Just say something like, "I'm Mrs. Jones and we're thinking about moving into 1234 Main Street. What school will my six-year-old attend?"

Ask what elementary school your child will attend and what middle school and high school. In Santa Clara County, many children attend elementary and middle school or junior high in one school district then move up to a high school in a different district.

Cal States Chosen by Public School Graduates

School	Cal Poly	Chico	Hay	Sac	S.D.	S.F.	S.J.	Son	Fres
Cupertino	2	0	0	1	4	3	7	0	0
Del Mar	4	3	1	0	0	1	21	0	0
Fremont	1	1	1	0	2	1	21	0	1
Gilroy	2	4	0	2	3	1	6	2	2
Gunderson	1	0	1	1	1	0	9	0	2
Gunn	2	2	0	0	2	1	2	0	1
Hill	1	0	0	0	5	0	41	1	0
Homestead	11	0	0	0	5	9	13	2	0
Independence	8	4	1	0	5	3	104	1	0
Leigh	0	0	0	0	0	0	0	0	0
Leland	8	4	0	2	7	0	22	1	5
Lick	0	0	1	0	2	3	26	0	0
Lincoln	3	8	1	0	1	0	20	0	0
Live Oak	6	6	0	0	7	3	15	3	4
Los Altos	4	6	1	0	2	4	12	0	0
Los Gatos	9	7	1	0	7	1	11	2	0
Lynbrook	4	1	1	1	1	0	7	0	0
Milpitas	5	0	6	0	2	8	35	1	1
Monta Vista	11	2	0	0	3	1	6	1	0
Mt. Pleasant	5	0	0	0	0	0	52	0	0
Mtn. View	3	4	0	0	3	0	7	3	0
Oak Grove	8	0	0	0	1	2	35	2	3
Overfelt	4	2	0	0	0	1	36	0	1
Palo Alto	7	9	0	0	1	1	1	2	0
Piedmont Hills	3	0	4	1	1	1	38	2	0
Pioneer	6	3	1	0	1	1	10	0	0
Prospect	1	5	0	0	1	1	15	1	1
San Jose	1	0	0	0	1	0	24	0	0
Santa Clara	4	1	0	1	0	1	21	1	0
Santa Teresa	4	3	0	0	1	1	43	0	0
Saratoga	5	5	0	0	4	4	4	0	0
Silver Creek	0	0	1	0	1	5	51	0	1
Westmont	2	1	0	0	0	0	11	2	0
Wilcox	3	2	0	1	0	0	35	0	0
Willow Glen	1	0	0	0	0	0	16	0	0
Yerba Buena	0	1	0	0	0	0	42	0	0

Source: California Dept. of Education. The chart shows the most popular choices of 1998 local public high school graduates. The chart does not include all Cal State universities. The state does not track graduates enrolling in private or out-of-state colleges. Continuation schools not included in list. **Key**: Cal Poly (San Luis Obispo), Hay (Hayward), Sac (Sacramento), S.D. (San Diego), S.F. (San Francisco), S.J. (San Jose), Son (Sonoma), Fres (Fresno).

Keep in mind that although a district scores high, not all the schools in the district may score high. In some districts, scores vary widely.

Several districts may serve one town, another reason to nail down your school of attendance.

Dropout Rates — High School Districts

District	*1996	*1997	*1998	**No.
Campbell	3%	3%	3%	222
East Side	8%	4%	6%	1,375
Fremont	2%	2%	1%	69
Gilroy	5%	3%	3%	73
Los Gatos-Saratoga	***0%	***0%	***0%	1
Milpitas	1%	2%	2%	68
Morgan Hill	4%	4%	3%	79
Mt.View-Los Altos	***0%	***0%	1%	29
Palo Alto	1%	1%	1%	21
San Jose	2%	1%	2%	147
Santa Clara	1%	1%	1%	44
County	4%	3%	3%	2,175

Source: California Dept. of Education. *Percentages are single-year dropout rate; includes grades 9-12. **No. is the actual number of dropouts in 1997. ***Less than 0.5%. NA (not available).

Transfers

If you don't like your neighborhood school, you can request a transfer to another school in the district or to a school outside the district. But the school won't provide transportation.

Transfers to schools inside the district are easier to get than transfers outside the district. New laws supposedly make it easier to transfer children to other districts. In reality, the more popular (high scoring) districts and schools, lacking space, rarely — very rarely — accept "outside" students.

A few parents use the address of a friend or relative to smuggle their child into a high-scoring school or district. Some districts make an effort to ferret out these students and give them the boot.

If your child has a special problem that may demand your attention, speak to the school administrators about a transfer to a school close to your job. If your child's ethnicity adds some diversity to a school or district, it might bend its rules. Never hurts to ask.

Does a Different School Make a Difference?

This may sound like a dumb question but it pays to understand some of the thinking behind choosing one school or school district over another. Two stories:

Researching earlier editions, we contacted a school district (not in this county) that refused to give us test results. This stuff is public information. By law, we (and you) should be able to obtain it routinely.

In so many words, the school administrator said, look, our scores are lousy because our demographics are awful: low income, parents poorly educated, etc.

(Continued on page 89)

School Accountability Report Card

Want more information about a particular school or school district?

Every public school and district in the state is required by law to issue an annual School Accountability Report Card. The everyday name is the SARC report or the SARC card. SARCs are supposed to include:

- The ethnic makeup of the school and school district.
- Test results. The results may be presented in several ways but almost without exception the formats follow the presentation methods of the California Dept. of Education.
- Dropout rates for high schools.
- A description of the curriculum and the programs.
- Class sizes, teacher-pupil ratios.
- Description of the teaching staff. How many have teaching credentials.
- Description of facilities.

To obtain a SARC, call the school and if the person answering the phone can't help you, ask for the superintendent's secretary or the curriculum department. Some schools want you to pick up the report in person; others will mail it to you. It sometimes helps if you mail the school a stamped, self-addressed envelope or simply $3 worth of stamps and a cover letter. If you don't know the name of the neighborhood school, start with the school district. Here are the phone numbers:

Alum Rock Union Elementary	(408) 928-6800
Berryessa Union Elementary	(408) 923-1800
Cambrian Elementary	(408) 377-2103

(Continued on page 89)

School Districts, next page. Unified school districts include elementary, middle and high schools, the whole ball of wax. Palo Alto, San Jose, Santa Clara, Morgan Hill and Gilroy run unified districts. In the other arrangements, elementary school districts, as individual political agencies, educate the children up to the eighth grade. Then the students move up to high schools run by high school districts, also politically independent. For example, students from Los Altos, Mountain View and Whisman elementary districts move up to high schools in the Mountain View/Los Altos High School District. Attendance policies vary by district. For information about attendance, call the school districts.

Santa Clara County

ELEMENTARY, HIGH SCHOOL & UNIFIED SCHOOL DISTRICTS

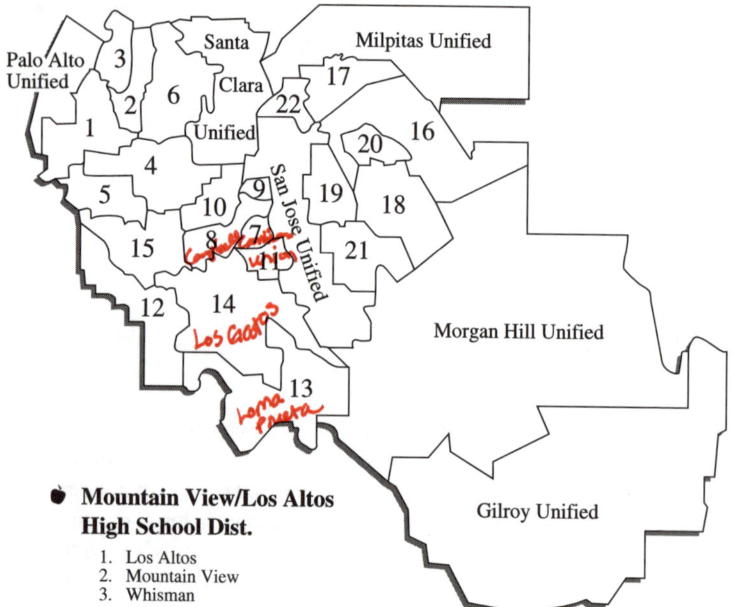

Mountain View/Los Altos High School Dist.

1. Los Altos
2. Mountain View
3. Whisman

Fremont Union High School Dist.

4. Cupertino
5. Montebello
6. Sunnyvale

Campbell High School Dist.

7. Cambrian
8. Campbell
9. Luthur Burbank
10. Moreland
11. Union

Los Gatos-Saratoga School Dist.

12. Lakeside
13. Loma Prieta
14. Los Gatos
15. Saratoga

Gilroy Unified School Dist.

East Side Union High School Dist.

16. Alum Rock
17. Berryessa
18. Evergreen
19. Franklin McKinley
20. Mount Pleasant
21. Oak Grove
22. Orchard

Palo Alto Unified School Dist.

San Jose Unified School Dist.

Santa Clara Unified School Dist.

Morgan Hill Unified School Dist.

Milpitas Unified School Dist.

*(**School Accountability Report Card**, Continued from page 87)*

Campbell Union Elementary	(408) 364-4200
Campbell Union High	(408) 371-0960
Cupertino Union	(408) 252-3000
East Side Union High	(408) 272-6400
Evergreen Elementary	(408) 270-6800
Franklin-McKinley Elementary	(408) 283-6000
Fremont Union High	(408) 522-2200
Gilroy Unified	(408) 847-2700
Lakeside Joint	(408) 354-2372
Loma Prieta Joint Union Elementary	(408) 353-1101
Los Altos Elementary	(650) 941-4010
Los Gatos-Saratoga Joint High	(408) 354-2520
Los Gatos Union Elementary	(408) 395-5570
Luther Burbank	(408) 295-2450
Milpitas Unified	(408) 945-2300
Montebello Elementary	(408) 867-3628
Moreland Elementary	(408) 874-2900
Morgan Hill Unified	(408) 779-5272
Mt. Pleasant Elementary	(408) 223-3700
Mountain View Elementary	(650) 526-3500
Mountain View-Los Altos Union High	(650) 940-4650
Oak Grove Elementary	(408) 227-8300
Orchard Elementary	(408) 944-0394
Palo Alto Unified	(650) 329-3700
San Jose Unified	(408) 535-6000
Santa Clara Unified	(408) 983-2000
Saratoga Union Elementary	(408) 867-3424
Sunnyvale Elementary	(408) 522-8200
Union Elementary	(408) 377-8010
Whisman Elementary	(650) 903-6900

(Continued from page 86)
But our programs and staff are great. I'm not giving out the scores because parents will get the wrong idea about our district and keep their kids out of our schools (He later changed his mind and gave us the scores.)

Second story, while working as a reporter, one of our editors covered a large urban school district and heard about a principal who was considered top notch. An interview was set up and the fellow seemed as good as his reputation: friendly, hardworking, supportive of his staff, a great role model for his students, many of whom he knew by their first names. But scores at the school were running in the 10th to 20th percentiles, very low.

The reason: the old failing of demographics, crime high, family structures weak, and so on.

Although neither person said this, the clear implication was that if the demographics were different, scores would be much higher. And they're probably right. If these schools got an influx of middle- and upper middle-class children, their scores would dramatically increase.

Why don't schools tell this to the public, to parents? Probably because socioeconomics is difficult to explain. Teachers want to work with parents, not alienate them with accusations of neglect. Some educators argue that even with poor socioeconomics, teachers should be able to do an effective job — controversy. Socioeconomics focuses attention on the problems of home and society to the possible detriment of schools (which also need help and funds). School, after all, is a limited activity: about six hours a day, about 172 teaching days a year (to be expanded to 180).

When you strip away the fluff, schools seem to be saying that they are in the business of schools, not in reforming the larger society, and that they should be held accountable only for what they can influence: the children during the school day, on school grounds.

For these reasons — this is our opinion — many teachers and school administrators think that scores mislead and that parents often pay too much attention to scores and not enough to programs and the background and training of personnel. This is not to say that teachers ignore scores and measurements of accomplishment. They would love to see their students succeed. And schools find tests useful to determine whether their programs need changes.

No matter how low the scores, if you, as a parent, go into any school and ask — can my child get a good education here — you will be told, probably invariably, often enthusiastically, yes. First, there's the obvious reason: if the principal said no, his or her staff and bosses would be upset and angry. Second, by the reasoning common to public schools, "yes" means that the principal believes that the school and its teachers have the knowledge, training and dedication to turn out accomplished students. And the programs. Schools stress programs.

Is all this valid? Yes. Programs and training are important. Many schools with middling scores do turn out students that attend the best universities.

But this approach has its skeptics. Many parents and educators believe that schools must be judged by their scores, that scores are the true test of quality.

Some parents fear that if their child or children are placed in classes with low-achieving or even middle-achieving children they will not try as hard as they would if their friends or classmates were more academic, or that in some situations their children will be enticed into mischief. In some inner-city districts, the children, for misguided reasons, pressure each other not to do well in school.

Some parents do not believe that a school with many low-scoring students can do justice to its few middle- and high-scoring students. To meet the needs of the majority, instruction might have to be slowed for everyone.

Discipline is another problem. Teachers in low-scoring schools might have to spend more time on problem kids than teachers in high-scoring schools.

There's much more but basically it comes down to the belief that schools do not stand alone, that they and their students are influenced by the values of parents, of classmates and of the immediate neighborhood.

To continue this logic, schools and school districts are different from one another and for this reason it pays to move into a neighborhood with high-scoring schools or one with at least middling-plus scores. Or to somehow secure a transfer to one of the schools in these neighborhoods.

To an unknown extent, the marketplace has reinforced this belief. It rewards neighborhoods and towns with high-scoring schools by increasing the value (the price) of their homes.

Woven into all this is the suspicion, held by many in California, that public schools have failed to dismiss incompetent teachers and have become inflexible and unable to address problems. California for decades has been wracked by arguments over the power of the teachers' union, and over testing and teaching methods, and curriculum.

For the first time in decades, the state in 1999 will have a Democratic governor, a Democratic legislature and a Democratic superintendent of education. Will the arguments disappear? Don't hold your breath.

The parents who seem to do best at this business find out as much as possible about the schools, make decisions or compromises based on good information and work with the schools and teachers to advance their children's interests. Each school should be publishing an "accountability report." Ask for it.

Year-Round Schools

Year-round schools are becoming popular, especially in fast-growing towns, as a way to handle rapidly increasing enrollments. Schedules, called "tracks," vary from district to district but all students attend a full academic year.

Traditional holidays are observed. One group may start in summer, one in late summer and so on. A typical pattern is 12 weeks on, four weeks off. One track is always off, allowing another track to use its class space. Some school districts run a "year-round" program called modified traditional: two months summer vacation, three two-week breaks in the school year.

Families with several children on different tracks are sometimes forced to do quite a bit of juggling for vacation and child care. A new game is being played: how to get the tracks you want. Call your school for information.

Ability Grouping

Ask about the school's advancement or grouping policy or gifted classes.

Without getting into the pros and cons of these practices, schools often tiptoe around them because they upset some parents and frankly because some children have to be slighted. Say the ideal in a middle school is three levels of math: low, middle and high. But funds will allow only two levels. So low is combined with middle or middle with high. If you know the school is making compromises, you might choose to pay for tutoring to bridge the gap.

Miscellaneous

- Because state spending on education was skimped for years, many school districts have asked their voters to approve parcel taxes or bonds, which require two-thirds of the votes cast. Within the last 10 years, many school districts in the county have won approval for at least one construction bond and a few have passed several financial measures. In 1998 voters passed a state bond to spend $9.2 billion on school construction and renovation. Of this, $6.7 billion will go to kindergarten-through-twelfth schools, and $2.9 billion for community colleges and universities. Voters in Year 2000 will decide whether to lower the bond approval cutoff from two-thirds to half.

- Private vs. public. A complex battle, it boils down to one side saying public schools are the best and fairest way to educate all children versus the other side saying public education is inefficient and will never reform until it has meaningful competition. The state is allowing up to 350 schools to restructure their programs according to local needs — an effort at eliminating unnecessary rules. These institutions are called charter schools. Generally, they are found in low-income neighborhoods. Much controversy and conflicting claims over these schools.

- Once tenured, teachers are almost impossible to fire, which opens schools to accusations of coddling incompetents. If your child gets a sour teacher, request a transfer. Better still, become active in the PTA or talk to other parents and try to identify the best teachers. Then ask for them.

- Educational methods. Arguments rage over what will work. In a recent lurch, California schools tilted back to phonics to teach reading.

- New math. A novel approach to teaching math gives students several ways to view problems and to get a "correct" answer. Supporters say it is much more effective than traditional methods. Opponents say that in the guise of boosting self-esteem, the program fails to teach math. Many districts, according to newspapers, mix the two methods.

- Over the past three years, the state Dept. of Education has adopted standards

Community College Transfers

ALTHOUGH PRIMARILY trade schools, community colleges are a major source of students for the University of California and for the California State universities. The students usually take freshman and sophomore classes at a community college, then transfer to a university.

Community colleges are cheap ($39 for average class) and, often, conveniently located. Many community colleges have worked out transfer agreements with local state universities and with the UCs. The data below shows how many students each sector advances.

Tracking All Santa Clara County Students to UCs & CSUs

By High Schools and Community Colleges

Student Sector	Graduates	To UC	To CSU
Public High School	12,739	1,399	1,351
Private High School	1,704	294	292
Community Colleges	NA	824	3,165

By Community College Campus

Community College	To UC	To CSU
De Anza College	394	1,122
Evergreen College	22	335
Foothill College	181	385
Gavilan College	15	185
Mission College	42	272
San Jose City College	36	296
West Valley College	134	570

Source: California Postsecondary Education Commission. **Note**: Enrolling students counted in fall 1998 by UCs and Cal States.

for science, history, math and reading. These standards define what the students are supposed to master at every grade level. Next to come are textbooks that reflect the new standards and after that tests based on the new standards. If students don't pass the tests, they may not be promoted. How much of this will be implemented remains to be seen. Testing is a touchy topic in California.

- Courts and school districts are sorting out Proposition 227, which curtailed non-English instruction in public schools. Parents can request a waiver, which under certain conditions allows instruction in the native language. Some school districts are asking to be exempted from the proposition's requirements.
- In well-to-do neighborhoods and rich towns, parents are informally "taxing" themselves to raise money for schools. If you are new to one of these districts, you might be approached by the parents' group — never the

school — and asked to contribute $100, $200 or $300 per child to the parents' group. Often the money is used to hire aides to help the teachers in the classroom.

- What if you or your neighborhood can't afford voluntary fees? Shop for bargains. Community colleges, in the summer, often run academic programs for children. Local tutors might work with small groups. Specific tutoring, say just in math, might be used to get the student over the rough spots. For information on tutors, look in the Yellow Pages under "Tutoring."
- Busing. School districts can charge and several do. Some low-income and special education kids ride free.
- High school changes. Many have switched to "block" instruction. The traditional six 50-minute classes are replaced by three blocks of 90 minutes.
- Uniforms. Schools have the discretion to require uniforms, an effort to discourage gang colors and get the kids to pay more attention to school than to how they look. "Uniforms" are generally interpreted to mean modest dress; for example, dark pants and shirts for boys, plaid skirts and light blouse for girls.
- Closed campus vs. open campus. The former stops the students from leaving at lunch or at any time during the school day. The latter allows the kids to leave. Kids love open, parents love closed.
- Grad night. Not too many years ago, graduating seniors would whoop it up on grad night and some would drink and then drive and get injured or killed. At many high schools now, parents stage a grad night party at the school, load it with games, raffles and prizes, and lock the kids in until dawn. A lot of work but it keeps the darlings healthy.
- T-P. California tradition. Your son or daughter joins a school team and it wins a few games or the cheerleaders win some prize — any excuse will do — and some parent will drive the kids around and they will fling toilet paper over your house, car, trees and shrubs. Damn nuisance but the kids love it.
- The number of teaching days is being increased, from about 172 to 180 but some of these days are coming at the expense of preparation time for teachers.
- Open Houses, Parents Nights. One study, done at Stanford, concluded that if parents will attend these events, the students, or at least some of them, will be impressed enough to pay more attention to school.
- Magnet Schools. Some school districts, notably San Jose Unified, use magnet or enriched schools to promote integration. With the enriched programs, educators open to draw the students out of neighborhood schools that have too many of one ethnic group and too few of another. For information about magnet programs, contact the school district.

Chapter 5

SANTA CLARA COUNTY
Private Schools

ALTHOUGH PRIVATE SCHOOLS often enjoy a better reputation than public, they are not without problems. The typical private or parochial school is funded way below its public school counterpart. In size, facilities and playing fields, and in programs, public schools usually far outstrip private schools. Private school teachers earn less than public school teachers.

"Typical" has to be emphasized. Some private schools are well-equipped, offer exceptional programs, pay their teachers competitively and limit class sizes to fewer than 15 students. Private schools vary widely in funding.

But even when "typical," private schools enjoy certain advantages over public schools.

The Advantages

Public schools must accept all students, have almost no power to dismiss incompetent teachers and are at the mercy of their neighborhoods for the quality of students — the socioeconomic correlation. The unruly often cannot be expelled or effectively disciplined.

Much has been said about the ability of private schools to rid themselves of problem children and screen them out in the first place. But tuition, even when modest, probably does more than anything else to assure private schools quality students.

Parents who pay extra for their child's education and often agree to work closely with the school are, usually, demanding parents. The result: fewer discipline problems, fewer distractions in the class, more of a willingness to learn.

When you place your child in a good private school, you are, to a large extent, buying him or her scholastic classmates. They may not be the smartest children — many private schools accept children of varying ability — but generally they will have someone at home breathing down their necks to succeed in academics.

The same attitude, a reflection of family values, is found in the high-

Work Can Be Child's Play

At Rainbow Montessori, our work has been child's play for two decades. At our Sunnyvale facility, we take child care and education to a new level.

Programs include computer education & gymnastics, a curriculum from infants to the sixth grade, music, dance, corporate child care programs, hot meals available and much more. Rainbow Montessori is the largest Montessori facility in the Bay Area, located in Sunnyvale, near Lawrence and Central Expressways, Highway 101 & Wolfe. We're currently accepting enrollment for all ages, so call us today for an appointment.

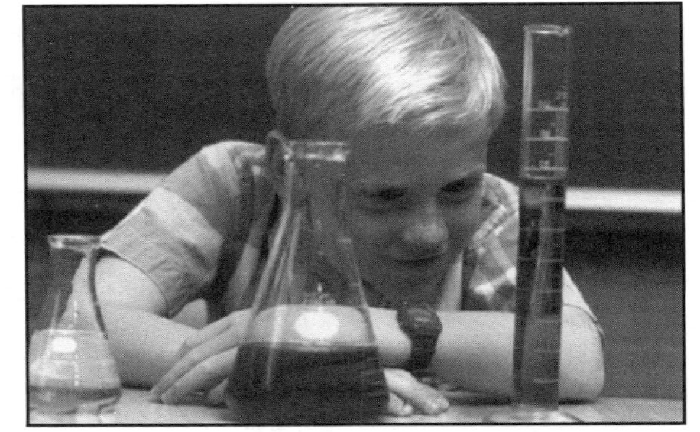

Rainbow Montessori
Child Development Centers
A B C

...Because You Care

Rainbow Montessori

790 E. Duane Ave.
Sunnyvale 408-738-3261

Public Colleges-Univ. Chosen by Private School Graduates

School	UC	CSU	Com	Total
Archbishop Mitty	53	88	63	204
Bellarmine	78	49	28	154
Castilleja	12	0	1	13
Mid-Pen. Ctr.	1	4	10	15
Mtn. View	0	1	5	6
Notre Dame	21	25	18	64
Pinewood	0	0	2	2
Presentation	35	22	13	70
St. Francis	72	42	48	162
St. Lawrence	5	4	14	23
Valley Christian	9	25	59	93

Source: California Dept. of Education. The chart tracks California public colleges or universities, and high school graduates from private schools. It shows how many students from these high schools enrolled as college freshmen in fall 1998. The state does not track graduates enrolling in private colleges or out-of-state colleges. **Key**: UC (University of California), CSU (California State University), Com (community college).

achieving public schools. When a child in one of these schools or a private school turns to his left and right, he will see and later talk to children who read books and newspapers.

A child in a low-achieving school, public or private, will talk to classmates who watch a lot of television and rarely read.

(These are, necessarily, broad generalizations. Much depends on whom a child picks for friends. High-achieving students certainly watch television but, studies show, much less than low-achieving students. Many critics contend that even high-scoring schools are graduating students poorly prepared for college.)

The Quality of Teaching

Do private schools have better teachers than public schools? Impossible to tell. Both sectors sing the praises of their teachers.

Private schools, compared to public, have much more freedom to dismiss teachers but this can be abused. The private schools themselves advise parents to avoid schools with excessive teacher turnover.

Although most can't pay as much as public schools, private institutions claim to attract people fed up with the limitations of public schools, particularly restrictions on disciplining and ejecting unruly children. Some proponents argue that private schools attract teachers "who really want to teach."

Religion and Private Schools

Some private schools are as secular as any public institution. But many are religious-oriented and talk in depth about religion or ethics, or teach a specific creed. Or possibly they teach values within a framework of western civilization or some other philosophy.

(Continued on Page 99)

A Profile of Catholic Schools

THE LARGEST PRIVATE school system in Santa Clara County, Catholic schools enroll 16,057 students. The following information is based on interviews with Catholic educators and reviewed by San Jose diocese. Data from 1997-98 school year.

- Statistics. 28 elementary schools, one kindergarten, six high schools.

  "The Catholic community values Catholic education, and they want it," according to a Catholic education administrator.

- All races, creeds welcome. Where schools are full, preference is given first to Catholic children from families active in parish. After that, to active Catholics unable to get into own parish schools.

  High schools recruit regionally for students. Admissions and placement tests but all accept average students. Standards vary by school. Recommendations by parish pastors, principals, eighth-grade teachers carry clout.

- Non-Catholic students for both elementary and secondary schools total 2,482 or 15 percent of system.

  Ethnic breakdown elementary: Asian, 7 percent ; Af. American, 2; Filipino, 12; Hispanic, 18; Causasian, 59 (percentages rounded).

  Ethnic breakdown secondary: Asian, 9 percent; Af. American, 3; Filipino, 7; Hispanic, 12; Causasian, 63 percent.

- Why parents send kids to Catholic schools. A survey: 1. Religious tradition, moral and spiritual values. 2. Academics. 3. Discipline.

- Curriculum. Elementary schools cover same basic subjects as public schools but weave in religious-moral viewpoint. "Philosophy based in Jesus Christ. Religious values are integral to learning experience." State textbooks often used. Each school picks texts from list approved by diocese. High school instruction, although varied, is greatly influenced by requirements of University of California. Strong emphasis on technology in elementary and secondary schools.

  Educators advise parents to approach high schools as they would any educational institution: ask about grades, what percentage of students go on to college.

- Non-Catholics. Get same instruction as Catholics, including history of Church and scripture. Attend Mass but not required to take sacraments. "We don't try to convert them," said one nun.

(Continued on Next Page)

Catholic Schools

(Continued from Previous Page)

- Corporal punishment. Thing of past. More aware now of child abuse. Stress positive discipline, name on board, detention, probation. Try to work problems through, few expulsions.
- Class sizes. Before 40, now 30 to 32. Somewhat smaller for high schools because of special classes, e.g. French.

  Would like smaller but point out that with well-behaved students, teachers can accomplish a lot. Matter of economics. If parents wanted smaller classes, they would have to pay more. "We want to keep affordable prices so all people can choose us, not just rich."
- Tuition. See directory of private schools at the end of this chapter.
- Schedule. Similar to public schools. 180 teaching days, minimum of five hours, 10 minutes a day. Many go longer.
- Ability grouping. In elementary grades (K-8) not done by class. Grouping within classes, advanced children working at one level, slow children at another. Tutoring after class. "You're not going to walk in and find 35 children on the same page."

  All high schools run prep programs, tend to attract prep students, but will accept remedial students, if they have remedial instruction. Admission standards vary by high school.
- Homework. Each school sets policy but diocese suggests guidelines: Grades one and two, 20 minutes; three and four, 30-45 minutes; five and six, 45 to 60 minutes; seven and eight, 60-90 minutes. None on weekends and vacations. High schools require more homework, may assign on weekends and holidays. Teacher's choice.
- Report cards. Four a year plus results of diocesan tests. Parents are expected to attend conferences, back-to-school nights.
- Teacher quality. Bachelor's degree required. Most credentialed. Hired for competence, commitment to Catholic educational philosophy. A few non-Catholic teachers but system tends to attract Catholic educators.
- Uniforms. Yes. Generally plaid skirts, blouses and sweaters for girls, collared shirts, sweaters and cords for boys.
- Extended care. Most schools offer before- and after-school care, 7 a.m. to 6 p.m. Ask.

(Continued on Next Page)

***CATHOLIC SCHOOLS** (Continued from Previous Page)*

- Drugs. "Not major problem but when it happens we do everything to work with student."
- Extracurricular activities. Although campuses small, schools try to offer variety of activities, sports, arts, music. At elementary school, much depends on work of parents. "Parents are expected to do a lot." High schools offer good variety: music, band, arts, intramural sports, many club activities, computers, science. Catholic high schools usually field very competitive football and basketball teams.
- For more information, admissions, call school directly. Most registrations in spring but earlier for high schools. Waiting list for many primary grades. Education office at diocese, (408) 983-0185.

(Continued from Page 96)

Until recently public schools almost never talked about religion or religious figures. They now teach the history of major religions and the basic tenets of each, and they try to inculcate in the children a respect for all religions.

It's hard, if not impossible, however, for public schools to talk about values within a framework of religion or a system of ethics. Often, it's difficult for them to talk about values. Some people argue that this is a major failing.

Many religious schools accept students of different religions or no religion. Some schools offer these students broad courses in religion — less dogma. Ask about the program.

Money

Private-school parents pay taxes for public schools and they pay tuition. Public-school parents pay taxes but not tuition. Big difference.

Ethnic Diversity

Many private schools are integrated and the great majority of private-school principals — the editor knows no exceptions — welcome minorities. Some principals fret over tuition, believing that it keeps many poor students out of private schools.

Money, the lack of it, weighs heavily on private schools. Scholarships, however, are awarded, adjustments made, family rates offered. Ask.

What's in Santa Clara County

Santa Clara County has more than 100 private schools. Here is a brief overview:

Many are one-family schools, mother and father teaching their own

UCs Chosen by Private School Graduates

School	Berk	Davis	Irv	UCLA	Riv	SD	SB	SC	Total
Archbishop Mitty	4	11	7	5	1	4	14	7	53
Bellarmine	19	9	5	13	5	11	9	8	79
Castilleja	3	1	0	4	0	2	0	2	12
Mid-Pen. Ctr.	0	0	0	0	0	0	0	1	1
Mtn. View	0	0	0	0	0	0	0	0	0
Notre Dame	5	1	2	4	4	0	0	5	21
Pinewood	0	0	0	0	0	0	0	0	0
Presentation	6	11	0	7	2	2	6	1	35
St. Francis	10	10	8	12	1	12	13	8	74
St. Lawrence	0	3	1	1	0	0	0	0	5
Valley Christian	1	0	0	0	1	3	1	3	9

Source: Calif. Dept. of Education. The chart tracks Universities of California and high school graduates from private schools. It shows how many students from these schools enrolled as UC freshmen in fall 1998. The state does not track graduates enrolling in private colleges or out-of-state colleges. **Key**: Berk (Berkeley), Irv (Irvine), SD (San Diego), SB (Santa Barbara), Riv (Riverside), SC (Santa Cruz).

children at home. A support network that supplies books and materials has grown up for these people.

Some regular private schools have low teacher-pupil ratios, fewer than 15 students per teacher, occasionally around 10 to 1. Public school classes usually go 25 to 30 per teacher, sometimes higher (new funding has reduced sizes in grades 1-3). Class sizes in Catholic schools, in the upper grades, run close to the public-school ratio, and in some schools higher. Catholic schools, nonetheless, are the most popular, a reflection in part of the high number of Catholics in Santa Clara County. Some Catholic schools have waiting lists.

Private schools in Santa Clara County come in great variety, Christian, Jewish, Montessori, Carden (schools with different teaching approaches), prep schools, schools that emphasize language or music, boarding and day schools, schools that allow informal dress, schools that require uniforms.

Choosing a Private School

1. Inspect the grounds, the school's buildings, ask plenty of questions. "I would make myself a real pest," advised one private school official. The good schools welcome this kind of attention.

2. Choose a school with a philosophy congenial to your own, and your child's. Carden schools emphasize structure. Montessori schools, while somewhat structured, encourage individual initiative and independence.

   Ask whether the school is accredited. Private schools are free to run almost any program they like, to set any standards they like, which may sound enticing but in some aspects might hurt the schools. A few bad ones spoil the reputation of the good.

   To remedy this, many private schools sign up for inspections by independent agencies, such as the Western Association of Schools and Colleges and the California Association of Independent Schools. These agencies try to make sure that schools meet their own goals. Some good schools do not seek accreditation.

3. Get all details about tuition carefully explained. How is it to be paid? Are there extra fees? Book costs? Is there a refund if the student is withdrawn or dropped from the school?
4. Progress reports. Parent conferences. How often are they scheduled?
5. What are the entrance requirements? When must they be met? Although many schools use entrance tests, often they are employed to place the child in an academic program, not exclude him from the school.
6. For prep schools, what percentage of the students go on to college and to what colleges?
7. How are discipline problems handled?
8. What are the teacher qualifications? What is the teacher turnover rate?
9. How sound financially is the school? How long has it been in existence? There is nothing wrong inherently with new schools. But you want a school that has the wherewithal to do the job.
10. Do parents have to work at school functions? Are they required to "volunteer"?
11. Don't choose in haste but don't wait until the last minute. Some schools fill quickly, some fill certain classes quickly. If you can, call the school the year before your child is to enter, early in the year.
12. Don't assume that because your child attends a private school you can expect everything will go all right, that neither the school nor the student needs your attention. The quality of private schools in California varies widely.

Susan Vogel has written "Private High Schools of the San Francisco Bay Area." (1999) Well researched. Comprehensive. Check with bookstores or call (415) 267-5978.

Directory of Private Schools

The directory contains the most current information available at press time but it may not include all the private school offerings. Some institutions mix day care with, say, a kindergarten program and come under the vague category of day care-private school. Consult the local phone directory.

In California, tuition ranges widely in private schools. Many Catholic elementaries charge from about $2,000 to $2,800. Some nondenominational schools go as high as $10,000. High schools range from $5,000 to $12,000, with the Catholic schools running from $5,000-$6,000 (plus fees and books).

Discounts are often given for siblings. If strapped, ask about financial help. Many schools offer family rates. Religious schools often charge more for nonmembers. Day care costs extra.

Campbell

Campbell Christian, 1075 W. Campbell Ave., (408) 374-7260, Enroll: 165, K-6.

Covenant Life Acad., 1300 Sheffield Ave., (408) 371-5141, Enroll: 64, K-8th.

Old Orchard Elem., 400 W. Campbell Ave., (408) 378-5935, Enroll: 212, K-8.

Pioneer Family Acad., 1799 S. Winchester Blvd. #100, (408) 265-4386, Enroll: 236, K-12th.

Primary Plus, 1125 W. Campbell Ave., (408) 379-3184, Enroll: 65, K-2nd.

San Jose Christian, 1300 Sheffield Ave., (408) 371-7741, Enroll: 210, K-8th.

St. Lucy's, 76 E. Kennedy Ave., (408) 378-7454, Enroll: 319, K-8th.

W. Valley Seventh-Day Adventist Elem., 95 Dot Ave., (408) 378-4327, Enroll: 116, K-8th.

Cupertino

Bethel Lutheran Elem., 10181 Finch Ave., (408) 252-8512, Enroll: 106, K-4.

Lutheran Sch. of Our Savior, 5825 Bollinger Rd., (408) 252-0250, Enroll: 105, K-8th.

Monarch Christian School Inc., 1196 Lime Dr., (408) 773-8543, Enroll: 122, K-4th.

One World Montessori, 20220 Suisun Dr., (408) 255-3770, Enroll: 85, K-6th.

St. Joseph of Cupertino, 10120 N. DeAnza Blvd., (408) 252-6441, Enroll: 318, K-8th.

Gilroy

Cornerstone Christian, 8457 Wren Ave., (408) 848-5895, Enroll: 87, K-12th.

Gavilan Hills Acad., 2080 Pacheco Pass Rd., (408) 842-7455, Enroll: 44, K-12.

Pacific West Christian Acad., 1575 Mantelli Dr., (408) 847-7922, Enroll: 180, K-6th.

St. Mary's, 7900 Church St., (408) 842-2827, Enroll: 309, K-8th.

Los Altos

Canterbury Christian Elem., 101 N. El Monte Ave., (650) 949-0909, Enroll: 104, K-6th.

Los Altos Christian, 625 Magdalena Ave., (650) 948-3738, Enroll: 232, K-6th.

Miramonte Elem., 1175 Altamead Dr., (650) 967-2783, Enroll: 179, K-8th.

Morgan Ctr., 201 Covington Rd., (650) 948-6834, Enroll: 48, Ungraded.

Pinewood Pvt. Sch. of Los Altos, 327 Fremont Ave., (650) 948-5438, Enroll: 175, 3rd-6th.

Pinewood Pvt. Sch.-Lower Campus, 477 Fremont Ave., (650) 941-2828, Enroll: 140, K-2nd.

St. Simon Elem., 1840 Grant Rd., (650) 968-9952, Enroll: 611, K-8th.

Waldorf Sch. of the Peninsula, 11311 Mora Dr., (650) 948-8433, Enroll: 216, K-8th.

Los Altos Hills

Pinewood Pvt.School of Fremont Hills, 26800 Fremont Rd., (650) 941-1532, Enroll: 311, 7th-12th.

St. Nicholas Elem., 12816 S. El Monte Ave., (650) 941-4056, Enroll: 285, K-8.

Los Gatos

Hillbrook, Marchmont Dr. at Englewood St., (408) 356-6116, Enroll: 256, K-8th.

Los Gatos Acad., 220 Belgatos Rd., (408) 358-1046, Enroll: 96, K-12th.

Los Gatos Christian, 16845 Hicks Rd., (408) 268-1502, Enroll: 541, K-8th.

St. Mary's Elem., 30 Lyndon Ave., (408) 354-3944, Enroll: 282, 1st-8th.

Valley Christian Elem., 220 Kensington Way, (408) 559-4400, Enroll: 401, K-5.

Yavneh Day, 14855 Oka Rd., (408) 358-3413, Enroll: 130, K-5th.

Milpitas

Milpitas Foothill Seventh-Day Adventist, 1991 Landess Ave., (408) 263-2568, Enroll: 131, K-8th.

Rainbow Bridge Ctr., 1500 Yosemite Dr., (408) 945-9090, Enroll: 363, K-8th.

St. John the Baptist Catholic, 360 S. Abel St., (408) 262-8110, Enroll: 305, K-8th.

Morgan Hill

Bridge Acad., 16131 Condit Rd., (408) 776-3340, Enroll: 81, 1st-12th.

South Valley Christian Elem., 145 Wright Ave., (408) 779-8850, Enroll: 291, K-8th.

St. Catherine Elem., 17500 S. Peak Ave., (408) 779-9950, Enroll: 306, K-8th.

Mountain View

Mountain View Acad., 360 S. Shoreline Blvd., (650) 967-2324, Enroll: 130, 9th-12th.

Southbay Christian, 1134 Miramonte Ave., (650) 961-9485, Enroll: 395, K-8th.

St. Francis High, 1885 Miramonte Ave., (650) 968-1213, Enroll: 1,454, 9th-12th.

St. Joseph's Elem., 1120 Miramonte Ave., (650) 967-1839, Enroll: 288, K-8th.

Palo Alto

Ananda Sch. on the Peninsula, 2171 El Camino Real, (650) 917-1140, Enroll: 50, Pre-8th.

Castilleja High, 1310 Bryant St., (650) 328-3160, Enroll: 385, 6th-12th.

Children's Int'l, 4000 Middlefield Rd., (650) 813-9131, Enroll: 60, K-5th.

Heads Up Elem., 445 E. Charleston Rd., (650) 424-1155, Enroll: 45, K-6th.

Int'l Sch. of the Peninsula, 3233 Cowper St., (650) 852-0264, Enroll: 318, K-7th.

Keys, 2890 Middlefield Rd., (650) 328-1711, Enroll: 176, K- 8th.

Mid-Peninsula Ed. Ctr., 870 N. California Ave., (650) 493-5910, Enroll: 121, 9th-12th.

Mid-Peninsula Jewish Comm. Day, 655 Arastradero Rd., (650) 424-8482, Enroll: 156, K-5th.

Palo Alto Prep., 4000 Middlefield Rd., (650) 493-7071, Enroll: 52, 8th-12th.

St. Elizabeth Seton Catholic Comm., 1095 Channing Ave., (650) 326-9004, Enroll: 228, K-8th.

Stanford Chinese, 2347 Williams St., (650) 813-1720, Enroll: 165, K-5th.

San Jose

Achiever Christian, 820 Ironwood Dr., (408) 264-6789, Enroll: 449, K-6th.

Almaden Country, 6835 Trinidad Dr., (408) 997-0424, Enroll: 361, K-8th.

Almaden Valley Christian, 6291 Vegas Dr., (408) 997-0290, Enroll: 44, K-12th.

Apostles Lutheran Elem., 5828 Santa Teresa Blvd., (408) 578-4800, Enroll: 194, K-8th.

Archbishop Mitty High, 5000 Mitty Ave., (408) 252-6610, Enroll: 1,428, 9th-12th.

Beacon, 5670 Camden Ave., (480) 265-8611, Enroll: 39, 5th-12th.

Bellarmine College Prep., 850 Elm St., (408) 294-9224, Enroll: 1,369, 9th-12th.

Casa Di Mir Montessori Elem., 220 Belgatos Rd., (408) 866-7758, Enroll: 53, 1st-6th.

Challenger, 2845 Meridian Ave., (408) 723-0111, Enroll: 408, K-8th.

Challenger, 880 Wren Dr., (408) 448-3010, Enroll: 205, K-5th.

Christ the King Acad., 2530 Berryessa Rd., (408) 298-2969, 114, K-12th.

Christian Comm. Acad., 1523 McLaughlin Ave., (408) 279-0846, Enroll: 285, K-12th.

De Young, 3001 Ross Ave. #3, (408) 445-2760, Enroll: 50, K-12th.

East Hills, 30 Kirk Ave., (408) 258-6595, Enroll: 30, K-3rd.

E. Valley Christian Sch., 2715 S. White Rd., (408) 274-6644, Enroll: 131, K-12th.

Excel Lrng. Ctr., 3278 Noble Ave., (408) 929-5617, Enroll: 31, 1st-8th.

Five Wounds Elem., 1390 Five Wounds Ln., (408) 293-0425, Enroll: 266, K-8.

For His Joy Christian, 228 Purple Glen Dr., (408) 578-9289, Enroll: 29, K-12th.

Gateway Acad., 3001 Ross Ave., (408) 264-1974, Enroll: 26, K-12.

Grace Ed. Ctr., 1228 Redmond Ave., (408) 997-7888, Enroll: 53, K-8th.

SAN JOSE (Continued)

Harker, 4300 Bucknall Rd., (408) 871-4600, Enroll: 498, K-4th. **See ad next page.**

Harker, 500 Saratoga Ave., (408) 249-2510, Enroll: 600, 5th-12th. **See ad next page.**

Holy Family Ed. Ctr., 4850 Pearl Ave., (408) 978-1355, Enroll: 607, K-8th.

Language Two Acad., 5965 Almaden Expressway, (408) 268-7361, Enroll: 40, K-8th.

Learning Acad., 5670 Camden Ave., (408) 723-1131, Enroll: 144, K-7th.

Liberty Baptist, 2790 S. King Rd., (408) 274-5613, Enroll: 483, K-12th.

Little Scholars, 3703 Silver Creek Rd., (408) 238-2500, Enroll: 66, K-4th.

Milpitas Christian, 3435 Birchwood Ln., (408) 945-6530, Enroll: 739, K-8th.

Montessori Acad., 1188 Wunderlich Drive, (408) 255-4710, Enroll: 30, K.

Montessori Acad., 495 Masser Ave., (408) 259-5736, Enroll: 30, K-1st.

Most Holy Trinity Elem., 1940 Cunningham Ave., (408) 729-3431, Enroll: 299, K-8th.

Mulberry, 1980 Hamilton Ave., (408) 377-1595, Enroll: 102, K-5th.

Notre Dame High, 596 S. Second St., (408) 294-1113, Enroll: 491, 9th-12th.

Olive Tree , 4586 Shadowhurst Ct., (408) 265-3621, Enroll: 63, K-12th.

Piedmont Hills Montessori, 1425 Old Piedmont Rd., (408) 923-5151, Enroll: 38, K-1st.

Piedmont Hills Montessori, 2995 Edison Dr., (408) 923-5151, Enroll: 34, K-4th.

Pine Hill, 1718 Andover Ln., (408) 978-7120, Enroll: 29, 1st-12th.

Pine Hill School, 1975 Cambrianna Dr., (408) 371-5881, Enroll: 48, 1st-12th.

Plantation Christian, 209 Herlong Ave., (408) 972-8211, Enroll: 137, 1st-12th.

Presentation High, 2281 Plummer Ave., (408) 264-1664, Enroll: 696, 9th-12th.

Primary Plus, 3500 Amber Dr., (408) 248-2464, Enroll: 385, K-8th.

Queen of Apostles Elem., 4950 Mitty Way, (408) 252-3659, Enroll: 302, K-8.

Rainbow Bridge Ctr., 750 N. Capitol Ave., (408) 254-1280, Enroll: 263, K-4.

San Jose Comm. Christian, 480 S. McCreery Ave., (408) 729-9300, Enroll: 47, K-12th.

South Valley Carden, 1921 Clarinda Way, (408) 879-1000, Enroll: 246, K-8th.

St. Christopher Elem., 2278 Booksin Ave., (408) 723-7223, Enroll: 626, K-8.

St. Elizabeth Day Home, 1544 McKinley Ave., (408) 295-3456, Enroll: 28, K.

St. Frances Cabrini, 15325 Woodard Rd., (408) 377-6545, Enroll: 672, K-8th.

St. John Vianney, 4601 Hyland Ave., (408) 258-7677, Enroll: 624, K-8th.

St. Leo the Great, 1051 W. San Fernando St., (408) 293-4846, Enroll: 298, K-8th.

St. Martin of Tours Elem., 300 O'Connor Dr., (408) 287-3630, Enroll: 362, K-8th.

St. Patrick Elem., 51 N. Ninth St., (408) 283-5858, Enroll: 314, K-8th.

St. Stephen's Elem., 500 Shawnee Ln., (408) 365-2927, Enroll: 217, K-6th.

St. Thomas More, 12000 Berryessa Rd., (408) 453-6086, Enroll: 133, K-12th.

St. Timothy's Lutheran, 5100 Camden Ave., (408) 265-0244, Enroll: 150, K-5.

St. Victor Elem., 3150 Sierra Rd., (408) 251-1740, Enroll: 316, K-8th.

Tower Acad., 2887 McLaughlin Ave., (408) 578-2830, Enroll: 85, K-4th.

Valley Christian High, 1570 Branham Ln., (408) 978-9950, Enroll: 772, 9th-12th.

Valley Christian Jr. High, 1570 Branham Ln., (408) 978-9830, Enroll: 333, 6-8th.

White Rd. Baptist Acad., 480 S. White Rd., (408) 272-7713, Enroll: 69, K-12.

Santa Clara

Adventures in Lrng., 890 Pomeroy Ave., (408) 247-4769, Enroll: 51, K-6th.

Carden El Encanto Day, 615 Hobart Ter., (408) 244-5041, Enroll: 432, K-8th.

Delphi Acad. of S.F. Bay, 890 Pomeroy Ave., (408) 260-2300, Enroll: 70, K-8th.

Granada Islamic, 3003 Scott Blvd., (408) 980-1161, Enroll: 300, K-8th.

Neighborhood Christian, 1290 Pomeroy Ave., (408) 241-8837, Enroll: 91, K-6th.

New Covenant Christian, 220 Blake Ave. #A, (408) 249-3993, Enroll: 67, K-5th.

Our Lady of Peace, 2800 Mission College Blvd., (408) 988-4160, Enroll: 40, K.

Pioneer Montessori, 400 N. Winchester Blvd., (408) 241-5077, Enroll: 101, K-6th.

Santa Clara Christian, 3421 Monroe St., (408) 246-5423, Enroll: 80, K-4th.

Sierra Elem. & High, 220 Blake Ave., (408) 247-4740, Enroll: 122, K-12th.

St. Clare Elem., 725 Washington St., (408) 246-6797, Enroll: 288, K-8th.

St. Justin's, 2655 Homestead Rd., (408) 248-1094, Enroll: 309, K-8th.

St. Lawrence Acad., 2000 Lawrence Ct., (408) 296-3013, Enroll: 321, 9th-12th.

St. Lawrence Elem. & Middle, 1977 St. Lawrence Dr., (408) 296-2260, Enroll: 419, K-8th.

Stanbridge Acad., 890 Pomeroy Ave., (408) 261-6610, Enroll: 77, K-12th.

Tican Institute, 220 Blake Ave., No. D, (408) 554-8787, Enroll: 51, K-6th.

Saratoga

Challenger, 18811 Cox Ave., (408) 378-0444, Enroll: 57, K.

Primary Plus, 18720 Bucknall Rd., (408) 370-0357, Enroll: 48, K-2nd.

Sacred Heart Elem., 13718 Saratoga Ave., (408) 867-9241, Enroll: 300, K-8.

St. Andrews , 13601 Saratoga Ave., (408) 867-3785, Enroll: 406, K-8th.

Sunnyvale

Challenger, 1185 Hollenbeck Ave., (408) 245-7170, Enroll: 513, K-8th.

French, 1510 Lewiston Dr., (408) 746-0460, Enroll: 82, K-4th.

Jubilee Acad., 560 Britton Ave., (408) 730-4777, Enroll: 31, K-3rd.

King's Acad., 562 N. Britton Ave., (408) 481-9900, Enroll: 536, 6th-12th.

Rainbow Montessori Child Dev. Ctr., 790 E. Duane Ave., (408) 738-3261, Enroll: 307, K-6th. **See ad on page 97.**

Resurrection Elem., 1395 Hollenbeck Ave., (408) 245-4571, Enroll: 264, K-8th.

S. Peninsula Hebrew Day , 1030 Astoria Dr., (408) 738-3060, Enroll: 243, K-8th.

St. Cyprian, 195 Leota Ave., (408) 738-3444, Enroll: 263, K-8th.

St. Martin's Elem., 597 Central Ave., (408) 736-5534, Enroll: 305, K-8th.

Sunnyvale Christian, 445 S. Mary Ave., (408) 736-3286, Enroll: 105, K-5th.

Chapter 6

SANTA CLARA COUNTY
Baby Care

FOR LICENSING, CALIFORNIA divides child-care facilities into several categories:

- Small family: up to 6 children in the providers's home.
- Large family: 7-12 children in the provider's home.
- Nursery schools or child-care centers.

A child is considered an infant from birth to age 2. No category at this time has been established for toddler.

Individual sitters are not licensed and neither are people whom parents arrange for informally to take care of their children but if a person is clearly in the business of child care from more than one family he or she should be licensed. Each of the three categories has certain restrictions. For example, the small-family provider with six children cannot have more than three under the age of 2.

In everyday reality, many of the larger facilities tend to limit enrollments to children over age 2, and some have even higher age limits.

The state and its local umbrella agencies maintain referral lists of local infant and day-care providers. All you have to do is call and they will send a list of the licensed providers and suggestions on how to make a wise choice.

The names of the agencies and their numbers are:

4 Cs Community Coordinated Child Care Development Council of Santa Clara County, Inc., 111 East Gish Rd., San Jose 95112. (408) 487-0747.

Community Coordinated Child Development Council of San Mateo County, Inc., 700 S. Claremont, No. 107, San Mateo. (650) 696-8787.

Here's some advice from one licensing agency:

- Plan ahead. Give yourself one month for searching and screening.
- Contact the appropriate agencies for referrals.
- Once you have identified potential caregivers, phone them to find out

about their services and policies. For those that meet your needs, schedule a time to visit while children are present.

- At the site, watch how the children play and interact with one another.
- Contact other parents using the programs. Ask if they are satisfied with the care and if their children are happy and well-cared-for.
- Select the program that best meets your needs. "Trust your feelings and your instincts."

This is a bare-bones approach. The referral centers can supply you with more information.

To get you started, we are listing here the names of the infant centers in the county. For the older children, please refer to the directory in the following chapter.

The infant centers:

Campbell

A Special Place-Camden, 1260 Erin Way, (408) 559-1566

Executive Sweet, 2323 S. Bascom Ave., (408) 559-6090

Kids at Play Presch., 124 Latimer, (408) 370-3745

Kinder Care Learning Ctr., 1806 W. Campbell, (408) 379-8152

Kinderwood Children's Ctr. #2, 1190 W. Latimer, (408) 374-4442

Noah's Ark, 560 N. Harrison Ave., (408) 378-3212

Primary Plus, 1125 W. Campbell Ave., (408) 248-2464 or 379-3198

Cupertino

Bright Horizons, 10253 Portal Ave., (408) 366-1963

Good Samaritan, 19624 Homestead Rd., (408) 996-8290

Gilroy

Countryside DCCtr., 8985 Monterey Rd., (408) 848-3448 or 848-3444

Gavilan College CD Lab, 5055 Santa Teresa Blvd., (408) 848-4815 or 848-4814

Goldsmith Seeds Ctr., 2280 Hecker Pass Hwy., (408) 847-7333

Happy Place Montessori, 7360 & 7350 Alexander St., (408) 848-3819

Ochoa Infant Migrant CDCtr., 915 Southside Dr., (408) 842-5066

Los Altos Hills

Foothill College Campus CCtr., 12345 El Monte Rd., (415) 941-7500 or 650-949-7500

Los Altos

Baby World, 1715 Grant Rd., (415) 988-8627

Early Horizons, 201 Covington Rd., (415) 941-2548

Pebbles, 211 Covington Rd., (650) 435-8823

Los Gatos

Addison Penzak Jewish Comm. Ctr., 14855 Oka Rd., Rm. 25, (408) 358-3636 or 358-1874

Kiddie Kampus DCCtr., 16330 Los Gatos Blvd., (408) 356-6776

Milpitas

Bright Beginnings, 1331 E. Calaveras Blvd., (408) 744-9280

Children's World, 860 Hillview Rd., (408) 263-0444

KinderCare Lrng. Ctr., 400 S Abel St., (408) 263-7212

Rainbow Bridge Ctr., 1500 Yosemite Dr., (408) 945-9090

Moffett Field

Ames CCCtr., Bldg. T20-D, (650) 604-4184

Morgan Hill

KinderCare Lrng. Ctr. , 605 E. Dunne Ave., (408) 778-1237

Linda's Place DC, 17535 Del Monte, (408) 779-7678

MORGAN HILL (CONTINUED)

Young Explorer, 25 Wright Ave., (408) 778-2529

Mountain View

Kiddie Acad. CC Lrng. Ctr., 205 E. Middlefield Rd., (650) 960-6900

Kidstown CDCtr., 180 N. Rengstorff, (650) 964-5006

KinderCare, 2065 W. El Camino Real, (650) 967-4430

Primary Plus, 333 Eunice Ave., (408) 967-3780

Walnut Grove CCtr., 84 Murlagan Ave., (650) 858-1601

Palo Alto

Children's Presch., 4000 Middlefield, T-1, (650) 855-5770

Covenant Children's Ctr., 670 E. Meadow Dr., (650) 493-9505

Good Neighbor Montessori, 4000 Middlefield Rd., (415) 493-2777

Headsup CDCtr., 4251 El Camino Real, Bldg. A, (650) 424-1221

Learning Ctr., 459 Kingsley, (415) 325-6683

Lilliput Infant Toddler Ctr., 3789 Park Blvd., (415) 857-1736

Mini Infant Ctr., 3149 Waverly St., (650) 424-9170

Neighborhhod Infant Toddler Ctr., 311 N. California Ave., (415) 321-3493

Palo Alto Infant Toddler Ctr., 4111 Alma St., (650) 493-2240

Sojourner Truth CDCtr., 3990 Ventura Ct., (415) 493-5990

Whistle Stop, 3801 Miranda Ave., #T6B, (650) 852-3497

San Jose

A Special Place-Williamsburg, 3124 Williamsburg Dr., (408) 374-4980

Action Day Nursery, 3000 Moorpark Ave., (408) 247-6972

Atypical Infant Motivation, 4115 Jacksol Dr., (408) 559-1400

Bright Horizons, 6120 Liska Ln., (408) 225-3276

Center for Employment Training-DCCtr., 701 Vine St., (408) 295-4566

CET Montessori, 1212 McGinness, (408) 929-4627

Children's Presch. Ctr.- Evergreen, 3403 Yerba Buena Rd., (408) 239-2633

Cory CDCtr., 897 Broadleaf Ln., (408) 296-5975 or 247-3938

Early Lrng. Ctr., 921 Fox Ln., (408) 944-0395

Emmanuel's CDCtr., 467 N. White Rd., (408) 272-9310

ESO CDCtr., 2055 Summerside Dr., (408) 971-0888

Familiar Footsteps, 301 Cottle Rd., (408) 225-0289

Future Assests CD, 7245 Sharon Dr., (408) 252-0203

Gardner Presch., 502 Illinois Ave., (408) 535-6083

Good Samaritan Hospital CDCtr., 2425 Samaritan Dr., (408) 264-1275

Headsup CDCtr., 2841 Junction Ave., (408) 424-1155

KinderCare Lrng. Ctr., 3320 San Felipe Rd., (408) 270-0980

KinderCare Lrng. Ctr.-Foxworthy, 1081 Foxworthy Ave., (408) 265-7380

Kinderwood Childrens Ctr., 5560 Entrada Cedros, (408) 363-1366

Montessori Acad., 1188 Wunderlich Dr., (408) 255-4710 or 2521488

Neighborhood Christian Presch., 2575 Coit Dr., (408) 371-4222

One World Montessori Sch., 5331 Dent Ave., (408) 723-5140 or 255-3770

Primary Plus, 801 Hibiscus Ln., (408) 248-2464

Rainbow Bridge Ctr., 750 N. Capitol Ave., (408) 254-1280

San Jose Day Nursery, 33 N. 8th St., (408) 295-2752 or 288-9667

San Jose Job Corps, 3485 East Hills Dr., (408) 923-1200 or 937-3276

San Juan Bautista CDCtr., 1945 Terilyn Ave., (408) 259-4796

Santa Teresa Village CDCtr., 7026 Santa Teresa Blvd., (408) 225-5437

St. Elizabeth's Day Home, 1544 McKinley Ave., (408) 295-3456

Tamian CCCtr., 1197 Lick Ave., (408) 271-1980

TLC Child Care Ctr., 2466 Almaden Rd., (408) 264-3707

Trinity Presbyterian CCtr., 3151 Union Ave., (408) 377-2342 or 377-8930

Valley Medical Ctr., 730 Empey Way, (408) 297-9044

Santa Clara County Births — History & Projections

Year	Births	Year	Births	Year	Births
1978	19,827	1988	26,274	1998	26,133
1979	19,827	1989	26,805	1999	26,218
1980	21,299	1990	28,080	2000	26,357
1981	21,902	1991	27,881	2001	26,520
1982	22,538	1992	27,481	2002	26,770
1983	22,698	1993	26,975	2003	27,000
1984	23,681	1994	26,639	2004	27,264
1985	24,110	1995	25,983	2005	27,577
1986	24,400	1996	26,646	2006	28,028
1987	24,518	1997	26,416	2007	28,600

Source: California Dept. of Finance, Demographic Research Unit.Projections start in 1997.

Voyager's DCCtr., 1590 Las Plumas Ave., (408) 926-8885

Wonder Years, 1411 Piedmont Rd., (408) 926-1234

YWCA-Eden Palms CCCtr., 5398 Monterey Rd., (408) 227-9858

YWCA-Villa Nueva, 375 S. 3rd St., (408) 295-4011

Santa Clara

Beautiful Beginnings Presch., 890 Pomeroy, (408) 247-4234

Happy Days CDCtr., 220 Blake Ave., (408) 296-5770

Kinder Care Lrng. Ctr., 840 Bing Dr., (408) 246-2141

MCA Granada Islamic Sch., 3003 Scott Blvd., (408) 980-1161

One World Montessori Sch., 2495 Cabrillo Ave., (408) 615-1254

YMCA-Millikin, 2720 Sonoma Pl., (408) 243-6577

Saratoga

My Preschool, 1472 Saratoga Ave., (408) 376-0385

Next Generation CDCtr., 19010 Austin Way, (408) 927-7250 or 395-4290

Primary Plus, 18720 Bucknall Rd., (408) 370-0357

Stanford

Children's Ctr. of Stanford, 695 Pampas Ln., (650) 853-3090

Stanford Arboretum, 211 Quarry Rd., (650) 725-6322

Sunnyvale

Calif. Young World #5, 1110 Fairwood Ave., (408) 245-7285

Caring Hearts CDCtr., 645 W. Fremont Ave., (408) 245-6356

Children's Creative Lrng. Ctr., 794 E. Duane Ave., (408) 732-2288

DeLor Montessori Sch., 1510 Lewiston Dr., (408) 773-0200 or 729-8809

Early Horizons, 1510 Lewiston Dr., (408) 746-3020

Little Rascals CCCtr., 494 S. Bernardo Ave., (408) 730-9900

Mothers Day Out, 728 W. Fremont Ave., (408) 736-2511

New World CDCtr., 730 E. Homestead Rd., (408) 720-9020

Prodigy CDCtr., 1155 E. Arquez Ave., (408) 245-3276

Rainbow Montessori, 790 Duane Ave., (408) 738-3261

Sunnyvale CDCtr., 1500 Partridge Ave., (408) 730-9600

Chapter 7

SANTA CLARA COUNTY
Day Care

SEE THE PRECEDING chapter on baby care for more information about how local baby and child care is provided and who provides it.

For insights on how to pick a day-care center or provider, here is some advice offered by a person who runs a day-care center.

- Ask about age restrictions. Many centers and family-care providers will not take care of children under age two or not toilet trained. See previous chapter for infant centers.
- Give the center or home a visual check. Is it clean? In good condition or in need of repairs? Is there a plan for repairs when needed?
- Find out if the person in charge is the owner or a hired manager. Nothing wrong with the latter but you should know who is setting policy and who has the final say on matters.
- Ask about the qualifications of the people who will be working directly with your child. How long have they worked in day care? Training? Education? Many community colleges now offer training in early childhood and after-school care.
- What philosophy or approach does the center use. The Piaget approach believes children move through three stages and by exploring the child will naturally move through them. The job of the teacher is to provide activities appropriate to the right stage. For example, from age 2-7, many children master drawing and language; from 7-11, they begin to think logically. For the younger child art and sorting and language games would be appropriate; multiplication would not.

  Montessori believes that if given the right materials and placed in the right setting, children will learn pretty much by themselves through trial and error. Montessorians employ specific toys for teaching.

  Traditional emphasizes structure and repetition.

  These descriptions are oversimplified and do not do justice to these approaches or others. Our only purpose here is to point out that day-care providers vary in methods and thinking, and in choosing a center, you also choose a distinct philosophy of education.

- For family day-care providers. Some set up a small preschool setting in the home. Often your child will be welcomed into the family as an extended member. Is this what you want?
- Discipline. Johnny throws a snit. How is it handled? Does the provider have a method or a plan? Do you agree with it?
- Tuition. How much? When it is due? Penalty for picking up child late? Penalty for paying late?
- Hours of operation. If you have to be on the road at 5:30 a.m. and the day-care center doesn't open until 6, you may have to look elsewhere or make different arrangements. Some centers limit their hours of operation, e.g., 10 hours.
- Holidays. For family providers, when will the family take a vacation or not be available? For the centers, winter breaks? Summer vacations?
- Communication. Ask how you will be kept informed about progress and problems. Regular meetings? Notes? Calls? Newsletters?
- Classes-Tips for parents. Opportunities to socialize with other parents? Activities for whole family?
- Field trips and classes. Outside activities. Your son and daughter play soccer, an activity outside the day-care center. How will they get to practice? What's offered on site? Gymnastics? Dance?
- Siestas. How much sleep will the children get? When do they nap? Does this fit in with your child's schedule?
- Activities. What are they? How much time on them? Goals?
- Diapers, bottles, cribs, formula, extra clothes. Who supplies what?
- Food, lunches. What does the center serve? What snacks are available?

Remember, day-care centers and providers are in business. The people who staff and manage these facilities and homes may have the best intentions toward the children but if they can't make a profit or meet payrolls, they will fail or be unable to provide quality care. Even "nonprofits" must be run in a businesslike way or they won't survive.

Some centers may offer a rich array of services but for fees beyond your budget. You have to decide the tradeoffs.

For licensing, the state divides child care into several categories, including infant, licensed family, child-care centers, and school-age centers for older children. The previous chapter lists the infant providers. This chapter will list the large day-care centers, for both pre-school and school-age children.

For a list of family-care providers, please call the Community Coordinated Child Development Council of Santa Clara at (408) 487-0747.

Alviso

George Mayne St. Presch., 5030 N. First St., (408) 983-2150

Campbell

A Special Place-Camden, 1260 Erin Way, (408) 559-1566

Aurora CDCtr., 995 Apricot Ave., (408) 371-2605

Bright Days CDCtr., 1675 Winchester Blvd., (408) 378-8422

Bright Ideas, 1063 Fewtrell Dr., (408) 371-9310

Campbell Comm. Ctr.-Creative Rec., 1 W. Campbell Ave., (408) 494-0550

Campbell Parents Nursery, 528 N. Harrison St., (408) 866-7223

Capri Extd. Day, 850 Chapman Dr., (408) 370-9646

Castlemont Sch.-Age CDCtr., 3040 E. Payne Ave., (408) 378-2143

Discoveryland, 600 W. Campbell Ave., (408) 379-6636

Early Years CDCtr., 3225 S. Winchester Blvd., (408) 378-9000

Executive Sweet, 2323 S. Bascom Ave., (408) 559-6090

Hazelwood Extd. Day, 775 Waldo Rd., (408) 370-9699

Hazelwood Head Start, 775 Waldo Rd., (408) 453-6900

Kids at Play Presch., 124 Latimer, (408) 370-3745

Kinder Care Lrng. Ctr., 1806 W. Campbell, (408) 379-8152

Kinderwood Children's Ctr. #2, 1190 W. Latimer, (408) 374-4442

Montessori Acad.-Campbell, 177 E. Rincon, (408) 378-9244

Moreland Area Comm. Ctr., 1125 W. Campbell Ave., Rm. 2, (408) 374-4103

New Generation, 1291 Elam Ave., (408) 446-3648

Noah's Ark, 560 N. Harrison Ave., (408) 378-3212

Primary Plus, 1125 W. Campbell Ave., (408) 248-2464 or 379-3198

Rosemary State Presch. and CDCtr., 401 W. Hamilton Ave., (408) 374-1158

San Jose Montessori Sch., 1300 Sheffield Ave., (408) 377-9888

Cupertino

Bethel Lutheran Nursery & Lrng. Ctr., 10181 Finch Ave., (408) 252-8512

Bright Horizons, 10253 Portal Ave., (408) 366-1963

Calif. Children's Comm.-Regnart, 1180 Yorkshire Dr., (408) 253-8820

Collins Sch. Age CDCtr., 10401 Vista Dr., (408) 446-5428

De Anza CDCtr., 21250 Stevens Creek Blvd., (408) 864-8822

Faria Sch. Age CDCtr., 10155 Barbara Ln., (408) 973-0325

Garden Gate CDCtr., 10500 Ann Arbor Ave., (408) 725-0269

Good Samaritan, 19624 Homestead Rd., (408) 996-8290

Little People Christian DCCtr., 20900 McClellan Rd., (408) 257-1212

Play and Learn, 10067 Byrne Ave., (408) 253-7081

Portal Sch. CDCtr., 10300 Blaney Ave., (408) 996-1547

Sedgwick CDCtr., 19200 Phil Ln., (408) 725-0909 or 252-3103

TLC, 10038 Bret Ave., (408) 996-1866

Vallco CDCtr., 10123 N. Wolfe Rd., (408) 446-4136

Villa Montessori Sch., 20900 Stevens Creek Rd., (408) 257-3374

Village Little, 10100 N. Stelling Rd., (408) 252-2050

YMCA-Lincoln, 21710 McClellan Rd., (408) 996-9260

YMCA-Northwest, 20803 Alves Dr., (408) 257-7160

YMCA-Stevens Creek, 10300 Ainsworth Dr., (408) 736-5041

Gilroy

Christopher Ranch Head Start, 305 Bloomfield Ave., (408) 847-3110

Countryside DCCtr., 8985 Monterey Rd., (408) 848-3448 or 848-3444

Creative Play Lrng. Ctr., 95 Fourth St., (408) 846-9551

Fourth St. Head Start, 7600 Church St., (408) 848-5093

Gavilan College CD Lab, 5055 Santa Teresa Blvd., (408) 848-4815 or 848-4814

Gilroy CDCtr., 8387 Wren Ave., (408) 842-8447

Gilroy Head Start Ctr., 7151 Hanna St., (408) 842-3022

Gilroy Unified State Presch., 475 W. Ninth St., (408) 842-4486

Goldsmith Seeds Ctr., 2280 Hecker Pass Hwy., (408) 847-7333

Happy Place Montessori, 7360 & 7350 Alexander St., (408) 848-3819

Medallion Sch. Partnerships, 8755 Kern Ave., (408) 847-1932

Medallion Sch. Partnerships, 9225 Calle Del Rey, (408) 842-7150

Medallion Sch. Partnerships, 930 3rd St., (408) 842-1093

Ochoa Infant Migrant CDCtr., 915 Southside Dr., (408) 842-5066

Vineyard Presch., 1735 Hecker Pass, (408) 842-2713

YMCA-Las Animas, 8450 Wren Ave., Portable, (408) 842-5245

Los Altos Hills

Foothill Coll. Campus CCtr., 12345 El Monte Rd., (415) 941-7500 or 650-949-7500

YMCA Kid's Place-Bullis, 25890 Fremont Rd., (415) 941-3876

Los Altos

Almond Extd. Day, 550 Almond Ave., (415) 949-4075

Altos Oaks Presch., 625 Magdalena, (650) 948-2907

Children's House of Los Altos, 770 Berry Ave., (408) 968-9052

Childrens Creative Lrng. Ctr., 2310 Homestead Rd., (408) 736-7400

Joan Bourriague's Presch., 1040 Border Rd., (408) 941-1662

Los Altos Unified Methodist Ch. CC, 655 Magdalena, (408) 941-5411

Los Altos-Mtn. View Children's Corner, 97 Hillview Ave., (415) 948-8950

Monarch Christian Sch., 2420 Foothill Blvd., (408) 773-8543

Montclaire Sch.-Age CDCtr., 1160 St. Joseph Ave., (415) 965-7169

Montecito Presch., 1468 Grant Rd., (415) 968-5957

Montessori Sch. of Los Altos, 201 Covington Rd., (415) 948-2329

New Horizons Presch., 201 Covington Rd., (650) 948-8265

Oak Extd. Day Prgm., 1501 Oak Ave., (415) 969-2751

Santa Rita Extd. Day, 700 Los Altos Ave., (415) 968-3756

Stepping Stones, 201 Covington Rd., (408) 435-8823

Los Gatos

Addison Penzak Jewish Comm. Ctr., 14855 Oka Rd., Rm. 25, (408) 358-3636 or 358-1874

Green Hills Presch., 16195 George St., (408) 356-8911

Growing Footprints & Growing Footsteps, 16575 Shannon Rd., (408) 356-4442

Harwood Hills Country Sch., 16220 Harwood Rd., (408) 266-2400

Hillbrook Presch., 16000 Marchmont Dr., (408) 356-6511

Holy Cross Lutheran CCtr., 15885 Los Gatos-Almaden Rd., (408) 356-6828

JCC Aftersch.-Kids Space, 14855 Oka Rd., Rm. 20 & 23, (408) 356-0814

Kiddie Kampus DCCtr., 16330 Los Gatos Blvd., (408) 356-6776

Little Oak Presch., 16837 Placer Oaks Rd., (408) 356-2444

Los Gatos Acad., 220 Belgatos Rd., #K2, (408) 358-1046

Oak Tree Children's Club, 17765 Daves Ave., (408) 395-6144

Open Doors CDCtr., 630 W. Parr Ave., (408) 370-7064

Peppertree Presch., 16035 Los Gatos-Almaden Rd., (408) 356-3211

Rinconada Hills Charmer Presch.-DC, 1975 Pollard Rd., (408) 378-7805

Shannon Nursery, 16575 Shannon Rd., (408) 356-6156

YMCA-Alta Vista, 200 Blossom Valley Dr., (408) 356-1866

Milpitas

Children's World, 860 Hillview Rd., (408) 263-0444

Day Star Montessori, 215 Dempsey Rd., (408) 263-1618

Elan Esprit Presch., 40 E. Carlo St., (408) 493-2441

First Years, 1400 S. Main St. , (408) 730-9900

Hands on Lrng. Ctr., 637 S. Main St., (408) 946-5622

KinderCare Lrng. Ctr., 400 S. Abel St., (408) 263-7212

MILPITAS (Continued)

Milpitas Christian Presch.-DC, 10 Dempsey Rd., (408) 957-0523

Milpitas Christian Presch.-DC, 200 Abbott Rd., (408) 946-5795

Milpitas Christian Sch., 1000 S. Park Victoria Dr., (408) 262-2630

Milpitas Discoveryland, 1991 Landess Ave., (408) 263-7626

Milpitas Montessori, 1500 Yosemite Dr., (408) 720-3913

Milpitas Parents Presch., 355 E. Dixon Rd., (408) 263-3950

Milpitas Rose Head Start, 250 Roswell Dr., (408) 262-1641

Monarch Christian, 1715 Calaveras Blvd., (408) 263-4840

Rainbow Bridge, 123 Corning Ave., (408) 946-2812

Rainbow Bridge Ctr., 1500 Yosemite Dr., (408) 945-9090

Randall Sch. Age, 1300 Edsel Dr., (408) 945-5583

Rose CDCtr., 250 A Roswell Dr., (408) 262-3535

Spangler CDCtr., 140 N. Abbott Ave., (408) 945-5591

St. John the Baptist Sch., 360 S. Abel St., (408) 262-8110

Sunnyhills CDCtr., 356 Dixon Rd., (408) 945-5577

Tomorrow Montessori Sch., 1905 N. Milpitas, (408) 719-1686

Tri-Cities Sunnyhills Children's Ctr., 297 Autry St., (408) 263-9576

YMCA Pomeroy, 1505 Escuela, (408) 298-3888

Moffett Field

Ames CCCtr., Bldg. T20-D, (650) 604-4184

Morgan Hill

Burnett CDCtr.-State Presch., 85 Tilton, (408) 779-6016

Countryside DC #2, 174 W. Main Ave., (408) 779-1220

El Toro CDCtr.-State Presch., 455 E. Main St., (408) 778-1402

Galvan Park CDCtr., 17666 Crest Ave., (408) 779-6553

KinderCare Lrng. Ctr., 605 E. Dunne Ave., (408) 778-1237

Linda's Place DC, 17535 Del Monte, (408) 779-7678

Little Sonshine, 16970 DeWitt Ave., (408) 779-6788

Montessori Lrng. for Living, 16900 De Witt Ave., (408) 358-2032

Morgan Hill Children's Ctr., 17720 Peak Ave., (408) 779-9924

Morgan Hill Parent-Child Nursery, 16870 Murphy Ave., (408) 779-4515

Morgan Hill Presch. Acad., 17780 Monterey Rd., (408) 226-2857

Noah's Ark, 18980 Monterey Rd., (408) 776-3262

Nordstrom State Presch. and CDCtr., 1425 E. Dunne Ave., (408) 778-2821

P.A. Walsh CDCtr., 353 W. Main St., (408) 778-2896

YMCA-Jackson, 2700 Fountain Oaks Dr., (408) 779-8854

YMCA-Paradise Valley , 1400 La Crosse Dr., (408) 778-5711

Young Explorer, 25 Wright Ave., (408) 778-2529

Mountain View

Abracadabra CCCtrs., 1120 Rose Ave, (650) 965-0695

Castro State Presch., 505 Escuela Ave., (650) 964-7555

Hobbledehoy Montessori Presch., 2321 Jane Ln., (650) 968-1155

Kiddie Acad. CC Lrng. Ctr., 205 E. Middlefield Rd., (650) 960-6900

Kidstown CDCtr., 180 N. Rengstorff, (650) 964-5006

KinderCare, 2065 W. El Camino Real, (650) 967-4430

Little Acorn, 1667 Miramonte Ave., (650) 964-8445

Mt. View Parent Nursery, 1299 Bryant Ave., (650) 969-9506

Mt. View Sch. Dist. State Presch., 325 Gladys Ave., (650) 526-3530

Oaktree III, 2100 University Ave., (650) 493-1905

Primary Plus, 333 Eunice Ave., (408) 967-3780

Southbay Christian Ctr., 1134 Miramonte Ave., (650) 961-5781

St. Paul Lutheran CDCtr., 1075 El Monte Ave., (650) 969-2696

St. Timothy's Nursery, 2094 Grant Rd., (650) 967-4724

Western Montessori Day Sch., 323 Moorpark Way, (650) 961-4131

Whisman Head Start, 750-A San Pierre Way, #1, (650) 960-3427
YMCA Kid's Place-Bubb, 525 Hans St., (650) 965-2922
YMCA Kid's Place-Castro, 505 Escuela, (650) 965-1436
YMCA Kid's Place-Landels, 115 W. Dana St., (650) 965-2008
YMCA Kid's Place-Monta Loma, 460 Thompson Ave., (650) 966-1120
YMCA Kid's Place-Slater, 325 Gladys Ave., (650) 965-8002
YMCA Kid's Place-Theuerkauf, 1625 San Luis Ave., Port. 18, (650) 961-7076
YMCA Kids Place-Huff, 253 Martens, (650) 567-9928
YMCA of the East Bay, 750 San Pierre Way, (650) 964-3809
YMCA Way To Grow-El Camino, 115 W. Dana St., (650) 965-2008

Palo Alto

Addison Kids Corner, 650 Addison Ave., (415) 323-6806
Albert L. Schultz Jewish Comm. Ctr., 655 Arastradero Rd., (650) 493-9400
Barron Park Presch., 3650 La Donna Ave., (415) 493-7597
Barrons Kids Club, 800 Barron Ave., (415) 856-3177
Besse Bolton CCtr., 500 E. Meadow Dr., (415) 856-0847
Besse Bolton CD, 4120 Middlefield Rd., (415) 856-0876
Casa dei Bambini, 463 College, (650) 858-0892
Children's Presch., 4000 Middlefield, T-1, (650) 855-5770
College Terrace Presch., 2300 Wellesley, (415) 858-1580
Community Assoc. for Rehab., 3864 Middlefield Rd., (650) 494-0550
Country Day Little Sch., 3990 Ventura Ct., (415) 464-8044
Covenant Children's Ctr., 670 E. Meadow Dr., (650) 493-9505
Discovery Montessori, 303 Parkside Dr., (415) 570-5038
Downtown Children's Ctr., 555 Waverly, (408) 321-9578
Duveneck Kids Club, 705 Alester Ave., (415) 328-8356
El Carmelo Kids Corner, 3024 Bryant St., (415) 856-6150
Ellen Thacher CCtr., 505 E. Charleston Rd., (415) 493-2361
Escondido Kid's Club, 890 Escondido Rd., (415) 855-9828
First Congregational Church Nursery, 1985 Louis Rd., (415) 856-6662
First School, 625 Hamilton Ave., (415) 323-6167
Good Neighbor Montessori, 4000 Middlefield Rd., (415) 493-2777
Grace Lutheran Presch., 3149 Waverly St., (415) 494-1212
Headsup CDCtr., 4251 El Camino Real, Bldg. A, (650) 424-1221
Heffalump Coop., 3990 Ventura Ct., (650) 856-4321
Int'l. Sch. of the Peninsula, 870 N. California, (415) 328-2338
Learning Ctr., 459 Kingsley, (415) 325-6683
Love-N-Care Christian Presch., 2490 Middlefield Rd., (415) 322-1872
Mid-Peninsula YWCA CCCtr., 4161 Alam St., (415) 494-0972
Midtown Nursery, 855 Bruce Dr., (415) 856-7461
Ohlone Kids Club, 950 Amarillo Ave., (650) 493-2361
Palo Alto Friends Nursery, 957 Colorado St., (415) 856-0744
Palo Alto Montessori, 575 Arastradero Rd., (415) 493-5930
Palo Verde Kid's Corner, 3450 Louise Rd., (415) 856-1337
Peninsula Day Care Ctr., 525 San Antonio Rd., (415) 494-1880
Piccolo, 888 Boyce Ave., (415) 322-9668
Redwood Enrichment Ctr, 445 E. Charlestown Rd., (650) 320-9001
Redwood Enrichment Ctr., 500 E. Meadow Dr., (415) 858-1006
Sojourner Truth CDCtr., 3990 Ventura Ct., (415) 493-5990
Walter Hayes Kids Club, 1525 Middlefield Rd., (415) 325-5350
Whistle Stop, 3801 Miranda Ave., #T6B, (650) 852-3497
Young Life Christian Presch., 687 Arastradero Rd., (415) 494-7885

San Jose

A Brand New World, 2174 Lincoln Ave., (408) 978-1116
A Place to Grow, 3001 Ross Ave., (408) 265-2994

SAN JOSE (Continued)

A Special Place-Williamsburg, 3124 Williamsburg Dr., (408) 374-4980

A.T.L.C. Presch., 1855 Curtner Ave., (408) 264-3151

A.T.L.C. Presch., 1975 Cambrianna Dr., (408) 371-2573

Achieve Therapeutic Presch., 3800 Blackbird Ave., (650) 494-1200

Achiever Christian, 800 Ironwood Dr., (408) 264-2345

Action Day Nursery, 2146-2148 Lincoln Ave., (408) 266-8952

Action Day Nursery, 3000 Moorpark Ave., (408) 247-6972

After School Adventures- Steindorf Play Society, 3001 Ross Ave., #12&13, (408) 264-8400

Almaden Head Start, 1200 Blossom Hill Rd., (408) 265-6251

Almaden Parents Presch., 5805 Cahalan Ave., (408) 225-7211

Almaden PreSch., 1295 Dentwood Dr., Rm. 17, (408) 535-6207

Alphabet Soup, 1191 DeAnza Blvd., (408) 253-6660

Anderson Head Start, 4000 Rhoda Dr., (408) 248-6697

Anderson Sch. Age CDCtr., 5800 Calpine Dr., (408) 972-5373

Andrew Hill CCtr., 3200 Senter Rd., (408) 226-5822

Arbuckle CDCtr., 1910 Cinderella Ln., (408) 259-8340

Arbuckle-Sunset Head Start, 1970 Cinderella Ln., (408) 251-4062

Astroland Presch., 3993 Will Rogers Dr., (408) 247-4510

Bachrodt CDCtr., 1471 Keoncrest Rd., (408) 453-0511

Bachrodt Sch. Age CDCtr., 102 Sonora Ave., (408) 453-7533

Ballard Montessori Sch., 2555 Moorpark Ave., (408) 260-1888

Berryessa CDCtr., 2760 Trimble Rd., (408) 923-1943

Berryessa Presch. Northwood Elem., 2760 Trimble Rd., (408) 923-1944

Bethel CCCtr., 1201 S. Winchester, (408) 246-6790

Blackford Sch.-Age CDCtr., 1970 Willow St., (408) 371-9900

Blackford State Presch., 3800 Blackford Ave., (408) 248-6661

Blossom Hill-Southside State Presch., 5585 Cottle Rd., (408) 225-6885

Bright Beginnings, 635 Calero Ave., (408) 227-1771

Bright Horizons, 6120 Liska Ln., (408) 225-3276

Building Blocks, 6350 Rainbow Dr., (408) 996-2477

C.A.R. Creative Rec., 780 Thornton Way, (408) 298-2009

Carter Ave. Nursery Sch., 5303 Carter Ave., (408) 265-3580 or 272-1963

CAS-Los Arboles Head Start, 455 Los Arboles Ave., (408) 363-9016

Cathedral of Faith Lrng., 2315 Canoas Garden Ave., (408) 267-4691

Center for Employment Training-DCCtr., 701 Vine St., (408) 295-4566

Central Nursery, 1177 Naglee Ave., (408) 287-0266

CET Montessori, 1212 McGinness, (408) 929-4627

Challenger Presch. #3, 4977 Dent Ave., (408) 266-7073

Challenger School, 19950 McKean Rd., (408) 377-2300

Challenger School, 711 E. Gish Rd., (408) 998-2860

Challenger School, 880 Wren Dr., (408) 448-3010

Challenger School, Meridian Ave., (408) 377-2300

Chandler Tripp/Thornton Head Start, 780 Thornton Way, (408) 293-8404

Cherrywood Extd. DCCtr., 2550 Greengate Dr., (408) 259-9739

Child Kingdom, 4160 Senter Rd., (408) 365-1236

Childcare Ctr. at Calvary Chapel, 1175 Hillsdale Ave., (408) 269-8331

Children's Presch. Ctr.- Evergreen, 3403 Yerba Buena Rd., (408) 239-2633

Church of the Chimes CCtr., 1447 Bryan Ave., (408) 723-3600

Clement Presch., 955 Branham Ln., (408) 256-2226

College of the Crayons CDCtr., 4390 Narvaez Ave., (408) 723-8650

Congregation Sinai, 1556 Willowbrae, (408) 264-8486

Cornerstone Presch., 6601 Camden Ave., (408) 268-7595

Cory CDCtr., 897 Broadleaf Ln., (408) 296-5975 or 247-3938
Crayon Ctr., 1590 Minnesota Ave., (408) 269-8026
Creative Beginnings, 14834 Leigh Ave., (408) 559-3247
Cupertino House of Montessori, 1211 D & E Kentwood Ave., (408) 255-8905
De Vargas Sch.-Age CDCtr., 5050 Moorpark, (408) 725-0278
Del Roble CDCtr., 5345 Avenida Almendros, (408) 371-9900
Dilworth Sch.-Age CDCtr., 101 Strayer Dr., (408) 446-5285
Discovery Ctr., 4645 Albany Dr., (408) 985-1460
Discovery Parent-Child Presch., 1919 Gunston Way, (408) 377-5390
Discovery School, 801 Hibiscus, (408) 874-3250
Early Learning Ctr., 921 Fox Ln., (408) 944-0395
East Hills Presch., 14845 Story Rd., (408) 923-8616
Easthills/Lyndale Head Start, 13901 Nordyke Dr., (408) 258-1523
Eastside CDCtr., 2490 Story Rd., (408) 251-7516
Eastside Parents Participating Nursery Sch., 935 Piedmont Rd., (408) 926-1264
Edenvale/Discovery Head Start, 285 Azucar Ave., (408) 363-1823
Eitz Chaim Acad., 1532 Willowbrae Ave., (408) 978-5822
El Rancho Verde CDCtr., 3l8 El Rancho Verde Dr., (408) 254-1717
Emmanuel's CDCtr., 467 N. White Rd., (408) 272-9310
Empire Gardens At Waston Park Annex, 550 N. 22nd St., (408) 535-6083
Enchanted Land Montessori, 667 N. First St., (408) 275-1720
Enchanted Land Montessori II, 712 Elm St., (408) 293-9669
ESO CDCtr., 2055 Summerside Dr., (408) 971-0888
Evergreen Valley College CDCtr., 3095 Yerba Buena Rd., (408) 270-6452
Evergreen Valley Presch., 3122 Fowler Rd., (408) 238-4001
Explorer Presch., 15040 Union Ave., (408) 879-0181
Familiar Footsteps, 301 Cottle Rd., (408) 225-0289
Familiar Footsteps, 420 Calero Ave., (408) 227-3464
Foothill Christian Presch., 5301 McKee Rd., (408) 258-8133
Forest Hill Extd. Day, 4450 McCoy, (408) 370-9697
Foxdale-Story Rd. Head Start, 1250 Foxdale Loop, (408) 251-8796
Frances Gulland CDCtr., 405 S. 10th St., (408) 924-6988
Frances Presley CDCtr., 1990 Kammerer Ave., (408) 258-1695
Franklin House Head Start, 451 Baltic, (408) 293-3558
Fred Marten Head Start, 14271 Story Rd., Rm. B-1, (408) 254-2035
Future Assests CD, 7245 Sharon Dr., (408) 252-0203
Gardner Children's Ctr., 611 Willis Ave., (408) 998-1343
Gardner Presch., 502 Illinois Ave., (408) 535-6083
Gardner's River Glen, 1610 Bird Ave., (408) 998-1343
Gloria Dei Lutheran, 121 S. White Rd., (408) 258-7563
Good Samaritan Hospital CDCtr., 2425 Samaritan Dr., (408) 264-1275
Goss Presch., 2475 Van Winkle Ln., (408) 258-4923
Grace Head Start, 2650 Aborn Rd., (408) 274-8193
Grant Presch., 470 E. Jackson St., (408) 293-7955 or 998-4204
Graystone CDCtr., 6982 Shearwater Dr., (408) 997-1980
Green Hills Presch. Downtown, 571 N. 3rd St., (408) 286-1533
Green Valley CDCtr., 302 Checkers Dr., (408) 923-1130
Green Valley CDCtr., 525 Giuffrieda Ave., (408) 371-9900
Grove CDCtr., 510 E. Branham Ln., (408) 226-3640
Hacienda Presch., 1290 Kimberly Dr., (408) 998-6259
Hayes CDCtr., 5035 Poston Dr., (408) 371-9900
Headsup CDCtr., 2841 Junction Ave., (408) 424-1155
Hellyer Head Start, 725 Hellyer Ave., (408) 225-8534

SAN JOSE (Continued)

Hillview Glen CDCtr., 880 Hillsdale Ave., (408) 265-8329

Holy Cross Lutheran CCtr., 5410 Taft Dr., (408) 356-4777

Holy Family Ed. Ctr., 4850 Pearl Ave., (408) 978-1355

Hubbard Presch., 1745 June Ave., (408) 258-4923

James Lick CCtr., 2955 Alum Rock Ave., (408) 251-8400

Jordan Presch., 5102 Alum Rock Ave., (408) 251-4152

Julian/26th St. Head Start, 333 N. 26th St., (408) 995-6735

K's Quality Children Ctr., 3621 Bercaw Ln., (408) 377-6660

Kennedy Presch., 1602 Lucretia Ave., (408) 536-0330

Kid Connection, 410 Sautner Dr., (408) 226-8600

Kiddie Kollege, 5386 Alum Rock Ave., (408) 259-1188

Kiddie Kountry, 2701 S White Rd., (408) 274-2040

Kids Extd. Care, 280 Martinvale Ln., (408) 926-6532

Kids Korner, 1515 Kooser Rd., (408) 267-3706 or 264-1846

Kidspark, 1600 Saratoga Ave., #431, (408) 374-2229

Kidspark, 2858 Stevens Creek Blvd., (408) 281-8880

Kidspark, 5440 Thornwood Dr., (408) 356-3721

KinderCare Lrng. Ctr., 3320 San Felipe Rd., (408) 270-0980

KinderCare Lrng. Ctr.-Foxworthy, 1081 Foxworthy Ave., (408) 265-7380

Kinderwood Childrens Ctr., 5560 Entrada Cedros, (408) 363-1366

Las Casitas Head Start, 14265 B Story Rd., Rm 8, (408) 937-6147

Las Plumas Head Start, 1590 Las Plumas Dr., (408) 926-8885

Latimer Head Start, 4250 Latimer Ave., #8, (408) 453-6900

Learning Co. #2, 5670 Camden Ave., (408) 723-1131

Linda Vista CDCtr., 65 Gordon Ave., (408) 258-4923 or 272-3666

Little Dino Lrng. Ctr., 3275 Williams Rd., (408) 260-2423

Little Friends, 2720 S. Bascom Ave., (408) 377-8541

Little Kiddles Swing Set Groups, 286 Sorrento Way, (408) 227-5758

Little Scholar Presch., 3560 Kettmann Rd., (408) 238-1474

Little Scholars Schools, 3703 Silver Creek Rd., (408) 274-4726

Los Alamitos Presch., 6130 Silberman Dr., (408) 998-6297

Lotus Presch., 639 N. Fifth St., (408) 293-9292

Luther Burbank CDCtr., 4 Wabash Ave., (408) 295-1731

MACSA Extd. DCtr., 848 E. Williams St., (408) 295-6054

MACSA Youth Ctr., 660 Sinclair Dr., (408) 929-1080

Mandala Children's House, 5038 Hyland Ave., (408) 251-8633

McGinness Head Start, 1212 McGinness, (408) 453-6900

McKinley Shea Presch., 651 Macredes Ave., (408) 283-6300

Medallion Sch. Partnerships, 6044 Vera Cruz Dr., (408) 997-9821

Meyer Presch., 1824 Daytona Dr., (408) 258-4923

Miller Presch., 1250 S. King Rd., (408) 258-4923

Minigym Explorations, 4115 Jacksol Dr., (408) 559-4616

Monte Alban Head Start, 1322 Santee Dr., (408) 298-2164

Montessori Acad., 1188 Wunderlich Dr., (408) 255-4710 or 2521488

Montessori Acad. III, 495 Massar Ave., (408) 259-5736

Montessori Acad. Saratoga, 480 Saratoga Ave., (408) 244-1420

Mt. Pleasant CCtr., 1650 S. White Rd., (408) 259-2331

Mulberry Coop. Nursery Sch. and Kinder., 1980 Hamilton Ave., (408) 377-1595

Neighborhood Christian Presch., 2575 Coit Dr., (408) 371-4222

New Frontier Presch., 1980 Fruitdale Ave., (408) 295-6687

Noble Extd. DC, 3466 Grossmont Dr., (408) 251-8952

Olinder Presch., 890 E. William St., Rm. K32, (408) 286-4198

One World Montessori Sch., 5331 Dent Ave., (408) 723-5140 or 255-3770
Over the Rainbow, 3001 Ross Ave., (408) 978-5454
Pacific Montessori Acad. #1, 4115 Jacksol Dr., (408) 246-5432
Park Ave. Presch., 1080 The Alameda, (408) 294-4807
Parkview CDCtr. and State Presch., 330 Bluefield Dr., (408) 371-9900 or 376-1901
Parkway CDCtr., 1800 Fruitdale Ave., (408) 297-7717
Phelan Tiny Tots, 801 Hibiscus Ln., (408) 446-4166
Piedmont Hills Montessori Acad., 1425 Old Piedmont Rd., (408) 923-5151
Pioneer Montessori Presch., 1010 University Ave., (408) 295-8140
Pioneer Montessori Sch., 3520 San Felipe Rd., (408) 238-8445
Play-n-Learn Presch., 3800 Narvaez Ave., (408) 269-9004
Precious Presch., 12360 Redmond Ave., (408) 268-9000
Presch. DC Dom Dinis, 1395 E. Santa Clara St., (408) 993-0383
Primary Plus, 801 Hibiscus Ln., (408) 248-2464
Rainbow Bridge Ctr., 750 N. Capitol Ave., (408) 254-1280
Rainbow McKinley Head Start, 651 Macredes, (408) 993-0403
Rainbow of Knowledge, 1718 Andover Ln., (408) 377-5730
Randol Sch.-Age CDCtr., 762 Sunset Glen Dr., (408) 224-4505
Redmond CDCtr., 11843 Redmond Ave., (408) 268-5165
Regard CCCtr., 2021 Lincoln Ave., (408) 971-2308
Rex and Lee Lindsey's CDCtr., 1315 McLaughlin Ave., (408) 279-1388
River Glen Presch., 1619 Bird Ave., (408) 998-6240
Rouleau Head Start, 1875 Monrovia Dr., (408) 270-4873
Sacred Heart Comm. Ctr., 1381 S. First St., (408) 278-2170
San Antonio Presch., 1855 E. San Antonio St., (408) 259-3020
San Jose City College, 2100 Moorpark Ave., (408) 288-3759
San Jose Day Nursery, 33 N. 8th St., (408) 295-2752 or 288-9667
San Jose Day Nursery, 890 East William, K33, (408) 288-7855
San Jose High 1&2 Presch., 275 N. 24th St., (408) 535-6083
San Jose Job Corps, 3485 East Hills Dr., (408) 923-1200 or 937-3276
San Jose Parents Participating, 2180 Radio Ave., (408) 265-3202
San Jose State University CDCtr., 1 Washington Sq., (408) 924-3727
San Juan Bautista CDCtr., 1945 Terilyn Ave., (408) 259-4796
Santa Familia CDCtr., 4758 Joseph Speciale Dr., (408) 264-1012
Santa Maria CCtr., 437 N. 10th St., (408) 729-1490
Santa Teresa CDCtr., 6200 Encinal Dr., (408) 972-4396
Santa Teresa Children's Ctr., 6150 Snell Rd., (408) 578-4510
Santa Teresa Village CDCtr., 7026 Santa Teresa Blvd., (408) 225-5437
Santee Sch.-Age CDCtr., 1313 Audobon Dr., (408) 280-6739
Seven Trees Head Start, 3975 Mira Loma, (408) 363-8944
Shea Pre-K Santee Sch., 1313 Audubon Dr., (408) 283-6450
Shepherd of the Valley Lutheran, 1281 Redmond Rd., (408) 997-4846
Shields Presch., 2851 Gay Ave., (408) 258-4923
Slonaker Extd. Day, 1601 Cunningham Ave., (408) 259-4796
Small World Athenour #A, 5200 Dent Ave., (408) 257-7320
Small World-Baker, 4845 Bucknall Rd., (408) 257-3757
Small World-Country Lane, 5140 Country Ln., (408) 379-3200
Small World-Latimer, 4250 Latimer Ave., (408) 379-7459
Small World-Noddin, 1755 Gilda Way, (408) 257-7320
Small World-Payne, 3750 Gleason Ave., (408) 246-1028
Small World-Strawberry Park, 730 Camina Escuela, (408) 379-2300
Small World-Valley Vista, 2400 Flint Ave., (408) 238-3525
Solari Park Head Start, 3590 Cas Dr., (408) 578-0283

SAN JOSE (Continued)

South Valley Children's Ctr. at Carlton Elem., 2421 Carlton Ave., (408) 356-1453

South Valley Children's Ctr. at Oster Elem., 1855 Lencar Way, (408) 269-1676

South Valley Children's Ctr., 4949 Harwood Rd. #19 & 20, (408) 448-1438

St. Elizabeth's Day Home, 1544 McKinley Ave., (408) 295-3456

St Frances Cabrini Sch., 15325 Woodard Ave., (408) 377-6545

St. Patrick Sch., 51 N. 9th St., (408) 283-5858

St. Stevens Sch., 500 Shawnee Ln., (408) 227-1235

St. Timothy's Lutheran, 5100 Camden Ave., (408) 265-0244

Steindorf Head Start, 3001 Ross Dr., Rm 5, (408) 266-0953

Strawberry Park Tiny Tots, 730 Camina Escuela, (408) 446-4166

Sunnymont Nursery, 1188 Wunderlich Dr., (408) 253-8125

Sunrise Kiddie Korral, 5860 Blossom Ave., (408) 227-0831

Tamian CCCtr., 1197 Lick Ave., (408) 271-1980

Tinytown, 1133 Piedmont Rd., (408) 923-0441

TLC Child Care Ctr., 2466 Almaden Rd., (408) 264-3707

Tom Thumb Presch., 668 N. First St., (408) 288-8832

Tower Acad., 2887 McLaughlin Ave., (408) 578-2830

Toyon Partners CDCtr., 995 Bard St., (408) 729-8239

Trace Presch., 651 Dana Ave., (408) 535-6257

Trinity Presbyterian CCtr., 3151 Union Ave., (408) 377-2342 or 377-8930

Tully Head Start, 420 Tully Rd., (408) 971-7362

Valley Medical Ctr., 730 Empey Way, (408) 297-9044

Villa San Pedro Head Start, 282 Danze Dr., (408) 453-6900

Voyager's DCCtr., 1590 Las Plumas Ave., (408) 926-8885

W.C. Overfelt CCtr., 1835 Cunningham Ave., (408) 258-3654

Westside Coop., 3257 Payne Ave., (408) 374-1232

Williams Sch.-Age CDCtr., 1150 Rajkovich Way, (408) 371-9900

Willow Glen Comm. Extd. Day, 1425 Lincoln Ave., (408) 286-6999

Willow Glen United Meth. Church., 1420 Newport Ave., (408) 294-9796

Willow Vale Christian CC, 1730- Curtner Ave., (408) 448-0656

Willow/Corazon/Edwards Head Start, 310 Edwards, (408) 286-8826

Winnie the Pooh, 1321 Miller Ave., (408) 996-0851

Wonder Years, 1411 Piedmont Rd., (408) 926-1234

Woolcreek Head Start, 645 Woolcreek Rd., (408) 283-6118

Yerba Buena CCtr., 1855 Lucretia Ave., (408) 279-2760

YMCA - Allen, 5845 Allen Ave., (408) 298-3888

YMCA - Brooktree, 1781 Olivetree Dr., (408) 923-1910

YMCA-Easterbrook, 4660 Eastus Dr., (408) 257-4505

YMCA - Lane View, Warmwood Ln., (408) 923-1920

YMCA - Schallenberger, 1280 Koch Ln., (408) 298-3888

YMCA-Anderson, 4000 Rhoda Dr., (408) 244-1962

YMCA-Autumn Wonderland, 505 W. Julian, (408) 298-1717

YMCA-Booksin, 1590 Dry Creek Rd., (408) 266-4454

YMCA-East Valley, 1975 S. White Rd., (408) 258-4419

YMCA-Fammatre, 2800 New Jersey Ave., (408) 370-1877

YMCA-Farnham, 15711 Woodard Rd., (408) 370-1877

YMCA-Hacienda Valley View, 1290 Kimberly Dr., (408) 978-1156

YMCA-Hester, 1100 Shasta Ave., (408) 295-1717

YMCA-Holly Oak, 2995 Rossmore Way, (408) 258-4419

YMCA-Lietz, 5300 Carter Ave., (408) 298-3888

YMCA-Los Paseos, 121 Avenida Grande, (408) 225-2686

YMCA-Lowell, 625 S. 7th St., (408) 287-8776
YMCA-Majestic Way, 1855 Majestic Way, (408) 923-1925
YMCA-Meyerholz, 6990 Melvin Dr., (408) 996-2308
YMCA-Muir, 6550 Hanover Dr., (408) 253-7440
YMCA-Reed, 1524 Jacob Ave., (408) 978-3002
YMCA-Ruskin, 1363 Turlock Ln., (408) 251-6222
YMCA-Sakamoto, 6280 Shadelands Dr., (408) 227-3319 or 227-3605
YMCA-Silver Oak, 1 Farnsworth Dr., (408) 258-4419
YMCA-Simonds, 6515 Grapevine Way, (408) 268-7125
YMCA-Terrell, 5925 Pearl Ave., (408) 226-9622
YMCA-Vinci Park, 1131 Vinci Park Way, (408) 259-0127
YWCA - Almaden, 1295 Dentwood Dr., (408) 295-4011
YWCA-Christopher, 565 Coyote Rd., (408) 578-1733
YWCA-Eden Palms CCCtr., 5398 Monterey Rd., (408) 227-9858
YWCA-Extd. Prog.–Lynhaven, 881 S. Cypress Ave., (408) 246-7538
YWCA-Frost, 530 Gettysburg Dr., (408) 578-4535
YWCA-Hillsdale, 3200 Water St., (408) 295-4011
YWCA-Kennedy, 1602 Lucretia Ave., (408) 286-2530
YWCA-O.B. Whaley, 2655 Alvin Ave., (408) 223-8952
YWCA-Villa Nueva, 375 S. 3rd St., (408) 295-4011
YWCA-West Valley, 4343 Leigh Ave., (408) 269-7543

San Martin

San Martin CDCtr., 100 North St., (408) 683-2808
San Martin Head Start, 13570 Depot Ave., (408) 683-2800

Santa Clara

A Special Place-Stevens Creek, 5041 Stevens Creek Blvd., (408) 248-0148
Action Day Nursery, 2001 Pruneridge Ave., (408) 244-2909
Alameda Day Nursery, 810 Washington St., (408) 296-7064
Angels Montessori Presch., 1000 Kiely Blvd., (408) 241-8434
Beautiful Beginnings Presch., 890 Pomeroy, (408) 247-4234
Bowers State Presch., 2755 Barkley Ave., (408) 983-2150
Bracher Center, 2401 Bowers Ave., (408) 983-2107
Briarwood Children's Ctr., 1940 Townsend Ave., Rms. 25-27, (408) 983-2095
Bright Beginnings Presch., 2445 Cabrillo Ave., (408) 247-7777
Carden El Encanto Day Sch., 615 Hobart Terr., (408) 244-5041
Christian Day Care, 3111 Benton Ave., (408) 241-8964
First Step Presch., 1515/1525 Franklin St., (408) 554-6692
Happy Days CDCtr., 220 Blake Ave., (408) 296-5770
Hughes State Presch., 4949 Calle de Escuela, (408) 983-2174
Joyful Noise Presch., 1700 Lincoln St., (408) 247-3600
Kids on Campus, Santa Clara University, (408) 554-4771
Kidsville Presch. & DCCtr., 1247 Benton St., (408) 296-7442
Kinder Care Lrng. Ctr., 840 Bing Dr., (408) 246-2141
Laurelwood Presch., 955 Teal Dr., (408) 554-1390
Little Lambs Christian Presch., 2499 Homestead Rd., (408) 736-3286
Martinson CDCtr., 1350 Hope Dr., (408) 988-8296
MCA Granada Islamic Sch., 3003 Scott Blvd., (408) 980-1161
Mission College Campus CC, 3000 Mission Collage Blvd., (408) 748-2712
Monroe & Pacific Head Start, 2383 Pacific Dr., Rm. 3 & 5, (408) 261-2701
Montague State Presch., 750 Laurie Ave., Rm. 12, (408) 983-2145
Monticello CDCtr., 3401 Monroe St., (408) 261-0494
Neighborhood Christian Presch., 1290 Pomeroy Ave., (408) 984-3418
One World Montessori Sch., 2495 Cabrillo Ave., (408) 615-1254
Pioneer Montessori Presch., 400 N. Winchester, (408) 241-5077

SANTA CLARA (Continued)

Pomeroy District Presch., 1250 Pomeroy Ave., (408) 249-9756

Santa Clara Christian Presch., 3421 Monroe St., (408) 246-5423

Santa Clara Parents Nursery, 471 Monroe St., (408) 248-5131

Scott Lane State Presch., 1925 Scott Blvd., (408) 249-3168

Small World-Sutter, 3200 Forbes Ave., #5, (408) 985-5990

St. Lawrence Presch., 1971 St. Lawrence Dr., (408) 248-1966

St. Mark's Episcopal Church, 1957 Pruneridge Ave., (408) 247-2223

Warburton Parent-CCtr., 2545 Warburton Ave., (408) 296-2774

YMCA-Eisenhower, 277 Rodonovan Dr., (408) 249-5330

Saratoga

Action Day Nursery, 13560 S. Saratoga-Sunnyvale Rd., (408) 867-4515

Challenger Presch. #2, 18811 Cox Ave., (408) 378-0444

Marshall Lane Sch.-Age CDCtr., 14114 Marilyn Ln., (408) 374-1156

My Preschool, 1472 Saratoga Ave., (408) 376-0385

Next Generation CDCtr., 19010 Austin Way, (408) 927-7250 or 395-4290

Notre Dame Montessori Presch., 15100 Norton Rd., (408) 867-1663

Primary Plus, 12211 Titus Ave., Rm. 19, (408) 996-1437

Primary Plus, 18720 Bucknall Rd., (408) 370-0357

Saratoga Presbyterian Presch., 20455 Herriman Ave., (408) 741-5770

St. Andrew's School, 13601 Saratoga Ave., (408) 867-3785

Village Presch., 20390 Park Pl., (408) 867-3181

West Valley College CDCtr., 14000 Fruitvale Ave., (408) 741-2007 or 741-2409

YMCA-Blue Hill, 12300 De Sanka Ave., (408) 257-7160

YMCA-Southwest Presch., 13500 Quito Rd., (408) 370-1877

Stanford

Bing Nursery, 850 Escondido Rd., (650) 723-4865

Children's Creative Lrng. Ctr., 1711 Stanford Ave., (650) 493-6006

Children's Ctr. of Stanford, 695 Pampas Ln., (650) 853-3090

Peppertree After Sch., 845 Escondido Rd., (650) 723-0217

Rainbow Sch. at Escondido Village, 845 Escondido Rd., (650) 723-0217

Stanford Arboretum, 211 Quarry Rd., (650) 725-6322

Sunnyvale

Appleseed Montessori, 1095 Dunford Way, #B, (408) 260-7333

Bishop CDCtr., 440 N. Sunnyvale Ave., (408) 739-2611

Calif. Young World #5, 1110 Fairwood Ave., (408) 245-7285

Calif. Young World-Ellis, 550 East Olive St., Rm. K1&K2, (408) 774-0405

Calif. Young World-Lakewood, 750 Lakechime, (408) 734-8400 or 245-7976

Calif. Young World-San Miguel, 777 San Miguel Ave., (408) 245-7285

Caring Hearts CDCtr., 645 W. Fremont Ave., (408) 245-6356

Challenger Sch., 1185 Hollenbeck Ave., (408) 245-7170

Cherry Chase Sch.-Age CDCtr., 1138 Heatherstone, (408) 736-0168 or 523-4887

Children's Creative Lrng. Ctr., 794 E. Duane Ave., (408) 732-2288

Community Presch., 1098 Remington Dr., Rms 2-9, (408) 739-2022

Cumberland Sch.-Age CDCtr., 824 Cumberland Ave., (408) 371-9900

Cupertino Coop., 563 W. Fremont Ave., (408) 739-8963

De Lor Montessori Sch., 1510 Lewiston Dr., (408) 773-0200 or 729-8809

Early Horizons, 1510 Lewiston Dr., (408) 746-3020

French-American Sch. of Silicon Valley, 1510 Lewiston Dr., (408) 746-0460

Fun Learning Presch., 1194 Fairwood Ave., (408) 735-1776

Jamil Islamic Ctr./ Silicon Valley Acad., 1095 Dunford Way, Bldg. C, (650) 326-0400

Jubilee Acad., 560 Britton Ave., (408) 730-4777

Lakewood Head Start, 750 Lakechime Dr., (408) 752-0409

Little Rascals CCCtr., 494 S. Bernardo Ave., (408) 730-9900

Maremont CDCtr., 1601 Tenaka Pl., (408) 732-0648

Monarch Montessori, 1196 Lime Dr., (408) 749-0239

Montessori House of Children, 582 Dunholme Way, #A, (408) 749-1602

Mothers Day Out, 728 W. Fremont Ave., (408) 736-2511

New World CDCtr., 730 E. Homestead Rd., (408) 720-9020

Nimitz Sch.-Age CDCtr., 545 E. Cheyenne Dr., (408) 736-6176

Ponderosa Dist. Presch., 804 Ponderosa Ave., (408) 736-7647

Presbyterian Early Lrng. Ctr., 728 W. Fremont Ave., (408) 245-2253

Prodigy CDCtr., 1155 E. Arquez Ave., (408) 245-3276

Rainbow Montessori, 790 Duane Ave., (408) 738-3261

Rainbow Presch., 878 Lakewood Dr., (408) 738-2737

Resurrection Sch., 1395 Hollenbeck Ave., (408) 245-4571

South Peninsula Hebrew Day Sch., 1030 Astoria Dr., (408) 738-3060

St. Martin Sch., 597 Central Ave., (408) 736-5534

Stocklmeir-Ortega Sch.-Age CDCtr., 592 Dunholme Way, (408) 732-2008

Sunnyvale CDCtr., 1500 Partridge Ave., (408) 730-9600

Sunnyvale Christian Sch., 445 So. Mary Ave., (408) 736-3286

Sunnyvale Parent Presch., 1515 Partridge Ave., (408) 736-8043

Sunnyvale Sch. Dist. Presch., 739 Morse Ave., (408) 522-8213

Triumphant Lrng. Ctr., 420 Carroll St., (408) 737-7450

Vargas Sch.-Age CDCtr., 1054 Carson Dr., (408) 736-0174

Village Campus CDCtr., 649 E. Homestead Rd., (408) 732-5611

Wedgwood Sch., 1025 The Dalles, (408) 720-9080

YMCA-West Valley, 1635 Belleville Way, (408) 245-0148

Chapter 8

SANTA CLARA COUNTY
Hospitals & Health Care

GOOD HEALTH CARE. You want it. Where, how, do you get it? The question is particularly puzzling these days because so many changes are taking place in medicine and medical insurance.

The "operations" of a few years ago are the "procedures" of today, done in the office not the surgery room, completed in minutes not hours, requiring home care, not hospitalization. Large insurance companies, through their health maintenance plans, are setting limits on what doctors and hospitals can charge, and — critics contend — interfering with the ability of doctors to prescribe what they see fit. The companies strongly deny this, arguing they are bringing reforms to a profession long in need of reforming.

Many hospitals are now setting up their own insurance plans, structured according to the needs of local residents. Many hospitals are also merging, the better to avoid unnecessary duplication and to save money by purchasing supplies and medicine in larger amounts.

The government is taking a more active role in health insurance. California recently passed a law making it easier for the clients to sue their health insurers.

This chapter will give you an overview of Northern California health care and although it won't answer all your questions — too complex a business for that — we hope that it will point you in the right directions.

For most people, health care is twined with insurance, in systems that are called "managed care." But many individuals, for a variety of reasons, do not have insurance. This is a good place to start: with nothing, all options open. Let's use as our seeker for the best of all health care worlds — on a tight budget — a young woman, married, one child. Her choices:

No Insurance — Cash Care

The woman is self-employed or works at a small business that does not offer health benefits. She comes down with the flu. When she goes into the doctor's office, she will be asked by the receptionist, how do you intend to pay? With no insurance, she pays cash (or credit card), usually right there. She

Population by Age & Sex

Santa Clara County

Age	Male	Female	Total
0-4	69,034	65,394	134,428
5-9	71,032	67,576	138,608
10-14	62,647	59,040	121,687
15-19	56,161	53,241	109,402
20-24	52,151	48,957	101,108
25-29	61,667	56,301	117,968
30-34	75,486	66,379	141,865
35-39	91,298	79,492	170,790
40-44	85,725	76,290	162,015
45-49	67,453	63,470	130,923
50-54	54,943	55,677	110,620
55-59	42,623	44,341	86,964
60-64	33,032	34,129	67,161
65-69	26,143	27,618	53,761
70-74	19,901	23,764	43,665
75-79	14,666	20,261	34,927
80-84	8,010	12,708	20,718
85-plus	4,976	11,666	16,642
All	896,948	866,304	1,763,252
Median age	35	36	35

Source: Calif. Dept. of Finance. Population projected to July 2000.

takes her prescription, goes to the pharmacy and pays full cost.

If her child or husband gets sick and needs to see a doctor, the same procedure holds. Also the same for treatment of a serious illness, to secure X-rays or hospitalization. It's a cash system.

Medi-Cal

If an illness strikes that impoverishes the family or if the woman, through job loss or simply low wages, cannot afford cash care, the county-state health system will step in. The woman fills out papers to qualify for Medi-Cal, the name of the system (it's known elsewhere as Medicaid), and tries to find a doctor that will treat Medi-Cal patients. If unable to find an acceptable doctor, the woman could turn to a county hospital or clinic. There she will be treated free or at very low cost.

Drawbacks-Pluses of Medi-Cal

County hospitals and clinics, in the personal experience of one of the editors — who has relatives who work at or use county facilities — have competent doctors and medical personnel. If you keep appointments promptly, often you will be seen with little wait. If you want immediate treatment for, say, a cold, you register and you wait until an urgent-care doctor is free.

If you need a specialist, often the county facility will have one on staff, or will be able to find one at a teaching hospital or other facility. You don't choose the specialist; the county physician does.

County facilities are underfunded and inconveniently located — a major drawback. Some counties, lacking clinics and hospitals, contract with adjoining counties that are equipped. You have to drive some distance for treatment.

County hospitals and clinics are not 100 percent free. If you have money or an adequate income, you will be billed for service. Some county hospitals run medical plans designed for people who can pay. These people can ask for a "family" doctor and receive a higher (usually more convenient) level of care.

Let's say the woman lacks money but doesn't want to hassle with a long drive and, possibly, a long wait for treatment of a minor ailment. She can sign up for Medi-Cal to cover treatment of serious illnesses, and for the colds, etc., go to a private doctor for treatment and pay in cash, ignoring Medi-Cal. There are many ways to skin the cat, and much depends on circumstances. For the poor and low-income, Medi-Cal is meant to be a system of last resort.

Medicare — Veterans Hospital

If our woman were elderly, she would be eligible for Medicare, the federal insurance system, which covers 80 percent, with limitations, of medical costs or allowable charges. Many people purchase supplemental insurance to bring coverage up to 100 percent (long-term illnesses requiring hospitalization may exhaust some benefits.) If the woman were a military veteran with a service-related illness, she could seek care at a Veteran's clinic or hospital.

Indemnity Care

Usually the most expensive, this insurance allows complete freedom of choice. The woman picks the doctor she wants. If her regular doctor recommends a specialist, she can decide which one, and if she needs hospital treatment, she can pick the institution. In reality, the choice of hospital and specialist will often be strongly influenced by her regular doctor but the patient retains control. Many indemnity plans have deductibles and some may limit how much they pay out in a year or lifetime. Paperwork may be annoying.

Managed Care

This divides into two systems, Preferred Provider Organizations (PPO) and Health Maintenance Organizations (HMO). Both are popular in California and if your employer provides health insurance, chances are almost 100 percent you will be pointed toward, or given a choice of, one or the other.

PPOs and HMOs differ among themselves. It is beyond the scope of this book to detail the differences but you should ask if coverage can be revoked or rates increased in the event of serious illness. Also, what is covered, what is not. Cosmetic surgery might not be covered. Psychiatric visits or care might be limited. Ask about drug costs and how emergency or immediate care is provided.

Preferred Provider

The insurance company approaches certain doctors, clinics, medical facilities and hospitals and tells them: We will send patients to you but you must agree to our prices — a method of controlling costs — and our rules. The young woman chooses her doctor from the list, often extensive, provided by the PPO.

The physician will have practicing privileges at certain local hospitals. The young woman's child contracts pneumonia and must be hospitalized. Dr. X is affiliated with XYZ hospital, which is also signed up with the PPO plan. The child is treated at XYZ hospital.

If the woman used an "outside" doctor or hospital, she would pay extra — the amount depending on the nature of the plan. It is important to know the doctor's affiliations because you may want your hospital care at a certain institution.

Hospitals differ. A children's hospital, for instance, will specialize in children's illnesses and load up on children's medical equipment. A general hospital will have a more rounded program. For convenience, you may want the hospital closest to your home.

If you need specialized treatment, you must, to avoid extra costs, use the PPO-affiliated specialists. The doctor will often guide your choice.

Complaints are surfacing from people who started out with a general physician, who was affiliated with their PPO, then moved on to a specialist who was not affiliated with the PPO. When the second doctor submits a bill, people are shocked. Each time you see a doctor you should ask if he or she is affiliated with your PPO.

Besides the basic cost for the policy, PPO insurance might charge fees, co-payments or deductibles. A fee might be $5 or $10 a visit. With co-payments, the bill, say, comes to $100. Insurance pays $80, the woman pays $20.

Deductible example: The woman pays the first $250 or the first $2,000 of any medical costs within a year, and the insurer pays bills above $250 or $2,000. With deductibles, the higher the deductible the lower the cost of the policy. The $2,000 deductible is really a form of catastrophic insurance.

Conversely, the higher the premium the more the policy covers. Some policies cover everything. (Dental care is usually provided through a separate insurer.) The same for prescription medicines. You may pay for all, part, or nothing, depending on the type plan.

The PPO doctor functions as your personal physician. Often the doctor will have his or her own practice and office, conveniently located. If you need to squeeze in an appointment, the doctor usually will try to be accommodating.

Drawback: PPOs restrict choice.

Health Maintenance Organization (HMO)

Very big in California because Kaiser Permanente, one of the most popular medical-hospital groups, is run as an HMO. The insurance company and medical provider are one and the same. All or almost all medical care is given by the HMO. The woman catches the flu. She sees the HMO doctor at the HMO clinic or hospital. If she becomes pregnant, she sees an HMO obstetrician at the HMO hospital or clinic and delivers her baby there.

With HMOs you pay the complete bill if you go outside the system (with obvious exceptions; e.g., emergency care).

HMOs encourage you to pick a personal physician. The young woman wants a woman doctor; she picks one from the staff. She wants a pediatrician as her child's personal doctor; the HMO, usually, can provide one.

HMO clinics and hospitals bring many specialists and services together under one roof. You can get your eyes examined, your hearing tested, your prescriptions filled, your X-rays taken within an HMO facility (this varies), and much more.

If you need an operation or treatment beyond the capability of your immediate HMO hospital, the surgery will be done at another HMO hospital within the system or at a hospital under contract with the HMO. Kaiser recently started contracting with other facilities to provide some of the services that it used to do in its own hospitals or clinics.

HMO payment plans vary but many HMO clients pay a monthly fee and a small ($5-$15) per visit fee. Often the plan includes low-cost or reduced-cost or free prescriptions.

Drawback: Freedom of choice limited. If HMO facility is not close, the woman will have to drive to another town.

Point of Service (POS)

Essentially, an HMO with the flexibility to use outside doctors and facilities for an extra fee or a higher deductible. POS systems seem to be popular with people who don't feel comfortable limiting themselves to an HMO.

They pay extra but possibly not as much as other alternatives.

Which is Better: a PPO, an HMO or a POS?

This is a competitive field with many claims and counter claims. In recent years, PPOs have signed up many doctors and facilities — increasing the choices of members. Kaiser Permanente, however, remains very popular.

Point of Service (POS) seems to be catching on but some experts predict it will fade when people become more familiar with HMOs.

If you are receiving medical insurance through your employer, you will be limited to the choices offered. In large groups, unions often have a say in what providers are chosen. Some individuals will base their choice on price, some on convenience of facilities, others on what's covered, and so on.

Many private hospitals offer Physician Referral Services. You call the hospital, ask for the service and get a list of doctors to choose from. The doctors will be affiliated with the hospital providing the referral. Hospitals and doctors will also tell you what insurance plans they accept for payment and will send you brochures describing the services the hospital offers.

For Kaiser and other HMOs, call the local hospital or clinic.

A PPO will give you a list of its member doctors and facilities.

Ask plenty of questions. Shop carefully.

Common Questions

The young woman is injured in a car accident and is unconscious. Where will she be taken?

Generally, she will be taken to the closest emergency room or trauma center, where her condition will be stabilized. Her doctor will then have her admitted into a hospital. Or she will be transferred to her HMO hospital or, if indigent, to a county facility.

If her injuries are severe, she most likely will be rushed to a regional trauma center. Trauma centers have specialists and special equipment to treat serious injuries. Both PPOs and HMOs offer urgent care and emergency care.

The young woman breaks her leg. Her personal doctor is an internist and does not set fractures. What happens?

The personal doctor refers the case to a specialist. Insurance pays the specialist's fee.

In PPO, the woman would generally see a specialist affiliated with the PPO. In an HMO, the specialist would be employed by the HMO.

The young woman signs up for an HMO then contracts a rare disease or suffers an injury that requires treatment beyond the capability of the HMO. Will she be treated?

Often yes, but it pays to read the fine print. The HMO will contract treatment out to a facility that specializes in the needed treatment.

The young woman becomes despondent and takes to drink. Will insurance pay for her rehabilitation?

Depends on her insurance. And often her employer. Some may have drug and alcohol rehab plans. Some plans cover psychiatry.

The woman becomes pregnant. Her doctor, who has delivered many babies, wants her to deliver at X hospital. All the woman's friends say, Y

Hospital is much better, nicer, etc. The doctor is not cleared to practice at Y Hospital. Is the woman out of luck?

With a PPO, the woman must deliver at a hospital affiliated with the PPO — or pay the extra cost. If her doctor is not affiliated with that hospital, sometimes a doctor may be given courtesy practicing privileges at a hospital where he or she does not have staff membership. Check with the doctor.

With HMOs, the woman must deliver within the HMO system.

Incidentally, with PPOs and HMOs you should check that the doctors and specialists listed in the organization's booklets can treat you. Some plans may restrict access to certain doctors. Some booklets may be out-of-date and not have an accurate list of doctors.

The young woman goes in for minor surgery, which turns into major surgery when the doctor forgets to remove a sponge before sewing up. Upon reviving, she does what?

Some medical plans require clients to submit complaints to a panel of arbitrators, which decides damages, if any. But the courts are taking a dim view of this policy. Read the policy.

The woman's child reaches age 18. Is she covered by the family insurance?

All depends on the insurance. Some policies will cover the children while they attend college. (But attendance may be defined in a certain way, full-time as opposed to part-time.) You should read the plan thoroughly.

At work, the woman gets her hand caught in a revolving door and is told she will need six months of therapy during which she can't work. Who pays?

Insurance will usually pay for the medical costs. Workers Compensation, a state plan that includes many but not all people, may compensate the woman for time lost off the job and may pay for medical costs. If you injure yourself on the job, your employer must file a report with Workers Comp. Ask also how emergency or immediate care is provided.

The woman wakes up at 3 a.m. with a sore throat and headache. She feels bad but not bad enough to drive to a hospital or emergency room. She should:

Many hospitals and medical plans offer 24-hour advice lines. This is something you should check on when you sign up for a plan.

While working in her kitchen, the woman slips, bangs her head against the stove, gets a nasty cut and becomes woozy. She should:

Call 9-1-1, which will send an ambulance. 9-1-1 is managed by police dispatch. It's the fastest way to get an ambulance — with one possible exception. San Jose Police Dept. has opened an easy-dial line for non-emergencies.

Phone 3-1-1.

What's the difference between a hospital, a clinic, an urgent-care center and a doctor's office?

The hospital has the most services and equipment. The center or clinic has several services and a fair amount of equipment. The office, usually, has the fewest services and the smallest amount of equipment but in some places "clinic-office" means about the same.

Hospitals have beds. If a person must have a serious operation, she goes to a hospital. Hospitals have coronary-care and intensive-care units, emergency care and other specialized, costly treatment units. Many hospitals also run clinics for minor ailments and provide the same services as medical centers.

Urgent care or medical centers are sometimes located in neighborhoods, which makes them more convenient for some people. The doctors treat the minor, and often not-so-minor, ailments of patients and send them to hospitals for major surgery and serious sicknesses.

Some doctors form themselves into groups to offer the public a variety of services.

Some hospitals have opened neighborhood clinics or centers to attract patients. Kaiser has hospitals in some towns and clinic-offices in other towns.

The doctor in his or her office treats patients for minor ailments and uses the hospital for surgeries, major illnesses. Many illnesses that required hospitalization years ago are now treated in the office or clinic.

Major Hospitals & Medical Facilities

Columbia Good Samaritan Hospital, 2425 Samaritan Dr., San Jose, 95124. Phone: (408) 559-2011. General and tertiary acute care services; 24-hour emergency care; cardiology, cardiovascular surgery; cancer care center; comprehensive women and children services including family birthing center, level III neonatal intensive care nursery, maternal transport program, perinatology services, diabetes screening, childbirth and parenting education, breastfeeding services; Center for Children's Surgery; surgery, including endoscopic surgery; orthopedics; critical care; adult psychiatric services, alcohol and substance abuse, skilled nursing unit; diagnostic imaging, including MRI, CT Scan; home health care. 511 beds. Outpatient surgery, Columbia Breast Center on the Mission Oaks Hospital Campus, 15891 Los Gatos-Almaden Rd., Los Gatos. For physician referral, call 1-800-COLUMBIA.

Columbia San Jose Medical Center, 675 E. Santa Clara St., San Jose, 95112. Phone: (408) 998-3212. ICU, CCU, OB, GYN, emergency services, county-designated trauma center with helicopter service, family health center, family birthing center, women's wellness services, cancer care center, neurosurgery center, comprehensive cardiology services, center for rehabilitation, skilled nursing facility, home health care, comprehensive diagnostic imaging and therapeutic services, pediatric ICU, outpatient surgery, replantation and microvascular surgery, physician referral service. 295 beds.

Community Hospital of Los Gatos, 815 Pollard Rd., Los Gatos, 95032. Phone: (408) 378-6131. ICU, CCU, 24-hour emergency care services, Family Birth Place, perinatal education program, physician referral services, pediatrics, Community Home Health, diagnostic imaging, Joint Care Program, acute and subacute rehabilitation, Center for Spinal Deformity & Injury, Arthritis Center, Physical Performance Institute, sports medicine program, occupational medicine, transitional care, outpatient surgery, comprehensive endoscopy, advanced surgical procedures, community education preventive medicine lecture program, Women's Cancer Center, dietary and nutritional services, diabetes services, Western Kidney Stone Center. 153 beds.

El Camino Hospital, 2500 Grant Rd., Mountain View, 94040. Ph: (650) 940-7000. 24-hour emergency services, ambulatory surgery, behavioral medicine, breast screening, cancer care, cardiovascular, chemical dependency, community health education, critical care, critical care nursery, dialysis services, emergency heart services, employee assistance programs, endoscopy, interventional diagnostic radiology, laser surgery, maternal child health services, MRI, nutritional therapy, occupational and physical therapy, Older Adult Resource Center, radiation therapy. 426 beds.

Kaiser Medical Center, 900 Kiely Blvd., Santa Clara, 95051. Phone: (408) 236-6400. Kaiser Permanente is a group practice prepayment plan which provides comprehensive medical and hospital services to its Kaiser Foundation Health Plan members. Full range of hospital services including alcohol and drug abuse program, CCU, craniofacial and pediatric surgery, CT scan and MRI, emergency services, gynecological oncology, hospice, ICU, neonatal intensive care, high risk OB, internal medicine, neurosurgery, pediatric ICU, pediatrics, plasmapheresis, sports medicine center, surgery. Kaiser Permanente is an affiliated teaching hospital for Stanford University School of Medicine and has independent residency programs in Internal Medicine, OB and GYN, podiatry and emergency medicine. 337 licensed beds.

Kaiser Permanente-Santa Teresa Medical Center, 250 Hospital Pkwy., San Jose, 95119. Phone: (408) 972-3000 Kaiser Permanente is a group practice prepayment plan which provides comprehensive medical and hospital services to its Kaiser Foundation Health Plan members. Full range of hospital services including cardiac catheterization, emergency services, genetics, ICU, CCU, internal medicine, OB, GYN, pediatrics, surgery. 228 licensed beds.

Kaiser Permanente Medical Offices—Gilroy, 7520 Arroyo Cir., Gilroy, 95020. Ph. (408) 848-4001. Outpatient medical office providing pediatrics, internal medicine, OB, GYN, allergy, dermatology, optometry, health education and urgent care.

Kaiser Permanente Medical Offices—Milpitas, 770 E. Calaveras Blvd., Milpitas, 95035. Ph. (408) 945-2900. Outpatient medical office providing pediatrics, internal medicine, OB, GYN, allergy, dermatology, optometry, health education and urgent care.

Kaiser Permanente Medical Offices—Mountain View, 555 Castro St., Mountain View, 94041. Ph. (650) 903-3000. Outpatient medical office providing pediatrics, internal medicine, OB, GYN, allergy, dermatology, optometry, health education and urgent care.

Lucille Salter Packard Children's Hospital at Stanford, 725 Welch Rd., Palo Alto, 94304. Phone: (650) 497-8000. Primary care and specialty outpatient clinics, child psychiatry, neonatology, oncology/bone marrow transplantation, kidney and liver transplantation, heart and heart/lung transplantation, intensive care, cardiology, pediatric general surgery, neurosurgery, orthopedics, and other full-service medical and surgical services for children. Pediatric diagnostic, treatment and support services. Home pharmacy service, rehabilitation engineering, Parent Information & Referral Center (PIRC), Kidcall program. 162 beds.

Mission Oaks Hospital, 15891 Los Gatos Almaden Rd., Los Gatos, 95032. Ph. (408) 356-4111.

O'Connor Hospital, 2105 Forest Ave., San Jose, 95128. Phone: (408) 947-2500. Heart center, family center, cancer care center, recovery center for alcohol and chemical dependency, mental health program for seniors, wound care center, transitional care center, ICU, surgical services, 24-hour emergency department, physical, occupational and speech therapy, O'Connor MRI and all other diagnostic imaging services. Home health, pharmacy, physician referral service, community education seminars and wellness programs. Member of Catholic Healthcare West. 360 beds.

Regional Medical Center of San Jose, 225 N. Jackson Ave., San Jose, 95116. Phone: (408) 259-5000. ICU, CCU, 24-hour emergency services, family birthing center, pediatrics, neonatal intensive care, outpatient surgery, physical occupational & speech therapy, radiology & laboratory services, diagnostic imaging, diagnostic & vascular ultrasound, home health care, community education seminar & wellness programs, maternal child health classes in English, Vietnamese and Spanish, parish nurse program, senior health center, pediatric Medi-Cal clinic, OB Medi-Cal clinic, community benefit programs, physician referral. 204 beds.

Saint Louise Hospital, 18500 Saint Louise Dr., Morgan Hill, 95037. Phone: (408) 779-1500. 24-hour emergency care, ICU, OB, GYN, surgical services, physical therapy, skilled nursing, birthing suites, outpatient surgery, Center for Life prenatal care and delivery program, comprehensive diagnostic imaging, community health education, home health care, physician referral service. Urgent care center, cancer care center, family clinic and MRI located on campus. Member of Catholic Healthcare West. 60 beds.

Saint Louise Regional Hospital, 9400 No Name Uno, Gilroy, 95020. Phone: (408) 848-2000 or (800) 423-2032. 24-hour emergency services with emergency helicopter, ICU/CCU, medical, surgical and pediatric services; outpatient surgery, family-oriented birth suites, breast-care center; physical, occupational and speech therapy; diagnostic services include X-ray services, MRI and CT scan, ultrasound, home-health services. Skilled nursing facility. 21 beds.

Santa Clara Valley Health & Hospital System, 751 S. Bascom Ave., San Jose, 95128. Phone: (408) 885-5000. Recently rebuilt, $197 million job. Surgical ICU, medical ICU, CCU, OB, GYN, Trauma Center, Emergency Care, Regional Burn Center, Physical Rehab including Brain & Spinal Injury Center, Physician Referral, Pediatrics, Psychiatry, Poison Center, Neonatal Intensive Care, Pediatrics Intensive Care. Outpatient clinics. Helicopter transportation. 302 beds.

Stanford University Hospital, 300 Pasteur Dr., Stanford, 94305. Ph: (650) 723-4000. ICU, CCU, OB, GYN, emergency care & prompt care, trauma center, cardiovascular, stroke center, epilepsy, bone marrow transplantation, psychiatric care, physician referral, radiology, home health care, cancer treatment, ambulatory surgery center, multi-organ transplant center, comprehensive rehabilitation center, helicopter transportation. 663 beds.

Veterans Affairs Palo Alto Health Care System, 3801 Miranda Ave., Palo Alto, 94304. Phone: (650) 493-5000. ICU, CCU, GYN, psychiatric care, physical therapy, skilled nursing, home health care, trauma center, physician referral, chemical dependency, radiology, geriatric services, emergency care, alcohol treatment, eating disorders, cancer treatment, MRI, PET, PTSD, blind rehab, BIRU, spinal cord injury center, 1,264 beds (Palo Alto, Menlo Park and Livermore facilities combined).

Key: ICU, intensive care unit; CCU, coronary care unit; OB, obstetrics; GYN, gynecology; MRI, magnetic resonance imaging; PET, position emission tomography; PTSD, post-traumatic stress disorder; BIRU, brain injury rehabilitation unit.

Chapter 9

SANTA CLARA COUNTY

Newcomers Guide

Voter Registration

You must be 18 years and a citizen. Go to post office and ask for a voter registration postcard. Fill it out and pop it into the mail box. Or pick up the form when you register your vehicle or secure a driver's license. Before every election, the county will mail you a sample ballot with the address of your polling place. For more information call the elections office (408) 299-8302.

Change of Address — Mail

The change-of-address form can also be picked up at the post office. To assure continuity of service, fill out this form 30 days before you move.

Dog Licensing-Spaying

If you live in a city, call city hall for information about dog licensing and pet vaccinations and spaying-neutering. City hall numbers are listed at the beginning of your phone book.

If you live in the county jurisdiction, phone (800) 215-2555.

For licensing, bring proof of rabies vaccination. Some jurisdictions will discount the license fee if Rover or Fifi has been fixed.

Driving

California has the most stringent smog requirements in the country. If your car is a few years old, you may have to spend a couple of hundred dollars to bring it up to code.

You have 20 days from the time you enter the state to register your vehicles. After that you pay a penalty, and face getting a ticket-fine.

For registration, go to any office of the Department of Motor Vehicles. Bring your smog certificate, your registration card and your license plates.

If you are a California resident, all you need to do is complete a change-of-address form, which can be obtained by calling (800) 777-0133 or visiting one of the following Dept. of Motor Vehicles offices:

- Campbell: 430 Darryl Dr.

- Los Gatos: 600 N. Santa Cruz Ave.
- Mountain View: 595 Showers Dr.
- San Jose: 111 W. Alma Ave.
- San Jose (south): 180 Martinvale Ln.
- Santa Clara: 3665 Flora Vista Ave.
- Gilroy: 8200 Church St.

Driver's License

To obtain a driver's license, you must be 16 years old, pass a state-certified Driver's Education (classroom) and Driver's Training (behind-the-wheel) course, and at Department of Motor Vehicles a vision test and written and driving tests.

Once you pass the test, your license is usually renewed by mail. Retesting is rare, unless your driving record is poor. High schools used to offer free driving courses but these have all but disappeared due to state budget cuts. Private driving schools have moved in to fill the gap, at a cost of $200 to $250.

Teenagers older than 15 1/2 years who have completed driver's training can be issued a permit. New law restricts driving hours for young teens to daylight hours and, unless supervised, forbids them for six months to drive other teens. Law also requires more parental training and extends time of provisional license. Purpose is to reduce accidents.

If no driver's education program has been completed, you must be at least 18 years old to apply for a driver's license. Out-of-state applicants must supply proof of "legal presence," which could be a certified copy of a birth certificate. Foreign applicants must supply other documents. Law is aimed at illegal immigrants. If going for a driver's license, ask to have the booklet mailed to you or pick it up. Study it. All the questions will be taken from the booklet.

Turning Rules. If signs don't say no, you can turn right on a red light (after making a full stop) and make a U-turn at an intersection.

Stop for pedestrians. Stop for discharging school buses, even if on opposite side of road. Must have insurance to drive and to register vehicle.

Earthquakes

They're fun and great topics of conversation, until you get caught in a big one. Then they are not so funny. At the beginning of your phone book is some advice about what to do before, during and after a temblor. It's worth reading.

Garbage Service

The garbage fellows come once a week. Rates vary by city and lately a lot of competition has been coming into this business. Figure $20 a month for one-can-a-week service. Besides the cans, almost every home will receive recycling bins for plastics, glass and cans.

Pickup weekly, usually the same day as garbage. Some garbage companies are switching to wheeled carts that can be picked up by mechanical arms attached to truck.

Don't burn your garbage in the fireplace or outside. Don't burn leaves. Against the law. To get rid of car batteries, motor oils and water-soluble paints, call your local garbage firm and ask about disposal sites. Or call city hall.

Property Taxes

The average property tax rate in California is 1.25 percent. If you buy a $300,000 home this year, your property tax will be $3,750. Once the basic tax is established, it goes up about 2 percent annually in following years.

"Average" needs to be emphasized. Some jurisdictions have tacked costs on to the property tax; some have not. Some school districts, in recent years, have won approval of annual parcel taxes.

Property taxes are paid in two installments, due by April 10 and December 10. They are generally collected automatically through impound accounts set up when you purchase a home, but check your sale documents carefully. Sometimes homeowners are billed directly.

Some cities, to fund parks and lights and other amenities in new subdivisions, have installed what is called the Mello-Roos tax. Realtors are required to give you complete information on all taxes.

Sales Tax

Varies by county. In Santa Clara County, it is 8.25 percent. If you buy something for $1 you will pay $1.08 and if the item costs $100, you will pay $108.25. Food, except when sold in restaurants, is exempted.

State Income Taxes

State income taxes range from 1% to 9.3%. A single person earning between $26,045 and $32,916 would pay $899.56 plus 8% of amount over $26,045. A married couple filing jointly with an income of $65,832 would pay $2,898 plus 9.3% of the amount over $65,832 .

Disclosure Laws

California requires Realtors to give detailed reports on every home sold, including information about earthquake faults. Megan's law applies: for home sales and rentals, sales agent must tell you where you can get names and addresses of registered sex offenders. Usually, this will be the local police department.

Grocery Prices

Item	Store one	Store two	Average
Apple Juice, 1 gallon	$3.29	$2.25	$2.77
Apple Pie, Mrs. Smith's, 37 oz.	$5.09	$4.59	$4.84
Apples, Red Delicious, 1 lb.	$1.19	$0.79	$0.99
Aspirin, cheapest, 250 ct.	$3.99	$3.99	$3.99
Bacon, 1 lb. Farmer John Sliced	$4.25	$2.99	$3.62
Bananas, 1 lb.	$0.49	$0.55	$0.52
Bayer's Children's Aspirin, 36 count	$2.75	$2.69	$2.72
Beef, top round boneless roast, 1 lb.	$2.19	$2.99	$2.59
Beef, ground round, 1 lb.	$1.36	$2.59	$1.98
Beer, Budweiser, 12-pack, cans	$8.49	$8.49	$8.49
Beer, Coors, 12-pack, cans	$8.49	$8.49	$8.49
Bisquick, 2lbs 8oz	$2.49	$2.39	$2.44
Bleach, Clorox, 1 gal.	$1.99	$1.89	$1.94
Bread, sourdough, Colombo, 1 lb.	$2.69	$2.19	$2.44
Bread, white, cheapest, 1 lb.	$1.69	$0.89	$1.29
Broccoli, bunch	$0.89	$0.89	$0.89
Butter, Tillamook, 1 lb.	$3.39	$3.79	$3.59
Cabbage, 1 lb.	$0.39	$0.39	$0.39
Cantaloupe, 1 lb.	$0.69	$0.50	$0.60
Carrots, fresh, 1 lb.	$1.00	$1.99	$1.50
Cat Food, store brand, small can	$0.39	$0.35	$0.37
Cereal, Wheaties, Kellogg, 18 oz.	$4.19	$4.23	$4.21
Charcoal, Kingsford, 20 lbs.	$8.49	$8.19	$8.34
Cheese, Mild Cheddar, 1 lb..	$3.89	$3.79	$3.84
Chicken, breasts, boneless skinless 1 lb.	$5.79	$5.89	$5.84
Chili, Stagg, with beans,15 oz. can	$1.79	$1.65	$1.72
Cigarettes, Marlboro Lights, carton	$31.99	$34.99	$33.49
Coca Cola, 12-pack, 12 oz. cans	$4.49	$4.49	$4.49
Coffee, Folgers, 1lb.	$3.49	$6.99	$5.24
Cookies, Oreo, 20 oz pkg.	$3.59	$3.49	$3.54
Diapers, Huggies, size 2	$13.99	$13.99	$13.99
Dishwasher Soap, Comet, 22 oz.	$0.99	$0.95	$0.97
Dishwashing Liquid, Dawn, 22 oz.	$3.49	$3.33	$3.41
Dog Food, Friskies, 22 oz.can	$1.19	$1.19	$1.19
Eggs, large, Grade AA, doz.	$2.33	$1.89	$2.11
Flour, Gold Medal, 5 lbs.	$1.99	$1.95	$1.97
Frozen Yogurt, Dreyers, half gal.	$5.29	$4.99	$5.14
Gerber's Baby Food, Fruit, 4 oz.	$0.49	$0.49	$0.49
Gerber's Baby Food, Vegetables, 4 oz.	$0.67	$0.49	$0.58
Gerber's Baby Food, Meat, 2.5 oz.	$0.75	$0.75	$0.75
Gerber's Baby Food, Cereal, 4 oz.	$0.49	$0.49	$0.49
Gerber's Baby Food, Turkey, 2.5 oz.	$0.75	$0.75	$0.75
Gin, Gilbeys, 1.75 Liter	$9.29	$16.99	$13.14
Grapes, Red Seedless, 1 lb.	$0.88	$1.49	$1.19
Grapefruit, each	$0.79	$0.49	$0.64
Grapenuts, Post, 24 oz.	$3.65	$3.99	$3.82
Ham, Armour, 1.5 lb. canned	$5.19	$5.19	$5.19
Ice Cream, Dreyers, vanilla half gal.	$5.29	$5.29	$5.29
Instant Lunch	$0.59	$0.59	$0.59
Jam, Mary Ellen, 18 oz.	$3.79	$3.69	$3.74
Ketchup, Del Monte, 40 oz.	$3.39	$2.85	$3.12

Grocery Prices

Item	Store 1	Store 2	Avg
Kleenex, 160 count box	$1.69	$1.39	$1.54
Kraft Macaroni & Cheese	$0.99	$0.95	$0.97
Laundry Detergent, Tide, 92 oz.	$8.79	$12.19	$10.49
Lettuce, Iceberg, head	$0.69	$0.69	$0.69
Margarine, Can't Believe It's Not Butter, 1lb. Tub	$1.65	$1.63	$1.64
Mayonnaise, Best Foods, 1 qt.	$3.59	$3.39	$3.49
Milk, Whole, half gal.	$1.85	$1.84	$1.85
M&M Candies, plain,1 lb.	$2.89	$2.99	$2.94
Mushrooms, sliced, per lb.	$2.79	$2.79	$2.79
Olive Oil, cheapest, 17 oz.	$3.49	$5.39	$4.44
Onions, yellow, 3 lb.	$0.99	$1.17	$1.08
Orange Juice, Tropicana, 64 oz. Original Style	$3.99	$3.99	$3.99
Oranges, Valencias, fresh, 4 lb.	$3.19	$3.69	$3.44
Paper Towels, single pack	$1.79	$1.45	$1.62
Peanuts, cocktail, Planter's, 12 oz. jar	$3.29	$2.79	$3.04
Peas, frozen, 10 oz.	$1.89	$1.19	$1.54
Peanut Butter, Jiff, 1 lb.	$3.89	$2.59	$3.24
Pork, chops, center cut, 1 lb.	$2.49	$1.49	$1.99
Potato Chips, Lays, 12.25 oz.	$2.99	$2.99	$2.99
Potatoes, 10 lbs.	$1.99	$1.99	$1.99
Raisins, bulk, 24 oz.	$3.45	$3.49	$3.47
Red Snapper, fresh, 1 lb.	$4.99	$4.99	$4.99
Reese's Peanut Butter Cups,10 pk.	$1.49	$1.39	$1.44
Rice, cheapest, 5 lbs.	$2.99	$2.89	$2.94
Seven-Up, 6-pack, cans	$2.59	$2.59	$2.59
Soap, bar, Zest, 3-pack, 5-oz.	$2.69	$2.59	$2.64
Soup, Campbell, Chicken Noodle, 10.5 oz. can	$0.99	$0.95	$0.97
Soy Sauce, Kikkoman, 10 oz.	$1.69	$1.65	$1.67
Spaghetti, cheapest, 2 lb.	$1.95	$2.19	$2.07
Sugar, cheapest, 5 lbs.	$2.15	$2.09	$2.12
Tea, Lipton's, 48-bag box	$2.69	$3.19	$2.94
Toilet Tissue, 4-roll pack, cheapest	$1.49	$1.39	$1.44
Tomatoes, extra large, 1 lb.	$1.49	$1.39	$1.44
Toothpaste, Colgate, 6.4 oz.	$2.39	$2.59	$2.49
Top Ramen	$0.29	$0.25	$0.27
Tortillas, cheapest, 12-count pack	$1.59	$1.19	$1.39
Tuna, Starkist, 6 oz.	$1.89	$1.99	$1.94
Turkey, ground, 1 lb.	$1.17	$2.89	$2.03
Vegetable Oil, store brand, 64 oz.	$3.79	$3.49	$3.64
Vegetables, frozen, 10 oz.	$1.99	$2.29	$2.14
Vinegar, store brand, 1 pint	$0.69	$0.69	$0.69
Whiskey, Seagrams 7 Crown,750 ml	$9.99	$9.99	$9.99
Wine, White Zinfandel, 750 ml.	$4.99	$4.99	$4.99
Yoplait Original Yogurt, single	$0.79	$0.75	$0.77
Young Chicken-Foster Farms 1 lb.	$1.29	$1.18	$1.24
Other Prices			
Baby Shampoo, Johnsons, 20 fluid oz.	$4.89	$4.89	$4.89
Babysitting (per hour)	$5.00	$6.00	$5.50
McDonald's Big Mac Meal	$3.49	$3.49	$3.49
Parental Stress Reliever (qt. Haagen Daz ice cream)	$5.39	$5.19	$5.29
Puppy (German Shepherd, pure bred, class. Ad)	$350.00	$400.00	$375.00

Cigarette-Tobacco Tax

Took effect in 1999. Adds 50 cents to a pack of cigarettes. Many Californians load up on cigarettes in Nevada or Mexico or order over Internet.

Gas and Electricity

Most homes are heated with natural gas. No one, or almost no one, uses heating oil. Pacific Gas and Electric reports that gas bills, year round, average about $30 a month, and electric bills $60 a month.

Almost never between May and September, and rarely between April and October, will you need to heat your home. Winter days are often balmy; no heating required.

Air conditioners are used throughout the summer but on many days they're not needed. PG&E, the utility, will give you advice on insulating your home.

Cable TV Service

Almost all East Bay homes are served by cable. Rates vary according to channels accessed but a basic rate plus one tier is $30 a month. Installation is extra. For clear FM radio reception, often a cable connection is required.

Bottled Water

If the direct source for your town's water is the Sierra, then you may not need bottled water. If the source is wells, many people take the bottled.

Tipping

It's not done in the Bay Area as much as it is done in other parts of the country. Tip the newspaper delivery person, cab or limo drivers, waiters and waitresses and, at the holidays, people who perform regular personal services: yard maintenance, child care, housekeeping.

Don't tip the supermarket employee who carries bags to your car. Don't tip telephone or cable TV installers. Your garbage collector will usually be a Teamster. No beer. No money. Maybe a little cake or box of candy at Christmas. If a garbage collector gets nailed for drunk driving, it will probably cost him his job. Some people give the mail carrier a little holiday gift; many don't. Let your conscience be your guide: The coffee shops. Many are sprouting "tip" cups at the counter.

Smoking

In 1998 a state law took effect forbidding smoking in saloons, one of the last bastions of smoking. Bars in restaurants generally comply. Neighborhood saloons sporadically enforce but many people refrain from smoking and those that do, often hide the cigarette under the table. In San Francisco, people routinely smoke in neighborhood bars.

If visiting socially, you are generally expected to light up outside.

Love and Society

San Francisco often flaunts its sexuality, hetero and homo. Except in rare instances, the suburbs don't but the cosmopolitan virtues apply. In the Bay Area, consenting adults, in sexual matters, are generally free to do what they want as long as it doesn't harm others.

In professional society in Santa Clara County and the Bay Area, same-sex couples attend office parties and social events, and no subterfuge is put up to disguise the relationship but what is accepted in San Francisco will often cock eyebrows in the suburbs. If you slobber over your loved one, no matter what the sexual orientation, you won't be stoned but you might be shunned.

If you want the society of men or the society of women or both, numerous groups exist to help to make connections.

Ages

You must be 18 to vote and smoke and 21 to drink alcohol. Watch the booze. California has a drunk-driving law so stringent that even a drink or two can put you in violation. Clerks are supposed to ask you for ID if you look under 27 for smokes and under 30 for booze.

Dress

Casual from the clerk to the CEOs making millions. But not universal. An older boss may dress more traditionally than a young.

If your job requires you to meet the public or to make a good impression, suits or sports coats are donned.

For almost all social occasions, even, in some circles, weddings and funerals, the dress is casual. The person who wears a tie to a restaurant on Friday or Saturday often stands out (depends a little on the town). San Jose and several towns throw Black-and-White balls to raise money for charity or schools. Break or rent out the tux; cut loose for that fabulous gown. These are the social events of the year.

Dress formal for dinner in San Francisco and the theater or opera (but even here, many men go in sports coats, no tie; women in slacks).

For the coast and San Francisco in the summer, bring a jacket or sweater. It's often chilly, even during the day.

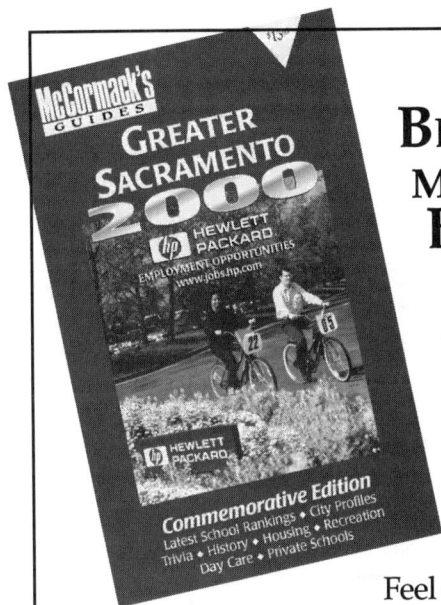

Chapter 10

SANTA CLARA COUNTY
Rental Housing

WITH THE ECONOMY BOOMING, rents unfortunately are also booming. The Bay Area over the past three years has seen a sharp but uneven rise in rents. Silicon Valley towns have posted some of the highest increases. See chart in this chapter for rents by town.

For those new to the region and shopping for homes, a hotel might do the trick — short term. The major chains have built large and small hotels in the suburbs, many of them near freeway exits and a few smack in the middle of residential neighborhoods. Prices range from below $70 to well over $100 a night, the higher amount buying more of the extras: pools, game rooms, etc.

Residency hotels offer a slightly different experience. They combine the conveniences of a hotel — maid service, continental breakfast, airport shuttle — with the pleasures of home: a fully-equipped kitchen and a laundry room (coin-operated). They may also have a pool, a spa, a sportscourt, a workout room. Some offer free grocery shopping and on evenings a social hour.

Residency hotels welcome families. Typically, guests remain at least five days and often much longer. At a certain stage, a discount will kick in.

In the Bay Area, apartments come in all sizes and settings. If you're strapped for funds, you can find single bedrooms and studios for under $600 a month. No pool, no spa, no extras. What goes for $1,400 in Palo Alto may rent for $1,100 in San Jose. If the neighborhood is safe and nice, if the apartment complex is close to light rail, you will probably pay extra.

Renters pay for cable service, electricity or gas and phone (in some instances, deposits may be required to start service.)

You will be asked for a security deposit and for the first month's rent up front. State law limits deposits to a maximum two months rent for an unfurnished apartment and three months for a furnished (this includes the last month's rent.) If you agree to a lease, you might get an extra month free. If you move out before the lease is up, you pay a penalty.

Some apartments forbid pets, some will accept only cats, some cats and small dogs. Many will ask for a pet deposit (to cover possible damage.)

Average Rents

City	1BR Apt.	2 BR Apt.	2 BR H,C,Twh.	3 BR H,C,Twh.
Campbell	$876	$1,201	$1,476	$1,942
Cupertino	$1,301	$1,724	$1,690	$1,901
Los Altos	$1,429	$1,706	$2,298	$2,405
Los Alltos Hills	NA	NA	$2,850	NA
Los Gatos	$1,113	$1,358	$1,842	$2,413
Milpitas	$995	$1,123	$1,475	$1,612
Mountain View	$1,023	$1,352	$1,664	$2.,197
Palo Alto	$1,353	$1,649	$2,182	$2,614
Saratoga	NA	NA	$1,941	$2,533
Santa Clara	$934	$1,235	$1,490	$1,791
San Jose	$895	$1,159	$1,411	$1,891
Sunnyvale	$1,041	$1,264	$1,522	$1,874

Source: Bay Rentals of San Jose, (408) 244-4900, www.bayarearentals.com. These rental prices, collected late in 1999 through Bay Rentals, are a good indication of average rents by selected towns.
Key: H=House, C=Condo, Twh.=Townhouse, NA=No listings.

To protect themselves, landlords will ask you to fill out a credit report and to list references. In one instance that made the newspapers, an apartment complex asked the prospective tenant for her parents' tax returns. With the shortage of apartments, the manager could afford to be choosy. The shortage has made apartment hunting more of an adventure than it should be. If you want help or are striking out with the classified ads, you might try a rental agency. Some complexes supposedly are renting only through agencies.

The Fair Housing laws will apply: no discrimination based on race, sex, family status and so on. But some complexes will be designed to welcome one or several kinds of renters.

A complex that wants families, for example, might include a tot lot. One that prefers singles or childless couples might throw Friday night parties or feature a large pool and a workout room but no kiddie facilities.

Some large complexes will offer furnished and unfurnished apartments or corporate setups, a variation of the residency hotel.

If hotels or apartments are not your cup of tea, you might take a look at renting a home or townhouse. See classified ads or Real Estate Rentals in Yellow Pages. Many owners turn the maintenance and renting over to a professional property manager.

In older towns, many of the cottages and smaller homes in the older sections will often be rentals. If you see a "For Sale" sign in front of a home that interests you, inquire whether the place is for rent.

What about rates? They will vary by town but in a middle-class town you often can rent a three-bedroom home for $1,100 to $1,600 a month. Older, smaller homes in some suburbs will go for about $900 a month but you might have to drive quite a way to job centers. In upscale towns, home rents are much higher.

Finally, there are shared rentals. Typically, they are most popular around colleges and universities. Berkeley, San Francisco, Palo Alto, San Jose, Hayward — where major universities are located — all possess a thriving market in shared rentals. For information, consult the campus housing office.

Some universities run housing departments that try to line up homes and apartments for single students, married students and staff and faculty. The larger universities have dorms.

Community colleges will sometimes support, just off campus, a small shared-rental neighborhood.

Newspapers routinely carry ads from people looking to share a rental. Preferences are stated: no smokers, women only, no pets, etc. If you really want to save the bucks and possibly pick up a friend or two, a shared rental might be just the thing.

A word on furniture. If you don't want to buy it, you can rent it. Check the Yellow Pages under furniture rental. For cheap furniture, check out the garage sales. They are usually advertised on weekends in the local newspapers.

When you're out scouting for a rental, check out the neighborhood, do a little research, and think about what you really value and enjoy.

If you want the convenient commute without the hassle of a car, pick a place near a light-rail line or bus stop. If it's the active life, scout out the parks, trails and such things as bars and restaurants and community colleges. Say the first thing you want to do when you arrive home is take a long run. Before you rent, get a map of local trails. City recreation departments will usually be able to give you information.

For parents, your address will usually determine what public school your child will attend. If you want a high-scoring school, see the scores in this book before making a decision. Always call the school before making a renting decision. Because of crowding, some schools are changing attendance zones. You may not be able to get your child into the "neighborhood" school. Ask also whether the school is year round. See the chapter on how public schools work. The same advice applies to day care. Make sure that it is available nearby before signing a lease.

Many of the larger apartment complexes offer some kind of security: parking lot lights, gates, guards. Happy hunting!

Rent Sampler from Classified Ads

Almaden Valley (San Jose)

Condo, 2 BR/2BA, A/C, frig., micro, D/W, pool, garage, $1,550.

Condo, 2 BR/1.5BA, patio, yard, $1,695.

Berryessa (San Jose)

Condo, 1 BR/1BA, gated, W/D, frig., pool, $1,050.

Condo, 2 BR/2.5BA, den, fireplace, 2-car garage, pool/spa, $1,500.

Blossom Valley (San Jose)

Condo, 3 BR/2BA, cat OK, $1,475.

Cambrian (San Jose)

Home, 3 BR/2BA, water/garbage, W/D. gardener incl., $1,850.

Townhome, 3 BR/2.5BA, fireplace, W/D, 2-car garage, $2,075.

Campbell

Townhome, 2 BR/1BA, pool, $1,290.

Townhome, 3 BR/2.5BA, 2-car garage, pool $1,675.

Cupertino

Condo, 2 BR/1.5BA, $1,400.

Condo, 2 BR/1BA, 2-car garage, pool/hot tub, $1,900.

East Valley (San Jose)

Home, 4 BR/2BA, family room, kitchen, large yard, $1,900.

Home, 4 BR/3BA, 2,500 sf, family room, 2-story, $2,000.

Evergreen (San Jose)

Home, 3 BR/2BA, fireplace, large yard, cov'd patio, $1,750.

Gilroy

Home, 1 BR, yard, pet OK, $600.

Home, 5 BR/3BA, frig., W/D, micro, landscaped, pool/spa, $1,950.

Los Altos

Home, 3 BR/2.5BA, 2 fireplaces, 2-car garage, $3,700.

Home, 3 BR/2BA, $4,000.

Los Altos Hills

Cottage, view, pool/spa, new kitchen, frig., garden, $1,200.

Home, 4 BR/2BA, on 2 ac., AEK, family room, no smokers, $3,800.

Los Gatos

Mountain retreat, 4 BR/3BA, 3,000 sf, office, den, $2,975.

Victorian 4 BR/4BA, walk to town, gardener incl., $6,500.

Milpitas

Apt., 1 BR, upstairs, no pets, $845.

Duplex, 2 BR/1BA, carport, $1,100.

Morgan Hill

Home, 3 BR/2BA, 3-car garage, fenced, security system, $2,500.

Home, 4 BR/3BA, 2,700 sf, on 1 ac., pool, $2,700.

Mountain View

Home, 2 BR/2BA, dining room, nr. downtown, $1,900.

Home, 3 BR/2.5BA, 2-car garage, high ceiling, gardener, $2,700.

North Valley (San Jose)

Home, 3 BR/2BA + den, $1,650.

Home, 4 BR/2BA, 2,084 sf, family room, $1,850.

Palo Alto

Cottage, with yard, $1,000.

Home, 3 BR/1BA, updated, $2,500.

Rose Garden (San Jose)

Home, 2 BR/1BA, studio garage, fireplace, hdwd floors, $750.

Home, 4 BR/2BA, $2,300.

San Jose (Downtown)

Home, 3 BR/1BA, remodeled, $1,395.

Home, 2 BRT/1BA, carport, $1,595.

San Jose (South)

Home, 3 BR/2.5BA, fireplace, 2-car garage, $1,750.

Home, 4 BR/2BA, no pets, $1,795.

San Jose (West)

Cottage, 1 BR, no smokers, no pets, util. incl., $900.

Home, 3 BR/2BA, pet OK, 2-car garage, new carpet, $1,650.

Santa Clara

Home, 3 BR/2BA, no smoke, no pets, carpet, gardener, $1,850.

Home, 4 BR/2.5BA, prime location, $2,300.

Saratoga

Studio cottage, near town, $775.

Home, 3 BR/2BA, fireplace, $2,500.

Sunnyvale

Duplex, 3 BR/2BA, gas fireplace, nr. community center, $1,700.

Home, 3 BR/2BA, fireplace, gardener, $2,300.

SANTA CLARA CITY & TOWN PROFILES

CAMPBELL

ROUNDED COMMUNITY, mix of bedroom, high-tech and the charms of modern suburban life, bookstores, restaurants, shops and parks. Welcoming the millennium by making the good life better by extending the farmers' market to year round and by adding the Buca de Beppo restaurant, a brew pub and another hotel. One of the older suburbs. Has done a nice job of restoring and preserving its downtown.

Close to the Silicon Valley job centers, which makes Campbell a good commute. Bisected by two freeways and one expressway and close to another expressway.

School scores generally high and much attention paid to schools. In recent years, voters approved bonds for school improvements and to open another elementary school. Served by Moreland and Campbell elementary districts and Campbell High School District, which also educate kids in other towns.

Some Moreland parents tried to disconnect Campbell High School from its district and attach it to the Moreland district. They contend that this would improve planning between the elementary schools and the high school. In 1999 voters said, Keep the status quo.

Crime rate low suburban average. FBI reported zero homicides in 1998, 1997, 1996, 1995, 1994 and 1993, one each in 1992 and 1991, zero in 1990 and 1989, one in 1988 and zero in 1987.

Increased its population by 33 percent in the 1980s, rising to 39,871 residents in 1999. Regional planners predict that in about 20 years Campbell will have 41,000 residents, a modest increase by county standards. The town is almost surrounded by San Jose.

Campbell, in times past, was famous for its prunes. The name "Sunsweet" was first used in reference to a local plant that processed dried fruit. Orchards all went in the building boom that started in the 1940s. Campbell remembers its past in diverse ways, among them The PruneYard, a picturesque shopping mall, remodeled in 1996, and an annual Prune Festival.

Residential units in 1999 numbered 16,159 of which 6,822 were single homes, 1,908 single attached, 7,032 multiples, 397 mobile homes.

Campbell's housing boom started in the 1940s when the town built about 1,200 residential units. In the 1950s, Campbell erected about 3,100 homes and apartments, in the 1960s about 4,100 units, and in the 1980s about 2,600 units. So far in the 1990s, the city has built about 800 units, an indication that Campbell now will slowly fill out.

The town was built for the middle class. Among owner-occupied units, two- and three-bedroom homes account for 77 percent of the total, with four-bedroom homes making up another 16 percent. In design, Campbell falls into the category of typical suburban but the neighborhoods differ. The homes east of Bascom Avenue are slightly older and more upscale and have more trees and foliage than the homes west of Bascom. Well-cared-for town. Residents mow the lawns, apply the paint and generally do a good job of keeping up appearances. Many of the apartments are located along Campbell Avenue, one of the main thoroughfares.

Campbell has upgraded its downtown, using that tax-capture plan that California cities love: redevelopment. The results are nice: buildings restored, streets spruced up, many small shops, restaurants, theater, and coffee houses, Barnes and Noble, Trader Joe's, brew pubs. City Hall is trying to position Campbell as a small-town schmoozer with (or close to) big-city ornaments (downtown San Jose, about 7 miles to east).

Campbell streets get a lot of traffic from adjoining towns. City Hall has upgraded lights to keep cars and trucks moving. Campbell was the first city in California to use photo radar to nab speeders. In 1998, police department killed the project. Chief said many judges tossed out the radar-tickets.

Light-rail is supposed to pull into town in three to five years. Tall office buildings near the downtown and a few high-tech businesses make the commute easy for some residents.

Many service clubs. High school, a 30-acre site, was converted into a community center (gyms, auditorium, track, tennis). John F. Kennedy University. Year-round pool. Fifteen parks. Old mansion was converted into a city museum. Bike trail along creek. You can pedal to Los Gatos or, if your job is close by, to work. One park features giant plastic tubes with water spigots. When the kiddies enter, the spigots kick into action, administering a good soaking. Many activities for kids and seniors. Exercise courses. Summer day camps. Fly-casting ponds. Scottish Highland games, Prune Festival (more wine than prunes), Easter Egg Hunt, Christmas Crafts Faire, Oktoberfest. Many restaurants Many shops. Staples, Home Depot.

Campbell is a mature suburb that has had the time to build a comfortable community life with much to do. It is an intimate town with many long-time residents who know each other. The politicians know what the residents will take in the way of development and work to build consensus for anything major. Chamber of commerce (408) 378-62529.

SANTA CLARA CITY & TOWN PROFILES

CUPERTINO

SILICON VALLEY town famous for the quality of its schools, particularly computer education. Passed bond, $71 million, in 1995 to improve elementary schools and rewire them for high tech. In 1999, the work was in its final stages.

Also becoming famous or notorious for its home prices. People love those high-scoring schools and the high-tech education. At one point in 1999, there was on the market an "as-is" home, 1,048 square feet, for $360,000.

Being almost in the heart of Silicon Valley, many Cupertino residents have a short but often sluggish commute. Town is served by Highway 85, Interstate 289, Foothill Expressway and on the east side by the Lawrence Expressway. Local streets also lead to the job centers. Shuttle bus to Caltrain, which travels up the Peninsula to San Francisco. Buses.

Heart of the town is De Anza Community College, lovely campus that includes a planetarium and the Flint Center for Performing Arts, which presents top talents — from San Francisco Symphony to Henry Kissinger to Beijing Acrobats and Mikhail Gorbachev. In 1994 the college opened an Advanced Technology Center to train students in math, physics, computers, programming. In 1995, the Flint Center was renovated.

Served mainly by Cupertino School District and Fremont High School District. The latter in 1998 won voter approval of a $144 million bond for more renovations and for equipment and lab and facilities improvements.

Schools score very high. Many schools have won state and national recognition for academic excellence. Homestead High was honored in ceremony at White House. In last round of SAT, Monta Vista High School in math came in second in the state.

Cupertino elementary district runs three "alternate" programs, each with a different approach to education: in one, students are grouped by age and stay with same team of teachers for up to three years; the second follows a traditional structure; the third requires parent participation, working in schools as aides and other positions. Of the remaining schools, some accept children from any address in the district, space permitting, some restrict to immediate neighborhood. Admission to some schools is determined by lottery.

John Muir Elementary offers some instruction in Mandarin and English.

School district encourages parents to work with children at home and at schools.

Cupertino is the headquarters city for Tandem and Apple, and has about 50 high-tech firms. Many businesses have gotten behind the schools and work with the kids to make them computer sharp.

Town is jammed with high-tech parents and the local newspaper reports that the town is famous in the Far East for the excellence of its schools. If a Realtor is selling a home in Cupertino, the first thing he or she will mention is school quality.

Local community-business foundation raises $300,000 annually for schools, a nice shot in arm. De Anza College offers "College for Kids" in summer and runs a high-school program during the regular school year. NASA, the space agency, is located nearby at Moffett Field. Its scientists occasionally pitch in on projects with the school kids. Bond passed in 1994 allowed library to stay open seven days a week and expand its book and CD collection.

Crime rate is low-average for suburban cities. Zero homicides in 1998, 1997, 1996, 1995, 1994. Counts for previous years are 1, 0, 3, 0, 0, 1, 2, 1.

In 1999 the state tallied 17,417 housing units: single homes 9,827, single attached 2,145, multiples 5,438, mobile homes 7. Population 47,668.

A farm village for most of its life, Cupertino started 1950 with fewer than 500 homes, and then was swept up in the great suburban boom. About three of every four homes and apartments were built between 1950 and 1980, census data shows. Although Cupertino has its mansions, the city was built almost entirely for the middle class. The last census noted that three-bedroom homes were the most popular style, followed closely by four-bedroom homes.

In the 1980s Cupertino constructed 2,134 residential units, a sharp drop from previous decades and, typical for upper-income towns running out of space, found itself becoming more concerned over what should be built on the remaining land. For the older homes, drive the neighborhoods east of DeAnza Boulevard. For the newer, cruise Phar Lap Drive and other neighborhoods west of DeAnza. Cupertino rises from flatlands to hills. Hill homes command higher prices. Pleasant-looking town in suburban way. Many trees. Well-kept lawns. Vallco Fashion Park, 180 shops and restaurants. Anchored by Sears, Penneys.

Baseball, gymnastics, girls softball. Over 200 activities, from painting to karate. Soccer draws over 1,000 kids. After-school music program. Shakespeare for the Kids. Thirteen parks, nature preserve, a winery, a racquet club. Loads of classes, events at De Anza, which has an art gallery. Two golf courses, seniors center, movies, community center, sports center, bowling alley, ice skating rink, YMCA, city museum, arts and wine festival, De Anza Days, Heritage parade, Oktoberfest, Dickens Faire, Cherry Blossom Festival. City is spending millions on bike paths. Chamber of commerce (408) 252-7054.

SANTA CLARA CITY & TOWN PROFILES

GILROY

SOUTHERN-MOST TOWN in Santa Clara County. Moving from rural to suburban. Has an old downtown that's picking up antique stores and one of the most successful outlet malls in the South Bay. Famous for its Garlic Festival but losing some of its farming luster. The last tomato cannery recently closed. Gated community with golf course going up on westside.

In percentages, one of the fastest-growing cities in Santa Clara County. Added 9,846 residents in last decade, a rise of 46 percent. Lots of playmates for the kiddies. In the 1990 census, 33 percent of the residents came in under age 18, unusually high. Countywide, the percentage was 24. State estimates population in 1999 to be 39,071.

Despite this, Gilroy has a lot of "country" in the farms that start on its outskirts and the hills and mountains to the east and west. City favors gradual growth and limits the number of homes that can be built. As the newcomers settled in, shops, supermarkets and stores opened to meet their needs. The Gilroy outlet mall draws about 4 million shoppers annually. Gilroy also has a Wal-Mart. All this raises revenue for the city and helps fund city programs.

Split by freeway, Highway 101. A long haul to Silicon Valley and job centers in north but Gilroy, with plenty of open land, would like to woo high-tech south. Neat streets, many tree-lined. Many sections plain old nice suburban, three- and four-bedroom homes, lawns mowed, shrubs trimmed. Median barrier is being erected on Highway 101 to Morgan Hill, a safety measure.

Housing units in 1999 numbered 11,558 — 7,375 single homes, 629 single attached, 3,185 multiples, 369 mobiles. Tract homes for commuters make up the great majority of the housing but you can find turn-of-the-century and early 1900s homes near the downtown and some nice custom homes. For tight budgets, modest homes east of the freeway. The new homes can generally be found west of the freeway, on the outskirts of the town. In 1994, a sewage treatment plant for Morgan Hill and Gilroy was opened. St. Louise Regional Hospital. Kaiser office-clinic offers outpatient services.

Traffic a problem as commuters have to crawl up Highway 101 to reach Silicon Valley. But there is an alternative: Caltrain, which runs up to San Jose, takes a left, and finishes in downtown San Francisco. Runs have been added

and schedules changed to attract commuters. More trains are being added. Historic train depot has been restored.

Bookstore, historical museum, golf course, kid sports, youth center, swimming, softball, bingo, dancing, roller-skating, athletic clubs, bowling, 10 parks, regional parks nearby, ice cream and yogurt parlors, poker parlor, movies, community theater, delis, restaurants — for a small town, Gilroy does all right in amusements. New county park, four miles west of town. Honors and calls attention to culture of Ohlone Indians.

To open in 2001, a horticultural theme park, 167 acres, expected to attract 1 million visitors. Trees, picnic benches and rides. Family oriented. County government, for parks and open space, in 1996 purchased 6,187 acres in east hills between Gilroy and Morgan Hill. In 1998, in the same area, another 9,234 acres were purchased for open space.

Annual Garlic Festival (last full weekend in July) draws about 130,000 who consume about 5,000 pounds of garlic. Gilroy also throws a Hispanic Cultural Festival, dancing, singing, cultural events, eating (food booths). Mexican Independence Day in September. Antique and Micro-Breweries Fest. Farmers market, called El Mercado, good for fresh vegetables. In the spring, flowers, grown commercially, light up the countryside. Voters in 1994 approved tax to extend library hours and buy books.

Gavilan Community College is located at the south end of town. Pretty place and a plus for Gilroy, many classes, activities.

Gilroy is trying to tap the tourist trade. Wineries and redwoods a short distance off. Picturesque city hall. About 16 antique stores in downtown.

Crime rate in suburban range. Three homicides in 1998 and 1997, one in 1996, two in 1995, zero in 1994, two in 1993, one each in 1992, 1991 and 1990, two in 1989, two in 1988, and none the three preceding years, reports FBI. Dress code at high school to discourage gang colors and activity. No hats. High school forbids students from leaving during school hours and has installed security measures.

Schools score low to middling, a few high. Portable classrooms. Year-round education at some schools. In 1994, school district spent $4 million to renovate elementary schools and junior highs, the money coming from a bond passed in 1993. Several schools have been built in recent years. Another elementary school is to open in year 2000.

School district uses magnet schools to blend kids by ethnicity. Magnet schools use special, attractive programs to draw kids away from their neighborhoods, thereby breaking down segregation based on housing patterns. One Gilroy junior high school stresses science, another humanities. Other schools stress bilingual instruction, math, classes for high achievers. "Block" method being used at high school — 90-minute classes. Visitors bureau-chamber of commerce (408) 842-6436.

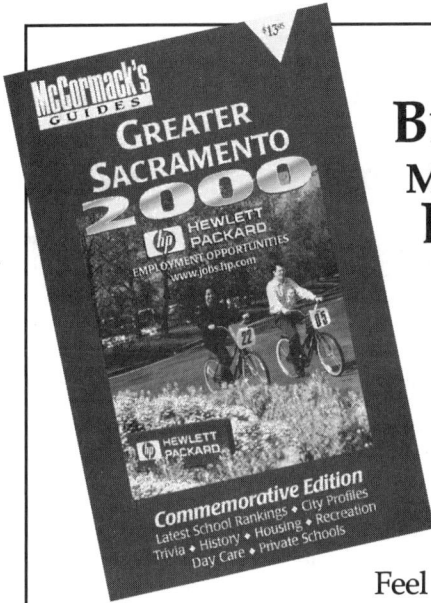

SANTA CLARA CITY & TOWN PROFILES

LOS ALTOS

PRESTIGE TOWN. School rankings are right at top in the state. Also among top in the state, its home prices, the median in 1999 about $750,000.

Quaint downtown. Streets lined with tall redwoods, pines and other trees. Police station and civic center hide behind apricot trees.

Sibling city to Los Altos Hills, the "top drawer" among the county's cities. They share the school district and shops and some civic projects. Community foundation raises money for worthwhile jobs in both towns.

One of the lowest crime ratings in the state. Only drawback: traffic congests on commercial streets.

Los Altos started 1999 with 28,488 residents. By the year 2010, predict regional planners, it should have 29,100 — essentially built out. Home to managers, administrators and professionals and, increasingly, retirees. About 31 percent of the residents are over age 55. About 21 percent are under age 18, reported 1990 census.

Seven shopping centers. Downtown has attracted first-class restaurants, bakeries, coffee shops, sidewalk cafes, boutiques and art galleries. Statues spotted here and there. At the corner of Main and State streets is a spic-and-span plaza decorated with bricks and stones and a large four-faced clock that looks like it stepped out of London. Town started as a summer vacation spot. When railroad arrived, Los Altos took off as second home of San Francisco wealthy, then as home for upper-middle class.

Single homes account for 89 percent of housing stock. Great majority built on about quarter-acre lots. In 1999 state counted 10,611 residential units — 9,386 single homes, 346 single-family attached, 876 multiples, 3 mobile homes. Many of the streets go without sidewalks, part of the country atmosphere that residents seem to love. Despite the name, Los Altos has few hills but it does slope gently toward the Bay.

School scores among highest in state. All six elementary schools have been designated "distinguished," meaning the state thinks they are well-run. Junior high and high schools received similar honors. Day care at elementary schools. Voters in 1989 passed a parcel tax to restore school programs and fix buildings and in 1993 renewed the tax, and in 1997 renewed it again with an

Home Price Sampler from Classified Ads

Almaden Valley (San Jose)

2 BR/2.5BA, 2 master suites, 14-yr-old complex overlooks pool, $179,500.

4 BR/2BA, FR & LR, cathedral ceiling, sep. DR, $465,000.

Berryessa (San Jose)

3 BR/2BA, big lot, $274,000.

5 BR/2.5BA, large lot, $350,000.

Blossom Valley (San Jose)

1 BR/1.5BA, master suite, walk-in closets, 1-car garage, $212,000.

3 BR/2BA, mountain views, large yard w/20+ fruit trees, $438,800.

Cambrian (San Jose)

3 BR/2.5BA, oak kitchen, inside lndry, $319,950.

4 BR/3.5BA, upgrades, on cul-de-sac near pond, view, 679,950.

Campbell

3 BR/2BA, great west-side neighbor-hood, $329,900.

4 BR/2BA, many upgrades, quiet, close to Saratoga, $469,900.

East Valley (San Jose)

2 BR/2BA, condo, A/C, fireplace, pool, tennis, $194,900.

3 BR/3.5BA, near SJ County Club, city lights view, on 1/2 ac., $525,000.

Evergreen (San Jose)

2 BR/2BA, den, many upgrades, $535,000.

5 BR/4BA, on 2.5 ac., 5,000 sf, high above city, $1,500,000.

Gilroy

3 BR/2BA, 2 yrs old, $389,000.

4 BR/3BA, elegant, designed for gracious living, $799,000.

Los Altos

2 BR/1.5BA, townhome, 1 blk to dwntwn, attchd garage, $499,900.

4 BR/3BA, at 10th tee of Los Altos CC, 2-story, all amenities, $2,285,000.

Los Altos Hills

2 BR/1BA, small, on .59 ac., "as is," $649,000.

4 BR/2.5BA, on 2.17 ac., across from Hewlett Packard Estate, $2,390,000.

Los Gatos

2 BR/2.5BA, condo, top floor, master suites, stroll to shopping, $359,000.

4 BR/4.5BA, 2-story, guest house, apt., on 1.98 ac., views, $3,900,000.

Milpitas

2 BR/2BA, downtown, large FR, $295,000.

5 BR/3BA, 2,670 sf, $419,500.

Monte Sereno

5 BR/3.5BA, sec. gate, on 1/2 ac., library, FR, $1,900,000.

4 BR/3BA, remodeled, on 1 ac., $1,600,000.

Morgan Hill

5 BR/3BA, beautiful yard, close to schools/shopping, $459,000.

4 BR/3.5BA, Town & Country villa, every convenience, big, $799,950.

Mountain View

2 BR/2BA, condo w/yard, fireplace, 1-car garage, $275,000.

increase to $264. Another tax measure for the elementary schools was passed in 1998, the money to be used to renovate all the schools in the district and to build schools. Well-run elementary district, its bond rating AA. This means that when it floats bonds, it gets a lower interest rate than districts that have paid perhaps less attention to financial soundness.

Los Altos High in 1993 added classrooms, new library. A $58 million bond to improve schools in the Mountain View-Los Altos High School District passed on the third try in 1995. The money was used to remodel and add classrooms, repair heating and plumbing, and add security lighting. Tax passed in 1994 to keep libraries in Los Altos and Los Altos Hills open longer.

Home Price Sampler from Classified Ads

4 BR/2BA, sunny, remodeled, pool/ spa, large yard, $795,000.

North Valley (San Jose)

4 BR/2BA, new roof/carpet/paint, A/C, pool/spa, $395,000.

3 BR/2BA, huge master suite, central air, big yard, many fruit trees, $420,000.

Palo Alto

1 BR/1BA, cottage, pvt backyard, near schools, parks, trans., $445,000.

3 BR/2BA, bright Eichler open floor plan, Palo Alto schools, $589,000.

Rose Garden (San Jose)

4 BR/3.5BA, Cape Cod, FR, LR, pool, music room, $874,000.

5 BR/3BA, custom, renovated, $1,400,000.

San Jose (Downtown)

4 BR/1BA, deep lot, fixer-upper, $250,000.

5 BR/2BA, LR, DR, $439,000.

San Jose (Central)

3 BR/1.5BA, Victorian, $308,000.

4 BR/2BA, 1,820 sf, $495,000.

San Jose (South)

2 BR/2BA, mobile home, large LR/DR, W/D incl., $57,000.

2 BR/1BA, condo, vaulted ceiling, tile entry, fireplace, $184,900.

San Jose (West)

3 BR/2BA, on 1/2 ac., remodeled, fruit trees, $429,000.

Santa Teresa (San Jose)

2 BR/2BA, condo, fireplace, 1-car garage, $221,500.

4 BR, on hillside, 2 yrs old, $499,000.

Santa Clara

3 BR/2BA, large FR, fireplace, screened patio, $330,000.

5 BR/3BA, dual-paned, hdwd flrs, fireplace, central air, sec system, $499,999.

Saratoga

2 BR/2BA, condo, upper end unit, clubhouse, pool, deck, $342,000.

6 BR/6.5BA, on 5 panoramic ac., vineyard, private, $4,999,998.

Sunnyvale

3 BR/2.5BA, condo, fireplace, attchd 1-car garage, $285,000.

3 BR/2.5BA, den, large lot, dual-paned, detached studio, $649,000.

Willow Glen (San Jose)

2 BR/1BA, bungalow, large yard, partial basement, $230,000.

4 BR/2.5BA, quiet, double-paned, new paint in & out, $569,000.

Parents raise $100,000 annually for physical ed, science, music classes.

Montclair Elementary is located in Los Altos but served by Cupertino School District, which in 1995 passed a renovation bond. About eight private schools are located either in Los Altos Hills or Los Altos.

Crime rate among the lowest in California. Zero homicides in 1998, 1997, 1996, 1995, 1994 and 1993, one in 1992, three in 1991, zero in 1990 and in 1989.

Commute pretty good. Foothill Expressway runs through town. Highways 280 and 101 are close by. Other freeways, Silicon Valley industries, within a short drive.

The problems: so many people shop the local stores and restaurants that traffic often creeps along the business streets — many traffic lights, delays. Every once in a while, residents throw a snit when someone tries to build a giant home; disturbs their artistic values.

Community Center, skateboard playground, 10 parks, including one with a redwood grove, adult education and recreation programs at the schools. Little theater. Art and wine festival, antique fairs, a lot to do in a small-town way. Baseball, soccer, drama, dance, many clubs. Seniors center. Youth center. Library recently expanded. Farmers market. Festival of Lights Parade draws 20,000-30,000. Annual pet parade, big hit with kids.

Los Altos Morning Forum secures pundits and celebrities for its talks. Nearby Foothill College attracts big-name speakers at its forums: George Bush, Jimmy Carter, Colin Powell and Gregory Peck, to name a few. For many people, a drive of 10 minutes brings them all that Palo Alto and Stanford offer. Arguments over quality of life. No gas-powered leaf blowers; only battery and electric.

Immigrants gather on El Camino Real looking for jobs. This disturbs some residents. Los Altos and Mountain View are working to get the workers to offer their services out of the St. Joseph the Worker Center. If you need help, the going rate appears to be $10 an hour. Chamber of commerce (650) 948-1455.

What's in a Name

- Campbell. After Benjamin Campbell, wagon-train pioneer.
- Cupertino. About the time of Spanish expeditions, Catholic Church canonized a priest from the Italian village, Cupertino. Camped beside a stream, Spanish honored the saint by calling the spot "Arroyo San Jose de Cupertino."
- Gilroy. John Cameron, Scottish seaman, jumped ship and took his mother's maiden name, Gilroy. He settled near that town, married into a Spanish land grant, gambled most of it away and left his name.
- Los Altos. After developing firm, Los Altos Land Company
- Los Gatos (The Cats). Several legends. The most popular: Men searching for water heard two wildcats fighting in the bushes.
- Milpitas. Obscure. May be Aztec for little cornfields.
- Monte Sereno. Peaceful Mountain.
- Morgan Hill. After early rancher, Hiram Morgan Hill.
- Mountain View. You can see mountains from this city.
- Palo Alto. Spanish for tall tree. Near city hall. A coast redwood, 1,048 years old, lost one of two trunks in 1909. Still alive.
- San Jose. After the patron saint of the second Spanish expedition.
- Santa Clara. At this site the Spanish built "Mission Santa Clara de Asis."
- Saratoga. Several versions, most popular: After Saratoga, New York, which has mineral springs, same as Saratoga, CA.
- Sunnyvale. Founding Realtor saw the sunshine.

SANTA CLARA CITY & TOWN PROFILES

LOS ALTOS HILLS

MOST PRESTIGIOUS CITY in Santa Clara County. Home to many of Silicon Valley's bosses and bigwigs. Small and essentially built-out. Located in hills and valleys above Silicon Valley. One of the lowest crime rates in state. Many mansions and custom homes. No business, no commercial. The Poor Clares, an order of nuns, run a cloistered monastery.

In 1999, the Associated Press analyzed STAR scores of fourth and eighth graders throughout the state. Los Altos Elementary District was first in reading in both grades, and first in math at the eighth grade, and second in math for the fourth grade. It then hired the principal of the school that came in number one. High schools also score very high. Bonds passed to improve schools. See Los Altos profile for more information on schools. Two private schools.

Minimum one-acre lots. Valley views. Trees overhang roads, creating tunnels of leaves and branches. Mansions hide behind walls and shrubs. Population increased by 93 in last decade; as of 1999 stands at 8,247. Large unincorporated neighborhood to south of town. Also upscale. Managed by residents through homeowner association.

Very picky about housing. City has issued handbook spelling out what Los Altos Hills would like to see — homes that fit in, heed neighbors' wishes, etc. Housing units in 1999 numbered 2,819, of which 2,760 were single homes, 24 single attached, 31 multiples, 4 mobile. Many homes go for millions. Not a town for the faint of wallet. Many homes have pools and tennis courts, some have horses grazing out back. Paths wander throughout town. Many dead-end streets. Ride-a-thons to save open space on ridges. Law protects redwoods, oaks, large trees. Fremont Hills Country Club: pool, 10 tennis courts, riding facility, golf. Two other golf courses nearby. Town started off as a place for wealthy San Franciscans to escape summer fog.

Foothill Community College adds life to cultural scenes and runs a speakers program, attracting top names, George Bush, Colin Powell, Jimmy Carter. Palo Alto borders Los Altos Hills. Short drive to movies, plays, delights of Stanford. Interstate 280 soothes the nerves, scenic freeway.

Zero homicides for 1998, 1997, 1996, 1995 and 1994. Stable, intimate. Residents know one another. One of lowest divorce rates in county, 4 percent of residents vs. 10 percent for county (1990 census). No chamber of commerce.

Why Is Paul Eckert The Area's
Number One Real Estate Broker?*
Enormous
Client Satisfaction
20 Years
Experience
ECKERT
& COMPANY
941-3333
Paul Eckert
(650) 941-6484
"Paul Eckert's Service Was Better than Shopping at Nordstrom!"
— Silicon Valley CFO
"Paul Eckert is simply the BEST!..."
— Executive, Intel Corporation
A Reputation for the
Highest Integrity
ECKERT
PROPERTIES INC.
RELOCATION DIVISION
100 University Ave., Los Altos, CA 94022
Call Paul Eckert at the office or at home anytime!
Office: (650) 941-3333 • Home: (650) 941-6484 • Toll Free: 1-800-655-2954
e-mail: paul@eckertproperties.com www.eckertproperties.com
*In the last five years, Paul Eckert has represented more
Buyers and Sellers in the Los Altos area than anyone else!

SANTA CLARA CITY & TOWN PROFILES

LOS GATOS

PRETTY, PRESTIGIOUS, LOVELY HOMES, charming old town. Crime low. School scores high. Great job of revamping its downtown into an inviting place to shop, stroll, dine and peruse (but some fear Yuppies have landed).

Flat lands rising to wooded hills and open hills. Many trees. Good views. Historic downtown. First city in county to adopt ordinance preserving historic buildings, and Los Gatos has reputation for being hyper sensitive about development and quality of life. For cat lovers, the name translates into "The Cats."

Between 1980 and 1990, Los Gatos added 451 residents and about 830 residential units, about three-fourths of them single homes or single attached. Many of the new homes jump up the scale but a good deal of the housing runs to well-done suburban with a high level of maintenance. Town is essentially built out. Association of Bay Area Governments, the regional planning agency, expects the population to increase by only 1,400 over the next 15 years. State estimated population in 1999 at 30,274.

Housing units in 1999 numbered 12,426, of which 7,108 were single homes, 1,722 single-family attached, 3,446 multiples, 150 mobile homes. Rentals in the downtown, which also has the older homes.

The commute, historically awful, got much better in late 1994 with the opening of Highway 85 to Cupertino and Saratoga and other Silicon Valley cities. One of these years light rail might connect Los Gatos to San Jose.

Los Gatos suffered major damage in 1989 quake, mostly to old structures, although chimneys and walls were cracked in newer homes. No one killed but many emotionally shaken. Building codes were revised to make reconstructed buildings better able to withstand earthquakes. Other safety measures taken. Town recovered quickly.

Zero homicides in 1998, one in 1997, zero in 1996, one in 1995, zero in 1994, 1993, 1992 and 1991, one in 1990, two in 1989, zero in 1988, two in 1987, and one in 1986.

Schools among the tops in the state. One study showed 85 percent of high school seniors going on to college. Los Gatos High in 1991 received national

honors for its programs. Fisher School received a similar award.

Computer labs, music, art at elementary. Foreign languages at junior high. Teen center next to high school.

Los Gatos Union School District voters in 1990 approved a $180-a-year parcel tax. Money is used to keep class sizes down, services up, to repair buildings and buy books and supplies. The tax was to have expired in 1994 but residents voted to renew it. Parents also fund elementary school programs through a foundation formed in 1982; have raised $1 million in about 15 years. Computer training emphasized. Steve Wozniak, a.k.a. "the Woz," co-founder of Apple, is a Los Gatos resident. He helped set up computer lab-arcade at Fisher school and trained many of the teachers. Also chipped in for a math lab at high school.

High school district in 1998 passed a $79 million bond. Money will be used to build a science wing at Los Gatos High, to add classrooms and to make general improvements, plumbing, wiring, air conditioning, etc.

Oak Meadows-Vasona Park, one of the nicest in the county (reservoir, miniature trains, playgrounds), is full on weekends with parents cooing over kiddies. Fifteen parks total, eight playgrounds, over 400 acres of open space, miles of trails for hiking and biking. Golf course on the northwest side of town.

Tennis, softball, soccer, rowing club, baseball, activities, classes. Concerts. Movie house. YMCA. Jewish Community Center with pool. High school pool used to teach young children and adults how to swim. Racquet and swim club. Banquet hall. Creek trail. Fitness clubs. Farmers market. Latest addition: bocce courts.

Summer concerts. Two historical museums. Library open seven days a week. Art galleries. Fiesta de Artes. Cats Festival. Quaint Old Town Shopping Plaza. More parking added recently. Carriage rides in downtown. Top-notch and diverse restaurants. Book stores. Community Foundation throws parties to raise money for parks, service groups and such endeavors as the high school band.

Many small towns can't or won't support a local newspaper. Los Gatos is an exception.

Among those who call or have called Los Gatos home: Peggy Fleming, Olympic ice skater; writer John Steinbeck; and Yehudi Menuhin, violinist.

A nice town to stroll. At Christmas, residents gather in old town for tree lighting and caroling and kids' parade. Stores go all out for holidays with lights and displays. Chamber of commerce (408) 354-9300.

SANTA CLARA CITY & TOWN PROFILES

MILPITAS

FAMILY TOWN MOVING UP THE SCALE as more high-tech professionals move in. School rankings on state comparison are landing in the top 25th percentile. Low crime rate. Good commute. Dynamic, changing town with one of the largest and most unusual shopping centers in the Bay Area.

Milpitas started out as an industrial community, home to the giant Ford auto plant, but switched gears in the 1980s. Wooed electronic high-tech firms and moved within the elastic boundaries of "Silicon Valley." Business parks scattered throughout the flatlands.

High-tech jobs and relatively low home prices attracted many professionals to Milpitas. The city added over 31,000 residents since the electronics boom. The state put the 1999 population at 64,325.

Housing in Milpitas has expanded to meet the demands of a growing population. Much of Milpitas is new or fairly new. The south and much of the middle of Milpitas are a mix of single homes (some upscale — two stories, three-car garages), townhouses and a few apartments. More apartments can be found east of Interstate 680, along with new tracts. Sound walls buffer the newer subdivisions from traffic noise. Arterial traffic is shunted around many neighborhoods and this makes the residential streets safer.

As you drive north, you encounter the old neighborhood, generally small single homes, somewhat faded, but many showing signs of care and attention. Here and there new tracts will be found. Further north, more new tracts. In the northeast hills, a gated golf course subdivision. In the winter rains of 1998, some new homes on Dixon Landing Road flooded.

City has established "urban boundary limit" to discourage housing in hills but the hills still get homes, usually posh.

Good housing mix, 17,437 residential units — 11,177 single homes, 2,051 single attached, 3,637 multiples, 572 mobile homes (1999 count). In the 1980s, Milpitas added about 3,600 residential units, increasing its housing stock by over 30 percent. Since 1990, it has added about 2,500 homes and apartments. Fast-growing towns generally mean many kids. The 1990 census found 27 percent of residents under age 18, only 11 percent above 55.

Overall academic rankings, compared to other schools in the state, land in the 60th to 90th percentiles. Indicates good support for education. School district runs morning and evening care programs for kids. New middle school.

For a middle-class suburban city, the overall crime rate is low. Zero homicides in 1998, two in 1997, 1996 and 1995, three in 1994, zero in 1993, one each in 1992 and 1991, zero in 1990, one in 1989, three in 1988, and two in 1987.

Lots of family activities in Milpitas. Twenty-one parks, 11 playgrounds. New community center and library. Aquatics center (four pools). Soccer, tennis, baseball, Little League, racquetball, waterslides, two golf courses in foothills, basketball, softball, volleyball, hang gliding, day camp, movies, bowling, roller skating, billiard parlor. On the unusual side: a string orchestra for children, a teen choir and kids' theater. Many fast-food and middling restaurants. Art and Wine Festival.

Milpitas has a solid commercial base to support its above-average amenities. Besides the high-tech industries located throughout the city, retail centers contribute much to the city coffers.

The old Ford assembly plant, which closed in 1983, was converted 10 years later into "The Great Mall of the Bay Area," one of the largest outlet malls in California. If plans pan out, it will hold nine to eleven "anchor" stores and 240 smaller stores. A big plus for Milpitas: providing not only tax revenues, but many entry-level and part-time jobs for local residents. Milpitas has also landed a Wal-Mart, located in another shopping complex. Great Mall to add a movie-plex, 20 screens.

The old downtown, lost in the shuffle, is tucked in near the train tracks but a new downtown — called Town Center — has risen to take its place. Anchored by civic complex, it's located off Calaveras and North Milpitas.

Few South Bay cities have great commutes but Milpitas has better than most. The town is divided north-south by Interstates 880 and 680 and east-west by Highway 237. The Interstates are usually a mess at peak hours, but the commute into downtown San Jose is only 7 to 10 miles. I-880 was widened and improved. Highway 237, also improved, shoots into the heart of Silicon Valley, 10 to 15 miles to the west. Short drive to Fremont and its jobs and relatively short haul across Dumbarton Bridge to Palo Alto and other Silicon Valley jobs. But even with road and freeway improvements, traffic often congests during peak hours, exasperating drivers. Close to San Jose Airport.

BART (commute rail) station located in nearby Fremont and one of these years, money permitting, either BART will be extended south from Fremont or the light rail north from San Jose.

Overall Milpitas is a middle-class town that delivers on many of the important aspects of suburban life. Chamber of commerce (408) 262-2613.

SANTA CLARA CITY & TOWN PROFILES

MONTE SERENO

SMALL CITY between Los Gatos and Saratoga, famous in a minor way for saying no to growth. Many custom homes on large lots. Built over gentle hills. Country feeling. Considered a prestigious address.

One of two Santa Clara cities in the last decade to lose population. It dropped 147 people. Population 3,443 (state count 1999).

When development galloped toward Monte Sereno in the 1950s, the town's leaders said, hell, no. They incorporated the hamlet as a city to keep planning under the control of the locals (through the city council), and since then have pretty much kept new construction down.

State tally (1999) showed 1,259 residences, of which 1,226 were single homes (many of them custom jobs), 25 single attached, 7 apartments, 1 mobile home.

Monte Sereno wines and dines in Los Gatos and Saratoga. Many kids attend Los Gatos schools. Scores very high. High school is adding a science wing and making other improvements. Lot of attention paid to schools. See Los Gatos profile. Los Gatos Police Department is paid to patrol the town, the assessment $100 to $125 per parcel. Crime low. Zero homicides in 1998, 1997 and 1996.

Commute improved in 1994 with the opening of Highway 85, which runs from South San Jose up to Mountain View (Silicon Valley).

City manager prepares budget, does planning and a host of other jobs. Every once in a while someone throws a snit over housing and appearances.

Golf course to north of city. Community college (many classes-activities) in adjoining Saratoga along with concerts and other events. Many parks and trails in region. Residents big on recycling; Monte Sereno a leader in this endeavor.

John Steinbeck, while living at Monte Sereno, wrote "Of Mice and Men."

Local paper calls town "Monte Snoreno," but residents want it that way, quiet and peaceful.

SANTA CLARA CITY & TOWN PROFILES

MORGAN HILL

SOUTH COUNTY TOWN, a mixture of country and suburbia. If San Jose epitomized the building spirit of 50 years ago, Morgan Hill captures the different mood of modern Santa Clara County.

San Jose said, "let 'er rip," and cheered as developers marched their tracts down the Santa Clara Valley.

A half century later, Santa Clara County is booming again. Silicon Valley, short of housing, is drawing its employees from bedroom communities as far east as Tracy, and Morgan Hill, surrounded by miles of open land, is saying, let's take it nice and slow — with a big exception: If you've got a high-tech firm and are shopping for a site, Morgan Hill would love to hear from you.

The result: a pretty town, population 31,896, a town that vows not to repeat the mistakes of yore but a town also in search of the right blend of elements to buy and sustain the amenities of modern life. Has added about 8,000 residents in the 1990s.

The town takes its name not from a local hill but from Hiram Morgan Hill who married into a pioneer family. But there is a striking hill to the west of town, called El Toro. Stately oaks grace a few lawns and trees planted around the city soften the housing lines. Hills to east and west. Most of town built on valley floor.

Served by Morgan Hill Unified School District, which has one major high school, Live Oak. About 10 years ago, Morgan Hill, at that time still fairly rural, was scoring in the 50th and 60th percentiles. Now the scores are landing in the 60th to 90th percentiles, a reflection mainly of the changing demographics of the town, more professionals, more high-tech people.

Renovation bond was passed in 1991. In 1999, another bond was passed, $72.5 million, to renovate Live Oak High School and build another high school and an elementary school. Morgan Hill district extends into San Jose and school officials want to build the new high school on land that San Jose has designated for a greenbelt. No way, says SJ but the matter is at the state of "we'll see." Several private schools.

Overall crime rate low. One homicide each in 1998 and 1997, zero in 1996 and 1995, the FBI reports. The counts for the previous years are one, one, one, zero, zero, zero, one, one, zero.

On many days, the commute to south and central San Jose is not bad. Both are a straight shot down Highway 101. Caltrain runs commute trains to both destina-

Santa Clara County Single-Family Home Prices

City	Sales	Lowest	Highest	Median	Average
Campbell	241	$27,500	$825,000	$350,000	$350,583
Cupertino	279	$113,000	$1,500,000	$570,000	$579,620
Gilroy	180	$25,000	$1,100,000	$297,000	$312,297
Los Altos	211	$71,000	$5,850,000	$925,000	$1,028,222
Los Gatos	286	$32,000	$6,931,000	$587,000	$689,719
Milpitas	290	$29,272	$1,127,500	$313,000	$339,374
Morgan Hill	309	$70,454	$1,210,000	$374,750	$395,650
Mountain View	354	$37,000	$2,995,000	$392,000	$435,492
Palo Alto	149	$105,000	$3,255,000	$639,000	$734,823
San Jose	4,604	$25,000	$3,500,000	$318,000	$346,945
San Martin	22	$41,000	$887,000	$455,000	$502,175
Santa Clara	368	$30,000	$780,000	$320,000	$317,044
Saratoga	175	$26,500	$4,700,000	$889,000	$1,004,930
Sunnyvale	468	$25,054	$860,000	$389,000	$402,559

Source: DataQuick Information Systems, LaJolla: Single Family residence sales from June 1999 through August 31, 1999. Median means halfway. In 100 homes, the 50th is the median.

tions and to other Silicon Valley cities, finishing up in San Francisco. Expanded parking at the train station.

For residents who have to travel by car to other towns in Silicon Valley the commute will often be an ordeal. More trains are being added to Caltrain line. Funding has been lined up to widen Highway 101 to three lanes, to and from San Jose.

Recreation offerings are plentiful but fragmented. About five years ago, Morgan Hill ran into money woes and scrapped its recreation department (but public works maintains the parks). Parent groups, the school district, the YMCA and other groups either stepped into the breech or had their own programs in place. Soccer, football, the typical kids' sports, swimming — all there but it has to be said that many other cities do a better job on recreation.

Large regional park and lake (reservoir) to east of town. Boating on lake.

To listen to many people, what San Jose did in the 1950s was a horror. It allowed (gasp!) developers to run free.

So did thousands of cities across the country. America was coming out of a world war and the Depression. Mobility had been stifled for almost 20 years.

Freeways were built, the car came into full flower and the great exodus was on, from city to suburbs, aided by developers but also enjoying great public support. A home in the suburbs — the American dream. Governments imposed few controls not only because they wanted the growth but because they didn't know what controls to impose.

This gave developers "free rein" but in reality they had to build to the discipline of the market. Still, corners were cut and stupid things done.

Morgan Hill missed this era. Until the 1980s, it was a hick hamlet in the middle of fields and orchards.

When its time came to develop, planners were in place, they had a much better idea of what worked and what didn't, the public was aware of environmental concerns, protecting open space was accepted — a different ball game.

If you buy into Morgan Hill, you are very much buying into a planned, controlled-growth community — which many people consider a plus.

And a community moving up the scale. The 1980s housing coincided with a period of prosperity in the South Bay. The same holds for the housing going up now.

In appearance, Morgan Hill traces the fortunes of Santa Clara County: small and modest, bungalows and cottages, in the old town. Three-bedroom, two-car-garage homes in the next ring and on the outer ring, two-story, four- to six-bedroom homes built in the modern style, creamy stucco and red-tile roofs, plenty of light, California Mediterranean. In the east hills, many of the homes were custom built along tract designs and positioned to command views of the valley or Lake Anderson. The town has one of the biggest supermarkets in the county.

The state in 1999 counted 10,306 residential units, of which 6,545 were single detached homes, 1,286 single attached, 1,623 multiple units and 852 mobile homes.

To pay for civic amenities and to shorten some commutes, city hall is wooing clean, high-tech firms. Several have been landed — Abbott Labs, Cidco, Anritsu and a number of smaller firms.

For information about opening a business, call the city's economic development office at (408) 779-7271.

San Jose may allow development of its south side. Cisco wants to build a large research complex. But a lot of land around Morgan Hill could remain in farming. The county has purchased 6,187 acres to the southeast for open space. In 1998, another 9,234 acres were secured.

Morgan Hill honors the mushroom with a festival. The town also has at least four wineries. The winter holidays are welcomed with a crafts fair, caroling and the lighting of a Christmas tree.

Downtown Morgan Hill, spruced up with trees and brick sidewalks and crosswalks, has attracted coffee shops, brew pubs and restaurants. Chamber of commerce (408) 779-9444.

SANTA CLARA CITY & TOWN PROFILES

MOUNTAIN VIEW

THE ONLY CITY in Santa Clara County where apartments outnumber single homes. Attracts many of the young and newcomers to the county. One of best night-lifes of county. Will finish 1999 with the opening of the light-rail extension from San Jose.

Crime suburban average on the low side. School rankings fairly high. Voters have approved higher taxes to rebuild schools. Commute good and soon to get better (the light rail).

Key player in Silicon Valley. Home to over 200 manufacturing and high-tech firms. About 70,000 jobs in town. Among the big guys: Silicon Graphics and Alza, a pharmaceutical firm, Netscape. More coming: Microsoft is consolidating its Silicon Valley operations in Mountain View. Alza and Silicon Graphics are expanding.

A city that's doing a lot of handwringing over what could be one of the region's biggest assets: Moffett Field, which borders Mountain View on land controlled by the county government. The Navy in 1994 said goodbye to its base in Moffett, a landmark because of its tall hangars that used to house dirigibles. NASA Ames Research Center took over Moffett, about 2,000 choice acres. NASA is researching computer systems for 21st century space exploration and hopes to find private partners for its projects.

In an advisory vote in 1996, Mountain View voters said no to opening Moffett to air cargo flights but many power people in Silicon Valley would like to keep this option open. The county's two other airports, San Jose and Reid-Hillview, are crowded, and many business leaders see air cargo from Moffett as quite important to the county's continued prosperity. In the planning fund-raising stage for Moffett Field: An Air and Space Center that would feature cutting-edge technology, and a Computer History Museum.

Apartments outnumber single homes two to one. Total housing units 32,987: single homes 9,127; 4,048 single attached; 18,623 multiple units; 1,189 mobile homes (state figures, 1999).

Apartments are not everyone's cup of tea but for the many people starting out in the computer business, they are quite acceptable.

A place for singles. Census in 1990 revealed that over half of Mountain View (55%) has never married or is either divorced, widowed or separated.

Most of the single homes can be found west of El Camino Real; most of the apartments, east of El Camino Real but this section also has many single homes. New homes and townhouses were recently opened on Whisman Road, near the Central Expressway and light-rail line. Innovative designs.

Many Mountain View homes sell in some instances well over $200,000 above what you would pay for similar homes in other parts of the Bay Area. Silicon Valley housing is hot. Signs of the times: BMWs, Volvos, SUVs parked in front of quite modest homes.

Many were built in the Fifties and Sixties and in size and design reflect what people wanted in those decades, generally three-bedroom units. In other Bay Area cities, older neighborhoods serve as way stations for people going up the scale or just marking time. Some homes are well-kept, some neglected.

In Mountain View (and Silicon Valley), home prices are so high and land so scarce that the old neighborhoods have increased their value, adding to stability and beauty. Lawns are well-tended, bungalows freshly painted and often remodeled, streets lined with trees. Older, smaller (two-bedroom) homes can be found south of City Hall.

City council recently approved two 10-story apartment buildings on El Camino Real. Council ordered some architectural and landscaping changes in response to opposition.

In the 1980s, Mountain View added 8,805 residents and 2,800 residential units. So far in the 1990s, it has added about 13,000 people. Population now 75,201 (1999 estimate). About 18 percent of residents are under age 18, which is low for Santa Clara County, but still amounts to 12,000 children and teenagers (1990 census).

Some of the recent arrivals are immigrants and Mountain View is trying to ease them into community life. Church group has opened a workers center to lessen complaints about men clustering on some street corners waiting for people to offer work.

Downtown overhauled: brick sidewalks, kiosks, pedestrian lighting, more trees. Choice of 50 restaurants (Asian cuisine popular). Nice place to stroll. Bookstore, free parking, monthly festivals, art. Ballet school. New city hall and Performing Arts Center (plays, musicals, dance, recitals) opened in 1991. Annual art and wine festival draws 200,000. City hall encourages public art. New library opened in 1997, pride of the city, holds up to 300,000 books.

Many activities. Tennis, swimming, boating, movies, theater, art and wine festival, sports — the typical offerings of well-managed town with some money in its pocket. City school districts have gone partners on playgrounds used by kids and community.

Big park on shore with golf course. Swim Center. Movie complex. Palo Alto and Stanford, and all they offer, are just up the road. Large shopping center off of El Camino Real on north side of town.

Shoreline Theater, managed by Bill Graham organization, draws top performers in U.S. Among recent performers, Bob Dylan.

Crime rate about suburban average. Zero homicides in 1998, one in 1997, zero in 1996, one in 1995, five in 1994, two in 1993 and 1992, zero in 1991, four in 1990, three in 1989 and 1988, and one in 1987 and 1986. Cops, through DARE program, work with schools to discourage drugs. Graffiti ordinance puts the burden of cleanup on property owner.

Academic rankings, in statewide comparisons, land mostly in the 70th to 90th percentile, which reflects well on parents and schools. Mountain View High School has been pronounced "distinguished," national award for good management, academic excellence. State "distinguished" awards to several elementary schools.

In 1995, a $58 million bond measure passed; money to be used to remodel high-school classrooms in the Mountain View-Los Altos High School District, repair heating and plumbing and add security lights.

Whisman elementary district, which serves part of Mountain View, in 1996 passed a $34 million bond to replace portable buildings with permanent and upgrade wiring, plumbing and heating. Mountain View Elementary District in 1998 won a $36 million bond to renovate all schools. Some people would like the two elementary districts to merge.

St. Francis High, a private school, was awarded a Blue Ribbon in 1991, a national honor, signifying that it's one of the best in the country.

Freeways crisscross town. In 1994, Highway 85 was opened, another connection with San Jose.

Being in the heart of Silicon Valley, Mountain View does much better in the commuting department than many other cities in the county. Caltrain to the City and down to Sunnyvale, Santa Clara and San Jose.

The light-rail line will end near downtown, where new transit center is being built. Should help downtown.

Chamber of commerce (650) 968-8378.

SANTA CLARA CITY & TOWN PROFILES

PALO ALTO

ONE OF THE MOST DESIRABLE ADDRESSES in the nation. Cultural center of Silicon Valley. Prestigious. Sophisticated. A financial powerhouse. What Wall Street is to New York, Sand Hill Road (which Palo Alto shares with Menlo Park) is to venture capital in computer projects.

Well-to-do, highly educated, cosmopolitan, built out. Added only 675 residents in last decade, increase of 1 percent. So far in this decade, it has added about 4,000 residents. Population 61,189 (state figures 1999).

"Home" of Stanford University, birthplace of Silicon Valley. The university is actually located just west of Palo Alto city limits.

In 1995, passed one the largest school-renovation bonds, $143 million, in the history of California, a great boost for local schools. All the schools have been renovated or rebuilt and equipped with modern technology. In 1998, the district opened another elementary school. Still, some schools are crowded.

Every year, the town's two high schools in the math SAT score among the highest in the state. The graduation rates at Gunn and Palo Alto High schools are hitting almost 100 percent and the schools advance students to the most prestigious universities in the country. Schools offer instruction in French, German, Spanish, Latin and Japanese.

In 1988 and 1991, the San Francisco Chronicle ranked Bay Area towns on such measures as crime, school quality, restaurants, commuting distances, cultural ornaments and more. In both rankings, Palo Alto was pronounced the best place to live in the Bay Area.

Tree-lined streets. Walls of ivy. Lovely campus. Excellent restaurants and coffee shops. Bookstores. First-run and foreign films near campus. Many cultural events on campus, theater, classical to rock music. French film festival. Big-time college football and basketball.

One of every four acres in parks, 4,233 acres total, 30 parks in all, including one, 1,400 acres in the Santa Cruz Mountains solely for Palo Alto residents. Swimming, libraries, community centers, farmers' market, playgrounds, bike and pedestrian trails, first children's theater in U.S., junior museum and zoo, teen center, ice-skating rink, skateboard bowl, golf, soccer,

baseball, many fitness and seniors classes. Summer concerts. Several years ago, it added a Bloomingdale's, a big deal among those who measure ooo-la-laah.

Some samplings from the city recreation program: T'ai Chi, Strollerrobics (usually moms and babies), lawn bowling, table tennis, chess, circuit training, drawing and painting (about dozen classes), bead making, photography, ceramics.

Also, indoor soccer, gym for boys and girls, rock climbing, skateboarding (several levels), Tae Kwon Do, tennis, tumbling, dance (including preschool ballet) and piano for kids, library readings, kinder science, children's theater.

Dance including classes in clog, country, folk, lindy, line, tap, salsa, swing and jitterbug, ballet, belly, Brazilian, Carribean, flamenco, jazz and tango. Other groups run soccer, baseball, football and basketball leagues. Annual ball draws thousands in tuxes and gowns and raises money for community recreation. Local firms donate food, wine, delicacies and other goodies for the ball, one of the big social events of the town. Stanford has a huge stadium and in the past has hosted a Super Bowl and World Cup soccer games.

Children's hospital opened in 1991. State-of-the-art. $100 million. Named for Lucille Salter Packard, late philanthropist.

Many arguments between libs and conservatives over policies of university and life in general. Stanford produces Supreme Court justices and rebels but overall the town has a healthy respect for the buck. Pro-choice, pro-gays in military, anti-discrimination.

Housing units number 25,952 — 15,538 single homes, 1,008 single-family attached, 9,293 multiples, 113 mobile homes (1999 state figures). Stanford is building about 1,000 apartments for students, faculty.

A fair number of older, modest homes — the postwar housing — but you pay for the Palo Alto address. Many expensive homes but also many Eichlers, homes built just after World War II. Open design, many windows; light.

Restrictions on building big homes on small lots, a practice of the late 1980s when real estate was booming. Height limits in some neighborhoods.

Much talk about housing prices. In mid 1999, on a real estate survey, Palo Alto showed up as the most expensive city in the nation, with an average price $843,500 for a four-bedroom home. Some residents are worried that the town is pricing out cops, teachers, firefighters, etc. Incidentally, Beverly Hills was second, $812,255. In Oklahoma City, similar homes were going for $111,875.

A lot of shaking during the 1989 quake but almost no damage to the town. The university, however, took a bad hit: damage well over $100 million. Cuts and bruises, no major injuries. Stanford library rebuilt; opened in 1999.

Crime rate low suburban average. More thefts than violence. Having shopping plazas and many stores, Palo Alto attracts the light-fingered. Three homicides in 1998, one in 1997, one in 1996, zero in 1995, one in 1994, zero in 1993, one in 1992 and 1991, zero in 1990 and 1989, one in 1988, zero in 1987, and two in 1986, reports FBI. In 1997, a NASA scientist, a young man with a family, was murdered on a downtown street, robbery the motive. Suspects captured. In 1998, father, who may have been upset about financial losses, is believed to have killed self, wife and son. City has curfew for young. For three decades, the cops patrolled in white cars. In 1999, they went back to traditional black and white.

Commute generally good, because of location. Two freeways to other Silicon Valley towns, several wide arterials, Caltrain up to San Francisco or down to San Jose, with stops along the way. Not too far from San Francisco International Airport. Express buses to East Bay. In 1999, city started free shuttle bus service around town. Cops are ticketing big cars parked in spaces designated for compacts.

A sizeable portion of Silicon Valley is located in Palo Alto — Hewlett-Packard, Varian, Syntex, Ford Aerospace. Historic tour shows the garage where Bill Hewlett and David Packard started out.

Supposedly the only city in California to own all its utilities, Palo Alto, thanks to clever decisions, enjoys unusually low power rates. Miscellaneous:

- To silence train whistles, the city may erect automatic gates at three street railroad crossings. With the gates, the train engineers would not have to sound their warning horns and whistles or not as much at they do now.
- Many arguments over limiting renovation on homes built before 1940. City has preservation ordinance.
- Beatles in 1965 spent two nights at Cabana Hotel in Palo Alto. In 1999, hotel opened and gussied up Room 810, the Beatles Room. Yes, you too can sleep where once slept the Fab Four.
- Palo Alto Middle School serves sushi. Unusual but tasty idea.
- On some occasions having to do with cloud cover, the music from the Shoreline Theater in Mountain View bounces into Palo Alto.
- Sand Hill project. Under way or soon to be, on Sand Hill Road, expanded shopping center, two four-story garages, 630 apartments, 338 apartments for elderly, the connection of Sand Hill Road with El Camino Real.
- Hindsight: In 1990s feds wanted to redraw maps of flood-prone areas to take in about 800 Palo Alto homes. This would have raised insurance rates. No way, said residents. In 1998, storms flooded about 400 homes in Palo Alto and Menlo Park. Some residents are sueing two cities, arguing bridges constricted flood waters, sent them over banks. Homes in Crescent Park.

Chamber of commerce (650) 324-3121.

SANTA CLARA CITY & TOWN PROFILES

SAN JOSE

LARGEST CITY IN SANTA CLARA COUNTY and Northern California. One of the high-tech giants. Suburban in nature, dynamic in action, especially in rejuvenating its downtown. Population 909,062.

Low crime, one of the defining characteristics of its nature. Unlike many major cities, San Jose has retained its middle class. It has its poor and its rich but it is not a town of great extremes. The great majority of residents land in the middle and practice the traditional middle-class habits of keeping appearances up, the kids under supervision and the schools focused on basics.

Often compared to San Francisco, San Jose lacks the zaniness and venality of its neighborhood to the north. In San Francisco, some one is always fiddling with the budget or putting friends and relatives on the municipal payroll or cutting some deal on the side. San Jose pressures its politicians to run a tighter ship, to stay to the straight and narrow.

Rare is the city in California these days that will interfere with consensual sex between adults. But San Jose doesn't dwell on sex; San Francisco gives college credit for mastering sado-masochistic techniques. San Francisco's unofficial motto is, "Whoopee!"

San Francisco has the lowest percentage of children of any county in the Bay Area, about 16 percent of all residents. San Jose runs to about 25 percent. It is much more of a family town. If San Jose had a motto, it would probably be, "Fire up the barbecue, Hubert!"

Several years ago, a study, probably still valid, gave San Jose the lowest crime rate of any metropolis (400,000 or more residents) in the country. The FBI reported 29 homicides in 1998, 43 homicides in 1997, 40 in 1996, 38 homicides in 1995, 33 in 1994, 41 in 1993, 43 in 1992, 53 in 1991, 35 in 1990, 39 in 1989, 37 in 1988, 24 in 1987, and 39 in 1986.

In 1995, the city implemented a 10 p.m-5 a.m. curfew for juveniles 15 and under; older juveniles have to be in by 11:30 p.m. If caught after hours, kids are dropped off at neighborhood centers and parents are called. Other measures: school gyms and swimming pools are being kept open longer, teen centers have been opened, after-school programs were expanded.

In appearance, suburban nice although critics call the town bland. San Jose has hills but much of the city is built on flat land. Outside of the downtown, very few buildings rise over three stories.

San Jose is not an "old" city with cosmopolitan traditions. Well into the 20th century, it was no more than the largest town in an agricultural region. The city's population in 1950 was only 95,000. When it grew, it grew rapidly, adding subdivision after subdivision, annexing almost everything in its path. Added 152,806 residents in the last decade, an increase of 24 percent, and in this decade, so far it has added about 160,000 which, in large measure, explains the traffic jams in Silicon Valley. As fast as freeways are erected and light rail extended, they are overtaken by more people.

Ethnically diverse, many Hispanics, Southeast Asians and Asians. Town, schools, churches and civic leaders work hard at helping people get along.

School rankings bounce all over the map in San Jose, but many are fairly high. School situation is confusing because San Jose is served by 19 separate school districts. The city grew up around established school districts, some of which serve other communities besides San Jose. If you have children, check with the local district to find out where your child will be attending school. Ask about hours and times of attendance. Some schools will offer buses, some will start later than others, some have year-round schedules with vacations in October.

In recent years, many bonds have been passed to improve schools. Some bond or tax winners: Fremont High School district, East Side Union district, Alum Rock district, Oak Grove, Union and Evergreen. In 1997, the largest district, San Jose Unified, passed a renovation-building bond for $165 million. Union Elementary School district in 1999 passed a $92 million bond to renovate all schools in the district (plumbing, electrical, roofs, etc.) and upgrade the wiring for computers. Local firms are "adopting" schools and getting more involved in civic causes.

Among homes, the tract look dominates — hence the accusation of bland. Many people put their creative energies into landscaping and gardening and interior decorating. And the bland label, which doesn't seem to bother residents in the least, is misleading. In cultural events, restaurants and quality of metropolitan life, the city has made great strides over the past 25 years.

The San Jose Arena opened in 1993, part of an effort that started 20 years ago to equip San Jose with the trappings of a big-time city. The Arena came with a professional hockey team, the Sharks, who have caught San Jose's fancy and support. The town is now a frequent stop when big-name singers, rock bands and opera stars tour the country.

Since 1982, well over $1.5 billion has been spent to make the downtown the great heart of the city. The jobs included a light-rail system (now extended to Mountain View), a convention center, the Fairmont Hotel, the Children's Discovery Museum, a retail mall, a highway and the arena. An international airport, located near the downtown, has been expanded. In 1998, San Jose opened a Tech Museum of Innovation.

The downtown also offers the cultural and recreational ornaments of metropolitan life: a symphony, an opera, light opera, ballet. Repertory theater opened in 1997. The opera company regularly visits elementary schools and sings for the students. San Jose State University, one of the largest in the state, is located in the downtown. Besides the state university, San Jose City College and Evergreen Valley College enhance the educational offerings of the town.

Although such cities as Sunnyvale have more high-tech firms than San Jose, the larger city is becoming to be viewed by many as true capital of the Silicon Valley. It is trying to provide the leadership to make the region prosper. And it has a fair amount of industry, especially on its north side, miles of sleek plants. Plus the airport. Good employment base.

Many commute into other areas of the Silicon Valley, a tortuous daily trek. In recent years, the opening of two freeway stretches —Highways 85 and 87— has greatly improved matters. Some neighborhoods are located next to employment centers; an easy commute. With additional light-rail transit, freeway widenings and additions, other neighborhoods don't have it so bad. Light rail is to be extended to Campbell and Southeast San Jose.

San Jose offers many activities. Little League, soccer, youth service organizations, libraries thrive. Museums, rose garden, many nice parks, water slide. Cinco de Mayo parade draws 100,000. The real strength of the city is in its neighborhoods, all sustained by their own shops, movies, restaurants, video outlets, churches and social organizations and activities, many of them organized around schools. The great majority of residents take their pleasures in the back yard or local park. City council members are elected by district, which gives the neighborhoods more clout in local politics.

Good choice of housing; a lot of the new, the great majority of it suburban tract, although some streets seem straight out of New England or the Midwest. San Jose in the 1980s added about 42,500 residential units, far more than any other city in the Bay Area and so far in the 1990s it has added about 24,000 units. Prices bounce all over. Although the housing falls into the category of suburban tract, variety is plentiful, housing styles having changed frequently over the past 50 years. Residential units in 1999 numbered 282,861, of which 160,977 were single homes, 25,487 single-family attached, 84,728 multiples, 11,669 mobile homes.

San Jose's Neighborhoods

San Jose is spread over 175 square miles of Santa Clara Valley floor and hillside. In some instances, the neighborhoods are distinct: they might contain housing from a certain era, or have a "look" that sets them apart from others, or contain many members of a particular ethnic group.

But in many places market forces have placed new subdivisions next to

station. From 7-11 miles to Santa Clara.

- South San Jose. Zone 11. South of downtown, east of Willow Glen. Housing tracts from '50s mixed in with newer housing. Older homes mean lower prices. Light rail accessible. Highway 87 extension opened in 1993; improved commute. Many apartments, mobile homes. From 8-12 miles to Santa Clara.

- Blossom Valley. Zone 12. South of South San Jose, north of Santa Teresa. Identifying street: Blossom Hill Road.

  Didn't start developing until '60s. Typical home is three-bedroom, two-bath, 1,400 sq. feet. Condos. Got its name from blossoming fruit trees. Middle America.

  Light-rail. Highway 82. Straight ride to downtown San Jose. From 10-14 miles to Santa Clara.

- Almaden Valley. Zone 13. West of Blossom Valley. Mix of housing, some very old, some from '60s, many new, custom, upscale. Scenic views from hill homes. Country feeling. Almaden Quicksilver Park. Almaden Country Club. Light-rail end of line. From 12-16 miles to Santa Clara.

- Cambrian. Zone 14. Borders Los Gatos and Campbell. Tract homes, many ranch style, built over last 10 to 30 years. Big trees. Stable. Many original owners. Some remodelings. Some townhouses, condos, duplexes.

  Commute made easier with the opening of Highway 85. Short drive to light-rail station. From 9-13 miles to Santa Clara.

  San Jose Chamber of Commerce (408) 291-5250. Convention and Visitors Bureau (408) 295-9600. Miscellaneous:

- Up and coming: Coyote Valley, on south side. Cisco wants to build 400-acre campus, which would employ 20,000; Calpine wants to build power plant, its smokestacks disguised as office building. Major improvements to freeways. Much argument expected.

- Free shuttle bus around downtown, between parking lots. Mayor Ron Gonzales is trying to revive plan to extend BART into downtown San Jose.

- San Jose Unified School District is changing attendance boundaries for about 16 schools. Check with district for more information.

- Downtown and airport areas drawing several more hotels. Good deal of work going on to make driving to and from the airport easier.

- Town and Country Village, 1960s mall on Stevens Creek Boulevard, is to be demolished and replaced with another mall (with twice the square footage), 1,200 housing units, two hotels, movie plex.

- City and San Jose State University are funding large library at downtown campus. Will be open to community.

SANTA CLARA CITY & TOWN PROFILES

THIRD-MOST POPULOUS city in the county. One of the high-tech heavyweights: many industries. An unusual mix of fun, commerce and education. Population 102,682.

Santa Clara firms and institutions employ about 140,000 people, or about 1.4 jobs for every man, woman and child in the town. The city borders the job centers of Sunnyvale and San Jose. If you are willing and able and can't find a local job (and a reasonable commute) in this burg, you may be uniquely hopeless.

School district in 1997 passed $145 million renovation bond. Served for the most part by the Santa Clara Unified School District. In comparisons on a national scale, the district scores about the 50th percentile, average, but individual schools score higher. Compared to other public schools in the state, Santa Clara's score generally in the top 25 percent. Some students attend Eisenhower Elementary School, part of the Cupertino School District. About 15 private schools complement the public schools.

Home to Santa Clara University, Jesuit institution. A pretty campus and the site of Mission Santa Clara De Asis. Also Mission College, a campus of West Valley Community College.

Triton Museum of Art is located in Santa Clara. The 49ers train in Santa Clara. Convention center, a testament to Santa Clara's importance in the Silicon Valley. Great America. Major amusement park serving the Bay Area.

Santa Clara dates back to 1777 when the first mission was erected and for almost 170 years it lived its life as a farming village. By 1940, the population had reached 6,650 residents, the great majority living in 1,400 homes and apartments in the downtown, around the university.

Came World War II and Santa Clara County blossomed as a military-industrial center. In the 1940s, the city more than doubled its housing units. Then came the real boom, fueled by veterans returning to sun-kissed California and an economy that sought to contain the Soviet Union (the Cold War).

In 1950s and 1960s, the city built about 21,000 homes and apartments and in the 1970s, about 7,500 more. In 1999, the state tallied in Santa Clara 39,231 residential units, of which 17,406 were single homes, 3,096 single attached, 18,608 multiples, 121 mobile homes. To state this another way, three of every four homes and apartments in Santa Clara were built between 1950 and 1980. For the middle class, this was the era of the G.I. Bill and the tract home, usually one story, three bedrooms, with a garage for one big fat car. And this is essentially Santa Clara in its housing.

The neighborhoods differ but usually in variations off the tract model: some homes will be slightly bigger, some slightly smaller, some will have many shrubs and flowers, some few. Almost nothing jumps up the scale, except for apartment complexes erected off of Lafayette Street on the east side.

Almost all cities say they want business, but few aggressively pursue it. Santa Clara went after and got a lot of high tech, and made itself into one of the silicon cities. Its industries include: Intel, Applied Materials, 3Com and Synoptics. In 1999 Sun Microsystems began work on a large complex located on one of sites that housed part of Agnews State Hospital. When completed, the complex will employ 4,000.

The payoff for a strong business sector comes in parks and recreation, and in ability to fill potholes, field cops, keep up appearances and perform dozens of jobs cities are supposed to do but often don't. When you look at a map of Santa Clara, you see parks spotted all around town.

Thirty-one parks and playgrounds. One city-owned golf course, plus private course. Tennis, baseball, basketball, adult classes, community theater and ballet, loads of activities. Santa Clara International Swim Center is famous for turning out Olympic winners. Restaurants, major hotels, bowling greens, seniors center, college basketball, movie complex, youth center, ample shopping and on and on.

Nice looking town in suburban way: lawns mowed, houses painted, streets clean, apartment complexes maintained.

Santa Clara has to be rated fairly good in commuting because of its central location. Freeways or parkways traverse the city. Caltrain up the shore to San Francisco with stops on the way or down to San Jose. Light rail starts at Great America, goes down to South San Jose and was extended to Mountain View.

Close to San Jose International Airport. Take-offs and landings are away from Santa Clara's residential sections but check out noise for yourself. San Jose is improving the access roads to the airport.

Crime rate about suburban average. One homicide in 1998 and 1997, zero in 1996, three in 1995, two in 1994, three in 1993, four in 1992, three in 1991, nine in 1990, six in 1989, five in 1988, and three in 1987 and 1986.

The Agnews Project, when rounded out, will also include 2,600 residential units, a park, a library and a school. Chamber of commerce (408) 244-8244.

SANTA CLARA CITY & TOWN PROFILES

SARATOGA

LOCATED ON THE EDGE of a valley that dotes on computer hardware and software and measures speed in nanoseconds, this city of 31,255 values the contrary intangibles of quiet and repose, grace and beauty.

Its school rankings are high, its crime low, its old town charming, its setting delightful, flatlands ascending into the foothills of the Santa Cruz Mountains. Residents in 1998 passed a bond to add library and science buildings to the high school and make general improvements.

On the downside, Saratoga, lacking many stores and therefore having a weak tax base, is struggling to fund city services but, please, no tears. If the shoe really starts pinching, residents have ample resources to relieve the pain. The average annual income for Saratoga, according to the Association of Bay Area Governments, is about $177,000. City is home to judges, doctors, computer chiefs, plus many middle and upper managers.

Served by six school districts, among which the most popular are Saratoga Elementary and the high school district, including Saratoga High. Overall rankings for Saratoga High and the Saratoga elementary schools are in the high 90s, among the tops in the state. In the 1996 math SAT, Saratoga High scored fourth highest in California; in 1997 it tied for third highest, in 1998, it tied for fifth highest. Three private schools, located in or near the town: Harker, St. Andrew's, Sacred Heart.

Saratoga Elementary district in 1997 passed a $40 million bond to renovate schools.

Overall crime, as tracked by the FBI, is low. Between 1985 and 1998, the most recent year reported by the state, Saratoga had zero homicides.

Compared to other Silicon Valley cities, the Saratoga commute falls into the range of "not that bad." The city borders or is close to the job centers of Cupertino, Sunnyvale, San Jose and Santa Clara. In 1996, Highway 85, which bites off a corner of Saratoga, was completed. This ties the town into the freeway network serving Santa Clara County. Walls muffle sounds from Highway 85 but some residents say the noise is irritating. Buses from Santa Clara Valley Transportation Authority. Caltrain to downtown San Francisco or San Jose can be picked up in Santa Clara.

Lovely town, one reason why its homes cost so much. Hill homes overlook the Santa Clara Valley. Much attention to preserving old town. Streets clean. Homes well-maintained. Many have custom landscaping. City codes restrict repairing cars in driveway or street, allowing junk to accumulate in yards, leaving cars parked on public street for more than three days.

Recreation, cultural ornaments, unusually bountiful. Concerts, art exhibits at Villa Montalvo, a mansion that was turned into an artists' residence and art museum. Jazz and pop concerts at the Mountain Winery. City hall runs recreation programs for kids and adults. About nine parks. Community theater. Hakone Gardens, created by a gardener who worked for the Emperor of Japan. Shakespeare festival.

In the middle of town sits West Valley, a community college, a cornucopia of facilities and activities, cheaply priced (average class $36), all open to local residents. West Valley has a library, a theater, a gym and workout rooms, a track and playing fields, plus many classes on arts, literature, computers and business subjects. Saratoga has a town band. To join, you sign up for a certain band class at the community college, an instance of a town shaping another institution to meet its interests. First-class restaurants in the downtown. Golf course-country club on the west side.

First a lumber town, Saratoga in last century evolved into a resort-farming community that attracted people of money who liked the mild climate, the mountain setting and possibly the mineral springs in the hills. In one version of how Saratoga got its name, civic leaders lifted it from Saratoga, New York, a wealthy town that also has mineral springs.

Among the early residents was James Phelan, a U.S. senator who built a palatial home (Villa Montalvo) in the Mediterranean style. Phelan was a patron of the arts and helped set the artistic tone of the town. The home was later deeded to the county for the benefit of artists. By 1940, the census counted about 350 homes. The war decade, when Santa Clara County developed its electronic muscles, saw the number of Saratoga homes more than double and in the 1950s, home construction boomed, 2,884 units. In 1956, Saratoga incorporated as a legal city. This took planning and zoning away from the county government, which was strongly pro-growth, and placed them in the hands of local residents. In the 1960s, Saratoga built 3,189 units, in the next decade, 2,264 units and in the 1980s, 908 units.

So far this decade, the town has built about 550 residential units. The town is not built out but its boom days are over. The state in 1999 counted 10,764 units, of which 9,648 were single-detached homes, 483 single attached, 628 multiples and 5 mobile homes. About one-third of the single homes have three bedrooms, about 40 percent have four bedrooms and 16 percent have five or more bedrooms (1990 census). If a tally were taken today, it would probably show more four-bedroom and five-plus-bedroom homes. In recent years, the trend has been to build larger homes. For the most part, the four-bedroom homes run to software engineer upscale: two-story structures built along enticing tract designs. The custom homes, many opulent, can be found west of city hall, around Villa Montalvo and in the hills off of Big Basin Way. If you have ever wondered where the wealth of Silicon Valley is invested, take a spin up Pierce Road.

Although considered part of Silicon Valley, Saratoga is not home to computer industries. The town has five small business sections and little else in way of stores that produce tax revenue. Proposals to add more stores (or parking) almost always run into town's wish to remain low-key and rustic. City restricts use of portable signs, streamers, banners, balloons in commercial district.

Saratoga has a formal government, the city council, and an informal one, the Good Government Group, a sort of watchdog, particularly sensitive to growth and aesthetics. If you like to argue about art, beauty and quality of life, this is the burg for you.

Local lasses who made good: the daughters of Lilian Fontaine, who under the umbrella of Adult Education ran a theater workshop and staged plays. Her daughters: Joan Fontaine ("The Women") and Olivia de Haviland ("Gone with the Wind"). Chamber of commerce (408) 867-0753.

SANTA CLARA CITY & TOWN PROFILES

SUNNYVALE

HIGH-TECH BEDROOM CITY located smack-dab in the middle of the original Silicon Valley. Bordered by Mountain View, Cupertino and Santa Clara, and on north side, San Francisco Bay and a wildlife refuge of marshes and salt ponds and trails.

For many residents great commute because the jobs are so close. Second-most populous city in Santa Clara County, 132,940 residents, and still adding homes and apartments. Although some housing can be found the north side, most residents live south of Highway 101.

Housing units in 1999 totaled 54,308 and included 21,042 single homes, 3,919 single attached, 25,126 multiples and 4,221 mobile homes.

From 1950 to 1960, Sunnyvale built 11,347 residential units; the following decade, 14,939; the next decade, 12,759. In the 1980s, construction dropped to 6,558. Sunnyvale in the 1990s will probably construct about 10,000 homes and apartments.

When Sunnyvale building boomed, the three-bedroom home was the rage. For owner-occupied homes, the 1990 census reported that 42 percent were three-bedroom, 25 percent two-bedroom, and 22 percent four-bedroom. Five or more bedrooms came in at 5 percent.

Sunnyvale offers a lot of choice in housing, across the price spectrum. With the exception of San Jose, it has the most mobile homes in the county, the great majority of them located in parks on the east side, north of Highway 101.

Homes, landscaping, generally well maintained. Nice-looking city in suburban way. As with many other Santa Clara cities in the last two decades, more diverse but still Middle America. Many homes have been remodeled or renovated in some way, a common practice in Silicon Valley. Home prices are so high that many owners can draw from their equity to make improvements.

Sunnyvale is home to hundreds of high-tech firms — semiconductors, software, telecommunications, global positioning equipment — and in recent years has been pushing into bio tech, which now fields about 30 firms. Also new: space satellites, a Lockheed Martin specialty. The firm in 1996 opened a giant clean-room manufacturing facility. Lockheed Martin employs about 8,300 in Silicon Valley, many of them at its Sunnyvale complexes.

Military presence in town is changing. The Navy in 1994 left Moffett Air Field, located on county unincorporated land between Sunnyvale and Mountain View. As a result, fewer planes fly over Sunnyvale enroute to the landing site.

Onizuka, formerly a secret Air Force base in Sunnyvale, appears to have escaped the post-Cold War knife and may emerge as an Air Force-private venture to track satellites.

The National Aeronautics and Aerospace Administration (NASA) took over Moffett Field from the Navy and is looking to attract private partners for its ventures. With so many scientists and so much technical knowledge, Sunnyvale, Mountain View and a few other towns hope to establish the region as a space center.

For a fairly large city, Sunnyvale has a low crime rate. Homicides totaled two in 1998, zero in 1997 and 1996, three in 1995, two in 1994, three in 1993, two in 1992, three in 1991, two in 1990 and 1989, ten in 1988, five in 1987, and four in 1986. In 1988, a man went on a rampage, killed seven.

In summer, cops patrol parks on bicycles. Graffiti Hotline; city tries to remove graffiti within three days of notice. Cops work with schools and counselors to keep kids straight. Neighborhood watches to discourage crime.

Served by Sunnyvale and Santa Clara School districts and, at high school, by Santa Clara and Fremont School districts, for the latter, mainly Homestead and Fremont High schools. Rankings on a statewide comparison for all come in well above the 50th percentile, some in the 80s and 90s, an indication of high parental interest in education. In recent years, distinguished school awards were given to Bishop, Cherry Chase, Columbia Community and Cumberland elementary schools.

Voters in Sunnyvale Elementary District in 1996 passed a renovation bond. In mid-1998, Fremont Union High School District passed a renovation-construction bond for $144 million. Fremont High School recently opened a science center.

Some Sunnyvale neighborhoods are in the Cupertino School District, which in 1995 passed a renovation bond.

Seventeen parks, tennis center with 13 courts, another 55 courts at other locations, two theater groups, 200-seat theater, dance company. Community center. Senior center. City has contracted with school district to make school facilities open to public: gyms, swimming pools, playing fields. Baseball, soccer, two golf courses (9 and 18 holes), Twin Creeks Softball Complex, 10 fields. Bowling alley, lawn bowling. Youth Family Center-sports complex at Columbia Middle School. Gymnastic center.

Baylands Park, 70 acres, opened in 1993. Trails to Bay, picnic grounds, playground, next to a 100-acre wildlife preserve. Part of effort is to run 400-mile trail around Bay Area.

Several shopping centers. Great variety of restaurants. Town Center Mall is being overhauled and will add outlets, restaurants and a 20-screen movie house. Old Del Monte building was gutted and rebuilt as bank-shopping complex. Home Depot. Night life showing some sizzle on Murphy Street. Palace night club popular. City for years has been working to revive downtown.

Four freeways, two expressways. Highway 237 at north end had its traffic lights removed, which speeded up traffic. Other improvements made. CalTrain up the shore to San Francisco or down to San Jose. Buses. San Jose Airport is within a drive of 10-15 minutes, when traffic is moving.

Light-rail line is being extended into Mountain View; also runs to downtown San Jose.

Sunnyvale has been singled out by Bill Clinton and Al Gore and ABC News as the city that knows how to make things work. Its officials are supposedly very efficient. Goals are set and met. Jobs priced out to the penny. Managers rewarded or penalized by how well they perform. Projects are completed ahead of schedule. Cops and firefighters are one and the same, public safety officers.

The payoff for residents: more services at less cost. Tax dollars that work harder.

City hall, to encourage entrepreneurs, runs a patent office-library located in what is called the Sunnyvale Center for Innovation, Invention and Ideas. Folks using the system can tap into the main patent database in Washington, D.C.

In the early Thirties, when Sunnyvale was orchard country, an employee of Libby, McNeil & Libby, the canner, scooped up leftover chunks of pears, pineapples, peaches and cherries to bring home to his children. Presto! The first fruit cocktail. Water tank at company was painted to resemble a fruit cocktail can. When the company closed the plant, the tank was retained and declared an historic monument.

Another Sunnyvale first: Rooster T. Feathers, a comedy club, was the first place to install a video game — 1972. Chamber of commerce (408) 736-4971.

Chapter 12

SANTA CLARA COUNTY *Fun & Games*

SANTA CLARA COUNTY is bulging with places to visit and things to do but, with some exceptions, it is not oriented toward tourists.

No battle monuments summon visitors simply because there were no battles. Only the Indians suffered catastrophe and they went quietly and quickly, mostly through disease, leaving little behind. The Spanish built a mission at Santa Clara, later destroyed and rebuilt — well worth a visit but little else of great interest remains from the ranchero era.

For most of its "American" history, the county has been run by farmers and shopkeepers — people who for the most part doted on grapes, raisins and prunes, welcomed settlers but saw little need to encourage tourism. Indeed, some of their actions — the cutting of great redwood groves — later worked against the tourist trade.

In recent decades, the county has built a few museums and amusements that attract outsiders. And such places as downtown San Jose and Palo Alto have put together clubs, galleries, restaurants and cultural events that have made the county much more palatable to the business visitor.

For its own residents, however, the county, in parks, culture, recreation and amusements, the county and its cities have done very well. Where there have been gaps, the county has inventively filled them. Of note are the celebrations of the stomach, the food festivals which flow nicely out of the county's history.

Here is some advice about making the most of local activities.

City Recreation Departments

Most cities have recreation departments that sponsor their own activities and coordinate or assist private groups. Chambers of commerce are excellent sources for club and activity lists. School districts occasionally run after-school programs and other activities. Adult schools and community colleges are loaded with recreational, exercise and cultural classes and activities.

Softball, possibly the most popular adult sport, thrives in many communities, complete with umpires, schedules, playoffs and trophies. Many teams are organized through jobs. Some live wire will recruit fellow employees and field a team. There are men's and women's leagues and mixed teams.

Private Classes and Clubs

What the public sector lacks, the private sector provides — racquetball, golf, bowling, tennis, movies, special-activity classes. Also shopping, an unsung, often-maligned pursuit but one that brings pleasure to thousands. Santa Clara County has some delightful malls and shopping centers.

Club life is varied and, as might be expected, computer clubs abound, great fun for the many enthusiasts. There are also model sailboat, powerboat, airplane and rocketry groups, water skiing, sailboating, powerboat racing, hiking, horseback and hunting trails, trap, skeet, pistol and rifle ranges, car clubs, even hang-gliding and hot-air balloon groups.

Church and Home

A number of people organize their lives around church activities.

Watching television is by far the most popular pastime in the county — or, for that matter, any other California county. Thanks to cable reception and satellite dishes, the stations are many and the diversity of choices great, from schlock to Stravinsky. Video recorders have spawned many video rental stores, another great source of entertainment. Libraries are plentiful, if not as popular as television.

City Parks, Sports, the Arts

Regional parks tend to get most of the attention, but city parks can be counted in the dozens and draw many people. Bicycle and jogging trails wind their way throughout the county.

Of the many children's activities, soccer is probably the most popular, attracting kids by the thousands, and a good deal of parental interest and screams. Little League, Pop Warner football, basketball, swimming — almost every town will have a league or several leagues. Girls participate in all these sports. Some sports — gymnastics — may attract more girls than boys.

Art guilds and galleries, dance schools, bands, a symphony, choral groups, college football and basketball, little theater — Santa Clara County has them.

And if the local offerings are not to your liking, San Francisco and Monterey are within an hour's drive and the Sierra Nevada (skiing, hiking and gambling) a few hours off.

Sorting It All Out

Sometimes hard to know just what to do. Here are suggestions to help with the sorting out.

- Find out who is organizing activities in your town and in nearby towns.

Usually this can be accomplished by calling or visiting the chambers of commerce, the city recreation departments and the school districts. Some activities take more digging than others.

Soccer and baseball leagues are occasionally put together by parents' groups with no connection to City Hall. A phone call to the city recreation department will usually turn up a phone number that will lead to another phone number that will pan out.

- Get on mailing lists. Adult schools and recreation departments change their classes about every three months. Theaters and orchestras issue calendars every season.
- Find out the rules. Some cities provide minimal support for certain activities. You may have to sign up players on your softball team and collect the fees and meet application deadlines. Baseball and soccer leagues usually guarantee the younger children, no matter what their skill, two innings or two quarters of play. But other sports (football) often go by skill. Ask about playing time.
- Ignore city boundaries. If you live in Campbell and want to take a class in San Jose, go ahead. A person with a Mountain View job might want to tackle an aerobics class in that city before hitting the freeway.
- Do a little investigation and spadework before making choices. This sounds obvious, but many people, to their unhappiness, do not.

  If you are new to the county and wish to make friends, almost assuredly you will mingle with people if you attend movies, art shows and concerts. But the opportunities for conversation may be few.

  The trick is to put yourself in a situation where you can meet and talk to people who share your interests or might in other ways make good friends. For a mother, this could be something as close as the PTA. For a person who delights in politics, it might be the local Democrat or Republican clubs.
- Subscribe to a local newspaper, of which there are many. Almost all will have calendars of events, lists of local attractions and hours of operation.
- Visit or call the San Jose Visitors and Convention Bureau, 333 West San Carlos St., San Jose. Phone (408) 295-9600. Maps and other information.

Places to Visit, Things to Do

Please phone ahead to find out hours of operation. Many of these places charge for admission.

Children's Discovery Museum. Hands-on exhibits with themes of "community, connection and creativity," with technology, science, humanities and the arts interwoven. Third-largest such museum in the nation, largest in the west. Purple building. 180 Woz Way, San Jose. Phone (408) 298-5437.

Great America. Located in city of Santa Clara, off Great America Parkway. First-class amusement park. Over 100 attractions, many of spine-tingling, stomach-churning variety.

Great place for kids. Enjoyable for adults. Entertaining musical reviews. When the kids poop out, take them inside for a show. (408) 988-1776.

Intel Museum. Located at Intel complex in the Robert Noyce Building at 2200 Mission College Blvd., Santa Clara. How computer chips are constructed and used and other aspects of high tech. Changing exhibits. Phone (408) 765-0503.

Lick Observatory. Atop Mt. Hamilton, southeast of San Jose, one of the most powerful observatories in the world, although in modern times its effectiveness has diminished because of background light from San Jose.

The history of Santa Clara County has been blessed by two benevolent screwballs, Sarah Winchester and James Lick. An adventurer and land speculator, Lick purchased a good deal of downtown San Francisco at the time of the gold rush and, as a consequence, became one of the richest men in the state.

Withdrawn, inclined to lawsuits and shabby dress, Lick was also an admirer of Tom Paine and determined to do good, particularly by encouraging education. Someone suggested a great telescope to study the heavens, to which Lick replied with the 19th century equivalent of "right on" and advanced the money to build the observatory, which was bequeathed to the University of California.

Scenic but slow and winding ride to the top. Tours. For schedules, phone (408) 274-5061.

Mission Santa Clara de Asis. Located on Santa Clara University campus, at 500 El Camino Real, Santa Clara. Old California, a good introduction to the Franciscan padres and what they tried to accomplish in pioneer days. Fires and other calamities destroyed early buildings. In 1929, Mission Santa Clara was rebuilt. While there, tour the university, a pretty campus. Phone (408) 554-4023.

Raging Waters. Your typical wild and wet water-slide and swimming park. Picnic areas, video arcade, shops, entertainment. Open May to September, exact dates depending on weather. In Lake Cunningham Park, San Jose, on the east side, at Tully Road and Capitol Expressway. Phone (408) 654-5450.

Rose Garden. Naglee and Dana avenues, in San Jose. Park planted with 5,000 rose bushes in 150 varieties.

Rosicrucian Museum. Park and Naglee avenues, San Jose. The Rosicrucians are a fraternal order of men and women who encourage the study of ancient learning. At their world headquarters in San Jose, the Rosicrucians built a striking museum that houses a large collection of ancient Egyptian artifacts. Highlights include a mummy gallery, a full-sized rock tomb, and exhibits on the Assyrians and the Babylonians.

The planetarium, one of the first in the U.S., explores the universe and pays particular attention to the mythologies and star lore of the ancients. Phone (408) 947-3636.

San Jose Flea Market. 12000 Berryessa Rd., between Highway 101 and Interstate 680, San Jose. One of the great bazaars of the West Coast. Open Wednesdays through Sundays. Draws 50,000 to 75,000 on weekends. Also includes farmers' markets and kiddie amusements. (408) 453-1110.

San Jose Historical Museum. 635 Phelan St., San Jose. Old Santa Clara County recreated at Kelley Park — an Indian acorn granary, the Pacific Hotel, a candy store, an electric tower, a 1920s gas station, a dental building, stables and more. Much memorabilia from the old days, also exhibits on Costanoan Indians, the rancheros, high-wheeler bicycles. Well worth a visit, especially with kids. Petting zoo nearby. Also nearby, the Japanese Friendship Park, six acres of waterfalls, stone bridges, bonsai plants — peaceful, restful, inviting. Phone 408-287-2290.

San Jose Museum of Art. Market and San Fernando streets. 20th century and contemporary art. Photography, paintings, sculpture, drawings. Many classes in art for children and adults. Taught by working artists. Phone (408) 294-2787.

San Jose Sharks. Professional ice-hockey team. San Jose Arena. For information on events and sports schedules, phone (800) 755-5050. Sharks tickets are sold at the arena and through BASS. Phone (408) 998-2277.

Stanford University. Palo Alto. A beautiful campus, a delight to tour. Spanish architecture. Hoover Tower (good view). Rodin Sculpture Garden, museums, galleries. Daily walking tours. For information on campus and group tours, and Hoover Tower, call (650) 723-2560. Palo Alto is also a good shopping town, lots to choose from.

Tech Museum of Innovation. San Jose, helped by Silicon Valley firms, opened a new tech museum. The museum features 250 exhibits divided into the following galleries, "Life Tech; The Human Machine"; "Innovation: Silicon Valley and Beyond"; "Communication: Global Connections"; "Exploration: New Frontiers." Located at 201 S. Market St., San Jose. For more info call (408) 279-7150.

Triton Museum, 1505 Warburton Ave., Santa Clara. Folk, contemporary, classic art. Pastoral scenes and wildlife of the early valley. Phone (408) 247-9340.

Villa Montalvo. Located just outside Saratoga on Saratoga-Los Gatos Road. Italian Renaissance villa built by politician with an artistic soul. James Phelan, a three-term mayor of San Francisco and a U.S. senator, was a patron of the arts. He left his beloved Villa Montalvo as a retreat for artists, writers and musicians. Many shows and programs on cultural subjects. The grounds, 175 acres, are maintained as a public arboretum. For information about programs, call (408) 741-3421.

Winchester Mystery House. 525 S. Winchester Blvd., San Jose. Sarah Winchester, heiress of the shooting Winchesters, pumped about $5 million into this four-story, 160-room house.

A reclusive, whimsical eccentric with a perverse eye for beauty, Mrs. Winchester ordered carpenters to build doors that opened to walls, staircases that lead nowhere and a window that peered out of a floor. Excellent rifle collection. Beautiful garden. Cafe. Banquet facilities. Tours. Phone (408) 247-2101.

Musical and Cultural Events

Music and culture buffs should get on mailing lists of four "must" places:

- Flint Center, De Anza College, 21250 Stevens Creek Blvd., Cupertino. Phone (408) 864-8816.
- San Jose Center for the Performing Arts. Almaden Boulevard and Park Avenue. Phone (408) 277-3900.
- Shoreline Amphitheater at Mountain View, phone (650) 967-3000.
- Stanford University, Palo Alto. Musical and cultural events, phone (650) 725-ARTS; athletic events, phone (650) 723-1021.

Regional Parks

- **Alum Rock Park.** Old favorite of San Jose. In east hills, via Penitencia Creek Road. Dappled sycamores. Hiking, bike trails, picnicking, falls and springs. A spa, now long gone, used to attract people to Alum Rock for the cure.
- **Anderson Lake County Park.** East of Morgan Hill, off East Dunne Avenue or Coyote Road. About 2,000 acres of park around north and east sides of Anderson Reservoir, which is occasionally drained. Views. Picnic tables.
- **Coe State Park.** A big one, 68,000 acres, east of Morgan Hill. Take East Dunne Avenue. Hiking, backpacking, about 100 miles of trails. Nature center.
- **Grant County Park.** 9,522 acres on the road to Mt. Hamilton, east of San Jose. Hiking, horseback riding trails. Many natural history exhibits. Four lakes.
- **Mount Madonna County Park.** West of Gilroy. Take Highway 152. Redwoods and bay, oak and large madrone trees among 3,093 acres of hilly land. Rewarding but strenuous trails.

Chapter 13

SANTA CLARA COUNTY
Job Training & Colleges

IF YOU ARE LOOKING for a job but need training or additional education, local colleges, public adult schools and private institutions have put together a variety of programs, ranging from word processing to MBA degrees.

Many institutions have devised programs for working adults or parents who must attend the duties of school and child rearing.

In many instances jobs and careers are mixed in with personal enrichment. At some colleges, you can take word processing, economics and music.

This chapter lists the major local educational and training institutes. All will send you literature (some may charge a small fee), all welcome inquiries.

Adult Schools

Although rarely in the headlines, adult schools serve thousands of Santa Clara County residents. Upholstery, microwave cooking, ballroom dancing, computers, cardiopulmonary resuscitation, aerobics, investing in stocks, art, music, Quicken, how to raise children — all these and more are offered in the adult schools.

These schools and programs are run by school districts and by cities. Many schools also run adult sports programs, basketball, volleyball, tennis. Call your local school or city for a catalog.

Older Students

As the public's needs have changed, so have the colleges. The traditional college audience — high school seniors — is still thriving but increasingly colleges are attracting older students and working people.

Many colleges now offer evening and weekend programs, especially in business degrees and business-related subjects. Some programs — an MBA — can take years, some classes only a day. The Bay Area is loaded with educational opportunities. Here is a partial list of local colleges. As with any venture, the student should investigate before enrolling or paying a fee.

Universities and Colleges

- San Jose State University. At 25,000 plus students, the largest university in

Santa Clara County and one of the largest in the Bay Region. Located in downtown San Jose. Bachelor's and master's degrees. Schools of Business, Education, Engineering, Applied Arts and Sciences, Science, Humanities and the Arts, Social Work, Social Science.

Regular program generally accepts high school students that score in top 35 percent. State universities are very popular with community college students: Two years at community college, last two years at state university. San Jose State offers day and evening classes, room and board.

What is the difference between the University of California schools and the state university schools? Both award bachelor's and master's degrees but only the UC schools award doctorates. Also, the UC schools have higher admission standards; e.g. the top 13 percent of high school students. UC schools also admit many community college grads.

The UC schools have the edge in prestige but there is much argument over which is academically superior. Critics charge that the UC schools do a better job on research than on undergraduate instruction.

State universities also run extension schools — one-shot classes or short programs generally aimed at building business skills but many cultural offerings are mixed in. These are cheap, often quite helpful classes for busy people.

For admissions information, call (408) 283-7500.

For a schedule of extension classes, call (408) 924-2630 or (408) 985-7578.

- Santa Clara University. Located in city of Santa Clara. Enrollment about 7,500, half undergrads. Run by Jesuits. Founded in 1851. One of the oldest

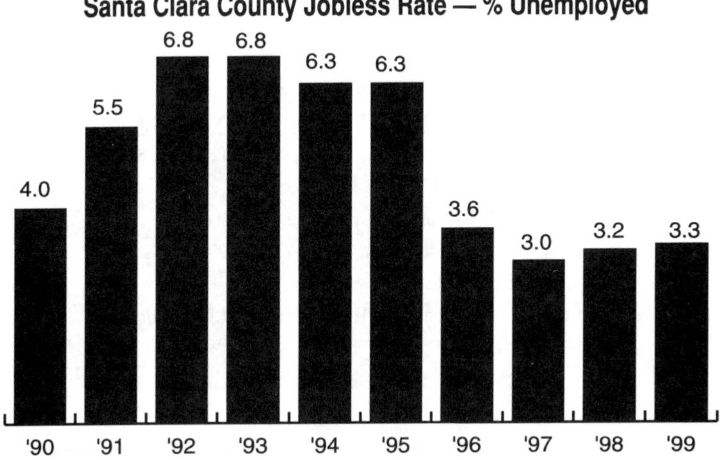

Source: California Employment Development Dept. 1999 percent is for July.

colleges in the state. Site of mission, which has been rebuilt. Pretty campus. Good scholastic reputation. Traditional university, bachelor to doctorate degrees. Undergraduate programs include engineering, business and arts and sciences.

Like many private colleges and universities, Santa Clara is tapping the market in education for mature adults, particularly for the strivers who want to stick an MBA in their resumes. Other graduate programs popular with the over-25 age group: Engineering, Counseling, Psychology, Education, Law, Catechetics-Liturgy-Spirituality. Phone (408) 554-4000 for information.

- Stanford. Located in Palo Alto. One of the great universities of the planet. About 13,500 students are enrolled in seven schools: Earth Sciences, Education, Engineering, Graduate School of Business, Humanities and Sciences, Law, Medicine. Continuing studies, (650) 725-2650. Well worth a visit even if you or yours don't stand a ghost of a chance of attending.

- University of California Extension. UC Extension in Santa Clara County is run by the University of California at Santa Cruz. Professional development classes are taken by about 30,000 adults each year at the Extension's facility at 3120 De La Cruz Blvd. in the city of Santa Clara (Trimble Road at Hwy. 101).

  Courses offered in computer science, engineering, business and management, environmental sciences, arts and humanities, English language, teacher education and behavioral sciences. Over 1,000 seminars annually. Also, courses and seminars leading to certificates in 25 professional programs. For schedule of courses, call (800) 660-4991.

- University of San Francisco. Jesuit University, based in San Francisco, but offers bachelor's and master's programs at its South Bay Center in Cupertino at 7337 Bollinger Rd. Aimed at working adults.

  Bachelor's degrees in Applied Economics, Information Systems Management, Organizational Behavior. Master's in Human Resources, Organization Management. Classes are also offered in Sunnyvale, Palo Alto, South San Jose and San Jose. For information call (408) 255-1701.

- Golden Gate University. Based in Los Altos. Phone (650) 961-3000. For working adults. Bachelor's degrees in Human Relations, Management, Telecommunications. Master's in Banking and Finance, Management, Human Resources Management, Information Systems, International Management, Marketing, Taxation, Telecommunications.

- St. Mary's College. Based in Contra Costa County but offers programs in Santa Clara County through its facility in San Jose. Degree programs scheduled for working adults. Phone 1-800-538-9999. Bachelor's and master's degrees in Health Services Administration, bachelor's in Management, master's in Procurement and Contract Management.

- National Hispanic University, 14271 Story Rd., San Jose, 95127. Phone (408) 254-6900. Associate and Bachelor's degrees in arts. Master's in education and business administration. English as second language.

Community Colleges

Three community college districts with campuses located throughout the county: San Jose-Evergreen, Foothill-De Anza and West Valley-Mission community college districts. Academic and vocational subjects, day and evening classes. Many students attend community colleges for first two years of college then transfer as juniors to four-year colleges.

- San Jose City College, 2100 Moorpark Ave., San Jose, 95125. Phone (408) 298-2181.
- Evergreen Valley College, 3095 Yerba Buena Rd., San Jose, 95135. Phone (408) 274-7900.
- De Anza College, 21250 Stevens Creek Blvd., Cupertino, 95014. Phone (408) 864-5678.
- Foothill College, 12345 El Monte Rd., Los Altos Hills, 94022. Phone (650) 949-7777.
- West Valley College, 14000 Fruitvale Ave., Saratoga, 95070. Phone (408) 867-2200.
- Mission College, 3000 Mission College Blvd., Santa Clara, 95054. Phone (408) 988-2200.

Tidbits

- With the boom in jobs, local universities have added classes to train students in high tech. San Jose State University in 1997 reported a 30 percent increase in enrollment in computer sciences.

Chapter 14

SANTA CLARA COUNTY

New Housing

SHOPPING FOR A new home? This chapter gives an overview of new housing under way in Santa Clara and nearby counties. Smaller projects are generally ignored. If you know where you want to live, drive that town or ask the local planning department, what's new in housing.

Prices change. Incidentals such as landscaping fees may not be included. In the 1980s, to pay for services, cities increased fees on home construction. Usually, these fees are included in the home prices but in what is known as Mello-Roos districts, the fees are often assessed like tax payments (in addition to house payments).

Nothing secret. By law, developers are required to disclose all fees and, in fact, California has some of the toughest disclosure laws in the country. But the prices listed below may not include some fees.

After rocketing in the 1980s, home prices, new and resale, stabilized and in many instances dropped. Some developers, particularly in towns with many new units, have gotten very competitive in pricing — a break for buyers. But in the last year or so, as employment has boomed, home prices and sales have increased. A lot depends on how far you are willing to commute.

This information covers what's available at time of publication. For latest information, call the developers for brochures.

If you have never shopped for a new home, you probably will enjoy the experience. In the larger developments, the builders will decorate models showing the housing styles and sizes offered. You enter through one home, pick up the sales literature, then move to the other homes or condos. Every room is usually tastefully and imaginatively decorated — and enticing.

An agent or agents will be on hand to answer questions or discuss financing or other aspects you're interested in. Generally, all this is done low-key. On Saturdays and Sundays, thousands of people can be found visiting developments around the Bay Area and Northern California. Developers call attention to their models by flags. When you pass what appears to be a new development and flags are flying, it generally means that units are available for sale.

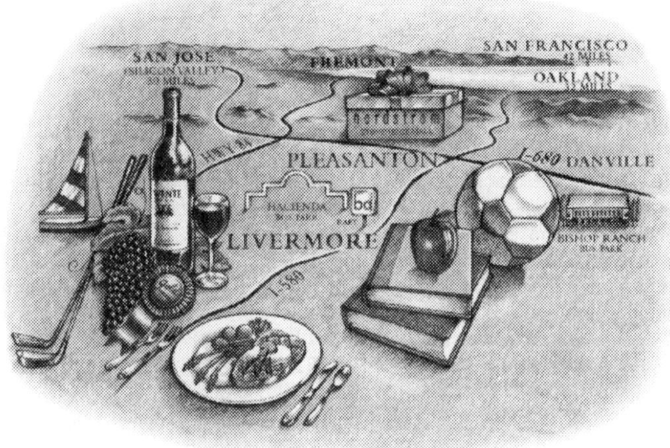

A TRADITION OF GREAT HOMES IN A GREAT PLACE TO LIVE.

Historic wineries. Great schools. Regional shopping. Hacienda Business Park. No other area in the East Bay offers this kind of livability. And no other homebuilder offers as many exceptional neighborhoods as Signature Properties. Visit us daily 10-5; Monday 12-5.

1. ASCONA AT RUBY HILL, PLEASANTON. 4 and 5 bedroom luxury homes from the mid $500,000's. (510) 417-2250.

2. RUBY HILL, PLEASANTON. A master-planned community featuring Northern California's first Jack Nicklaus golf course. Custom lots from the $200,000's. Custom homes from the mid $800,000's. (510) 417-2250.

3. COVENTRY AT STRATFORD PARK, LIVERMORE. 3, 4 and 5 bedroom single-family homes from the $300,000's. (510) 447-1314.

4. VALENCIA II AT HACIENDA, PLEASANTON. 3, 4 and 5 bedroom single-family homes from the mid $300,000's. (510) 227-1819.

5. SIENA AT HACIENDA, PLEASANTON. 2 and 3 bedroom townhomes from the high $180,000's. (510) 227-1817.

6. AVILA AT HACIENDA, PLEASANTON. 3 and 4 bedroom European courtyard-style single-family homes from the $270,000's.(510) 734-9569.

7. GARIN RANCH, BRENTWOOD. 3, 4 and 5 bedroom single-family homes from the low $200,000's. (510) 513-1057.

Prices effective as of publication deadline. Map not to scale.

BROKER CO-OP INVITED

SANTA CLARA COUNTY

Cupertino

Oak Valley, O'Brien Group, (650) 988-2555, single-family detached, 4-5 bedrooms, from $900,000s.

Oak Valley Estates, O'Brien Group, (650) 988-2555, single-family detached, 1/2 acre estates, from high $2,000,000s.

Gilroy

Oak Crest at Eagle Ridge, Standard Pacific Homes, Club Dr., (408) 847-0051, single-family detached, 2,580-4,561 sq ft, 4-5 bedrooms, from upper $500,000s.

Santa Fe, Western Pacific Housing, Ronan Ave., and Church St., 1-800-3300-WPH, single-family detached, 3-4 bedrooms, opening soon, high $200,000s.

The Villas, Orchard Valley Communities, Thomas Rd., (408) 846-5868, single-family detached, 1,525-2,027 sq ft, from low $300,000s.

The Woodlands at Eagle Ridge, Shapell, Club Dr., 1-877-81-EAGLE, single-family detached, 4-6 bedrooms, from $500,000s.

Hollister (San Benito County)

Canterbury, Ryder Homes, Sunnyslope Rd., (831) 636-2756, single-family detached, 1,490 to 2,500 sq ft, 3-5 bedrooms, from low $200,000s.

Grey Hawk, Award Homes, Inc., Union Ave., (831) 638-9650, single-family detached, 1,950-2,500 sq ft, 4-6 bedrooms, from upper $200,000s.

Kentfield at Quail Hollow, Standard Pacific, off Hwy 25, (831) 636-2934, single-family detached, 2,307-3,309 sq ft, 3-4 bedrooms, high $300,000s.

Sundance, Standard Pacific, Union Ave., (831) 634-0750, single-family detached, 2,105-2,718 sq ft, from high $200,000s.

Symphony Grove, Shea Homes, Sunnyslope Rd. and McCray St., (831) 637-1599, single-family detached, up to 3,256 sq ft, up to 5 bedrooms, low $300,000s.

Valley View, Kaufman & Broad, Fairhaven Dr., (831) 638-0404, single-family detached, up to 3,059 sq ft, 3-6 bedrooms from $250,000s.

Los Gatos

Heritage Grove, SummerHill Homes, Blossom Hill Rd., 1-800-585-0085, single-family detached, 2,700-3,600 sq ft, 3-5 bedrooms, from $800,000s.

Milpitas

Parc Metropolitan, RGC/Calprop, Curtis Ave., (408) 934-5800, single-family attached, 1,012- 1,764 sq ft, from the mid-$200,000s.

Morgan Hill

Kendal Wood, Warmington Homes, Main Ave., (408) 782-7559, single-family detached, 2,332-3,386 sq ft, up to 5 bedrooms, low $500,000s.

Mission Ranch, Coyote Estates, Cochran Rd. (408) 782-1458 or 782-8685, single-family detached, starting $400,000s.

Monte Verde, Kaufman and Broad, Del Monte Ave., (408) 776-1849, from $380,000s.

St. James Place, Warmington Homes, St. James Dr., (408) 778-1521, from $400,000s.

Mountain View

Montelena, Regis Homes of N. California, Del Medio Ct., (650) 917-9677, single-family detached and townhomes, up to 1,650 sq ft, 3 bedrooms, from mid-$400,000s.

Whisman Park, Whisman Rd., (650) 938-8880, townhomes, 1,300-1,440 sq ft, 2-3 bedrooms, low $400,000s.

Woodhaven in Mountain View, Greenbriar Home Communities, 650 Leksich, (650) 965-7600, single-family detached, 2,000-3,000 sq ft, 4-5 bedrooms, from mid-$600,000s.

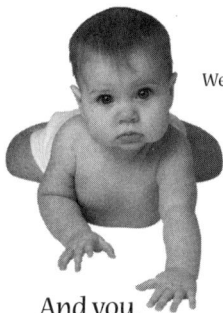

San Jose

Arbor Lane, Braddock & Logan, single-family detached, 3-4 bedrooms, coming in spring 2000.

Briar Creek, Ryland Homes, Keyes St., (408) 279-5262, single-family detached, 3-4 bedrooms, from mid-$300,000s.

Brookwood Homes, William and Eleventh St., (408) 297-3131, single-family detached, 1,813-1,831 sq ft, 3-4 bedrooms, low $400,000s.

Cambridge Park, Pulte Homes, Nieman Rd., (408) 364-0533, single-family detached, 3-4 bedrooms, mid-$500,000s.

Carnelian Heights at Bel Aire, Greenbriar Homes Communities, 2528 Bentley Ridge Dr., (408) 532-0600, single-family detached, from high $900,000s.

Creekside, Pinn Brothers, Silicon Valley Blvd., (408) 281-4426, single-family detached, up to 2,500 sq ft, 4-5 bedrooms, high $400,000s.

Enchantment at Evergreen Hills, Citation Homes Central, Yerba Buena Rd., (408) 528-0987, single-family detached, 2,611-3,518 sq ft, up to 6 bedrooms, from mid-$500,000s.

Jasmine Heights, Yerba Buena Rd., (408) 270-2239, 1,037-1,545 sq ft, 2-4 bedrooms, from mid-$200,000s.

Kaufman & Broad at Branham Village, Kaufman & Broad, Hwy 87 and Branham, (408) 266-4700, single-family detached, up to 5 bedrooms, from $400,000s.

Kaufman & Broad at the Willows, Kaufman & Broad, (408) 266-8900 or 266-8940 or 266-8956, three styles of homes, from the $280,000s to $460,000s.

Lancaster Gate, Western Pacific Housing, Hillsdale Ave., (408) 269-3635, townhomes, up to 1,741 sq ft, 2-3 bedrooms, high $260,000s.

The Masters at Palmia, Brookfield Homes, Cottle Rd., single-family detached, 2,116-2,884 sq ft, low $500,000s.

Montecito at Bel Aire, Greenbriar Homes Communities, 2596 Bentley Ridge Dr., (408) 532-0886, single-family detached, from mid-$700,000s.

Ponderosa Orchard, Ponderosa Homes, Delta Rd., (408) 223-8230, single-family detached, 4-6 bedrooms, from high $500,000s.

Ponderosa Ridge, Ponderosa Homes, Delta Rd., (408) 223-8230, single-family detached, 4-6 bedrooms, from mid-$700,000s.

Ryland Centerpointe, Ryland Homes, (408) 937-1481, single-family detached, up to 1,875 sq ft, 3-4 bedrooms, from mid-$200,000s.

Ryland Dove Hill, Ryland Homes, Yerba Buena Rd. and Dove Hill Rd., (408) 532-7331, single-family detached, up to 2,127 sq ft, 4 bedrooms, from upper $300,000s.

Ryland Silver Ridge, Ryland Homes, 1-888-646-6888, single-family detached, up to 2,800 sq ft, 4-5 bedrooms, from high $400,000s.

Silvercrest, Braddock and Logan, Yerba Buena and Neiman, (408) 270-3182, single-family detached, 4-5 bedrooms, anticipated prices from $895,000s.

Silver Oak Estates, Braddock and Logan, Silver Creek area, (925) 274-2555, single-family detached, 5-6 bedrooms, coming in spring 2000.

Tesora, Braddock and Logan, Union and Foxworthy, (408) 371-9804, single-family detached, 3-4 bedrooms, upper $400,000s.

Tuscan Hills, Pinn Brothers, Yerba Buena Rd. to Nieman Blvd., (408) 279-6285, single-family detached, starting at $765,000.

Woodbridge at Evergreen, Standard Pacific, Quimby Rd., (408) 532-1455, single-family detached, 1,822-2,022 sq ft, 3-4 bedrooms, mid-$400,000s.

San Martin

Corde Valle Vineyard Estates, O'Brien Group, Corde Valle Golf Club, (650) 377-0300, lakefront vineyard estates, 3 acre sites, from high $1,000,000s.

Santa Clara

Santa Inez at Mission Park, Citation Homes, near Lafayette Rd. and Agnew Rd., (408) 919-2992, single-family detached, 3-4 bedrooms, from low $400,00s.

SAN FRANCISCO COUNTY

Bayshore Heights, Bayshore Blvd. to Lois Lane, (415) 864-7800, ext. 571, single-family detached, 3-4 bedrooms, from $422,000-432,000.

SAN MATEO COUNTY

Brisbane

Altamar at The Ridge, Brookfield Homes, (415) 468-7447, attached homes, 2-3 BR, 1,070-1,663 sq ft, from high $200,000s.

Viewpoint at The Ridge, Brookfield Homes, Warbler Ln., (415) 468-4445, townhomes, up to 4 BR, 1,413-2,718 sq ft, from high $300,000s.

Daly City

Bay Vista, Western Pacific Housing, 1-800-3300-WPH, single-family detached, 1,548-2,360 sq ft, 3-5 bedrooms, from $400,000s.

Foster City

Meridian Bay, SummerHill Homes, (650) 638-1100, 880 Meridian Bay Ln., condos, 2-3 bedrooms, from mid-$300,000s.

Pacifica

Ryland Elite, Ryland Homes, Skyline Blvd., (650) 355-0811, single-family detached, up to 2,598 sq ft, 3-5 bedrooms, low $500,000s.

Redwood City

Gossamer Cove, Ponderosa Homes, Redwood Shores Pkwy., (650) 631-9732, single-family detached, 3-5 bedrooms, from high $500,000s.

San Mateo

111 St. Matthews, SummerHill Homes, St. Matthews Ave., 1-800-585-0085, condos, 1,355-1,881 sq ft, 2-3 bedrooms, from $400,000s.

Humboldt Square, Regis Homes of Northern California, Humboldt St. and Third Ave., (650) 558-1766, townhomes, up to 1,550 sq ft, 3 bedrooms, from high $300,000s.

Ryland Marble Bay and Ryland Cedar Bay, Ryland Homes, (650) 356-1046, single-family detached, up to 2,150 sq ft, 3-4 bedrooms, from high $300,000s.

South San Francisco

El Rancho Highland, Sunstream Homes, Chestnut Estates Subdivision, (650) 583-3651, single-family detached, 4-6 bedrooms, high $500,000s.

The Grove at Promenade, Greystone Homes, 6 Cymbidium, (650) 869-6887, single-family detached, 1,609-1,880 sq ft, 3-4 bedrooms, mid-$400,000s.

The Meadows at Promenade, Greystone Homes, 27 Amaryllis Ct., (650) 869-6225, single-family detached, up to 2,501 sq ft, 3-5 bedrooms, starting in high $500,000s.

Parcplace, SummerHill Homes, (650) 553-9040, single-family detached, 3-4 bedrooms, from mid-$400,000s.

Sunnyvale

Heritage of Sunnyvale, Regis Homes of N. California, Fair Oaks and Duane Ave., (408) 991-9386, single-family detached, 3-4 bedroom, from $400,000s.

ALAMEDA COUNTY

Alameda

The Gardens, Schuler Homes, Buena Vista from Webster Tube, (510) 521-5347, single-family detached, 3-4 bedrooms, from low $300,000s.

Castro Valley

Amber Ridge, Kiper Homes, Crest Ave. and Sheffield Rd., (510) 582-5151, single-family detached, 2,245-2,490 sq ft, 4-5 bedrooms, anticipated prices from low $400,000s.

Five Canyons, Centex Homes, (510) 886-7745, single-family detached, 4-6 bedrooms, from low $400,000s.

Palomares Hills, Regency II, Shapell, Villareal off Castro Valley Blvd., (510) 728-9292, single-family detached, 4-5 bedrooms, from mid-$400,000s.

Castro Valley (Continued)

Palomares Hills, Sunset Series, Shapell, Villareal off Castro Valley Blvd., (510) 733-3286, single-family detached, 1,944-2,277 sq ft, 3-4 bedrooms, from low $400,000s.

Whispering Oaks, Centex Homes, south east of Five Canyons Pkwy. and Hwy. 580, (510) 886-7745, single-family detached, 4-6 bedrooms, 1,900-3,500 sq ft, high-$400,000s.

Dublin

Dublin Ranch, Standard Pacific Homes, Centex, Shea Homes, Tassajara Rd. north of Hwy 580, 1-1-877-LIVE-AT-DR, single-family detached, 3-5 bedrooms, from mid-$300,000s.

The Estates at Emerald Park, Pulte Homes, (925) 551-7830, Hibernia off Dublin Blvd., single-family detached, 4-5 bedrooms, 2,459-3,900 sq ft, from high $400,000s.

Merrion at Emerald Park, Richmond American Homes, north east of Dougherty and Hwy. 580, (925) 829-8029, single-family detached, up to 5 bedrooms, up to 2,200 sq ft, from high $300,000s.

The Ridge at Hansen Hill, Warmington Homes, 1198 Inspiration Cir., (925) 556-9612, single-family detached, up to 6 bedrooms, 3,445-3,788 sq ft, from low $600,000s.

Starward, Schuler (925) 875-1060, Starward off Amador Valley, 3-4 bedrooms, from low $300,000s.

Stonecrest at Dublin Ranch, Centex Homes, Tassajara Rd. north of Hwy. 580, (925) 875-1561, single-family detached, 3-5 bedrooms, low $500,000s.

SummerGlen at Emerald Park, Kaufman and Broad, Hacienda Dr. at Gleason Blvd., (925) 829-9630, 3-6 bedrooms, mid $400,000s.

Tassajara Meadows, The Mission Peak Co., Tassajara Rd. north of Hwy. 580, (925) 875-0001, 1-888-754-0000, single-family detached, 3-5 bedrooms, 1,656-2,128 sq ft, from $300,000s.

Fremont

Avalon Estates, The Mission Peak Co., end of Green Valley Rd., (510) 226-9122, single-family detached, 3,000-4,750 sq ft, from $800,000.

Cameron Meadows, Western Pacific Homes, Mission Blvd. north of Durham Rd., (510) 657-5171, single-family detached, up to 5 bedrooms, 2,606-3,524 sq ft, from low $700,000s.

Fremont/Centerville Station, Kaufman & Broad, at Niles Station, (510) 818-1100, single-family detached, 3-4 bedrooms, up to 2,380 sq ft, from high $380,000s.

Glenmoor Village, SummerHill Homes, Eggers Dr., (510) 574-0826, single-family detached, 3-5 bedrooms, mid-$500,0000s.

Liberty Commons, Shapell, Liberty St., (510) 353-9052, town homes, from mid-$200,000s.

Niles Glen, Greystone Homes Inc., 35309 Terra Cotta Circle, (510) 505-0405, single-family detached, 3-5 bedrooms, 2,027-2,462 sq ft, from mid-$400,000s.

Niles/Centerville Station, Kaufman & Broad, Fremont Blvd. , (510) 818-1100, single-family detached, 3-5 bedrooms, from $370,000s.

Palomar, Delco Bldrs., off Murdell Ln. at Alden Ln., (510) 333-1434, 1,905-2,574 sq ft, from mid-$400,000s.

Rockland Court, 3500 block Mission Blvd., 1-800-331-4669, single-family detached, 4-5 bedrooms, 2,400-2,565 sq ft, from high $400,000s.

Hayward

Bailey Ranch, Signature Properties, in the Hayward Hills, 1-800-300-4123, single-family detached, 4 bedrooms, coming soon, call for prices.

Canterbury, Summerhill Homes, Taylor at Industrial, (510) 259-6297, single-family detached, 3-5 bedrooms, 2,000-2,400 sq ft, from low $300,000s.

Hayward (Continued)

Highlands at Clearbrook, Standard Pacific Homes, (510) 583-9542, Mission Blvd. to Garin Ave., single-family detached, 3-5 bedrooms, 2,500-3,300 sq ft, from mid-$400,000s.

Magnolia Place, Citation Homes Central, Whitman St., 1-800-8-BUY-NEW, single-family detached, 1,940-2,127 sq ft, 4-5 bedrooms, from low $300,000s.

Orchard Park, Greystone Homes, 103 Orchard Ave., 1-800-794-1926, single-family detached, 1,624-2,088 sq ft, 3-4 bedrooms, start in $300,000s.

Springfield Park, Greystone Homes, 28290 Capitola St., 1-510-266-0641, single family detached, 3-4 bedrooms, 1,625-2,088 sq ft, start in $300,000s.

Twin Bridges, Standard Pacific Homes, (510) 475-0367, 475-5585 and 487-0500, 3 groups, single-family detached, 3-5 bedrooms, from high $300,000s.

Livermore

Capistrano, Greenbriar Homes, (925) 447-9964, 633 Alden Ln., single-family detached, up to 4,400 sq ft, from low $600,000s.

Copper Hill, Ryland, (925) 425-5012, N. Canyons Pkwy. at Collier Canyon Rd., townhomes, up to 1,385 sq ft, 2-3 bedrooms, upper $100,000s.

Coventry at Stratford Park, Signature Properties, (925) 447-1314, 5720 Arlene Way, single-family detached, 3-5 bedrooms, up to 3,149 sq ft, from the $300,000s.

The Oaks, Pulte Homes, Alden Ln., (925) 449-1637, single-family detached, up to 6 bedrooms, from upper $500,000s to mid-$600,000s.

RavensWood, (925) 449-5458, Emily off south Vasco Rd., single-family detached, 4 bedroom, 2,554-3,246 sq ft, from upper $400,000 to $510,000.

Ridgecrest, Richmond American Homes, Portola off N. Livermore, (925) 371-6648, single-family detached, 4 bedrooms, up to 2,273 sq ft, from mid-$300,000s.

Saddleback, Schuler, Dalton west off Vasco north, (925) 294-9980, single-family detached, 3-4 bedrooms, 1,368-1,840 sq ft, from low $300,000s.

Sonterra, Standard Pacific Homes, north east of Vasco Rd. and Hwy. 580, (925) 294-9222, single-family detached, 4-5 bedrooms, from low $400,000s.

Vintage Collection, Delco Bldrs., Vasco Rd. south of Portola, (925) 606-5505, single-family detached, from low $600,000s.

Vintner Place, Castle Homes, south east of Portola and Hwy. 580, (925) 373-9100, single-family detached, 3-4 bedrooms, low $400,000s.

Newark

Main Street at Carter Station, Western Pacific Housing, (510) 668-0250, single-family detached, 3-4 bedrooms, 1,546-2,003 sq ft, from high $200,000s.

Pleasanton

Ascona at Ruby Hill, Signature Properties, (510) 417-2250, single-family detached, 4-5 bedrooms, from the mid-$500,000s.

Avila at Hacienda, Signature Properties, (510) 734-9569, single-family detached, 3-4 bedrooms, from $270,000s.

Bridal Creek, Greenbriar Sycamore Valley Company, Sycamore Rd., 1-888-800-8988, single-family detached, single-family detached, up to 4,455 sq ft, 4-5 bedrooms, opens fall 1999, call for prices.

The Preserve, Presley Homes, near Vineyard Avenue in south hills, (925) 737-0223, single-family detached, 3,424 to 4,345 sq ft, from $800,000s.

Rivasco, Signature Properties, Off Vineyard Ave., (925) 417-5808, single-family detached, 5-6 bedrooms, from high-$900,000s.

Ruby Hill, Signature Properties, (510) 417-2250, single-family detached, from the mid-$800,000s.

Siena at Hacienda, Signature Properties, (510) 227-1817, townhomes, 2-3 bedrooms, high $180,000s.

Stoneridge Square, Standard Pacific Homes, Bernal at Hopyard Rd., (925) 462-2711, single-family detached, up to 2,013 sq ft, 3-4 bedrooms, from high $300,000s.

Valencia II at Hacienda, Signature Properties, (510) 227-1819, single-family detached, 3-5 bedrooms, from mid-$300,000s.

San Leandro

Bay Walk at Heron Bay, Roberts Landing, Inc., near Lewelling Boulevard at the waterfront, (510) 351-1179, single-family detached, 3-4 bedrooms, from upper $200,000s.

Ryland Medallion, Ryland Homes, (510) 614-7050, single-family detached, up to 2,004 sq ft, 3-4 bedrooms, from upper $200,000s.

Stillwater Cove at Heron Bay, Greystone Homes, Inc., Anchorage Dr. off Lewelling Blvd., (510) 352-8920, single-family detached, 3-4 bedrooms, from low $400,000s.

View Point at Heron Bay, Robert's Landing Inc., Lewelling Blvd., (510) 895-9614, single-family detached, 4-5 bedrooms, 1,923-2,300 sq ft, from the mid-$300,000s.

San Lorenzo

Cottage Square, Centex Homes, north of Grant Ave. between Washington Ave. and Hesperian Blvd., (510) 276-2300, single-family detached, 1,300-1,700 sq ft, 3-4 bedrooms, from high $200,000s.

Union City

Ashford Place, Greystone Homes, O'Connell Ln. and Willow Ln., 1-800-794-1926, single-family detached, 1,978-2,244 sq ft, 4-5 bedrooms, start in $400,000s.

Heritage Pointe, Pulte Homes, Alvarado-Niles Rd., (510) 475-1847, single-family detached, 4-5 bedrooms, from mid-$400,000s.

Inspirations at Foothill Glen, Citation Homes Central, Decoto Rd. at 7th St., (510) 475-1853, single-family detached, 4-5 bedrooms, 1,875-2,300 sq ft, from low $400,000s.

Ryland Portico, Ryland Homes, Whipple Rd. at Bettencourt Way, (510) 475-6046, single-family detached, up to 2,450 sq ft, 4-5 bedrooms, from low $400,000s.

Ryland Woodberry, Ryland Homes, Alvarado-Niles Rd., (510) 429-7170, single-family detached, up to 2,100 sq ft, 4 bedroom, from high $300,000s.

Seabreeze Classics, Standard Pacific Homes, west of Dyer St. and Union City Blvd., (510) 487-2383 and 489-9300, single-family detached, 4-5 bedrooms, 2,530-2,813 sq ft, from mid-$400,000s.

Splendor, Citation Homes Central, Decoto Rd., (510) 475-1853, single-family detached, 2,169-2,609 sq ft, 4-5 bedrooms, from low $400,000s.

SAN JOAQUIN COUNTY

Manteca

Providence at Chadwick Square, Frontiers, London and Lathrop Rd., (209) 239-1648, single-family detached, up to 2400 sq ft, 3-5 bedrooms, from the mid- $100,000s.

Trophy Club, Raymus Development, Airport Way, (209) 825-5510, single-family detached, 3-5 bedrooms, call for prices.

Wildflower Collection at Woodward Park, (209) 823-9006, single-family detached, 1,732-3,300 sq ft, 4 bedrooms, low $170,000s.

Tracy

Crown Pointe & Ridgeview, Kaufman & Broad, off Linne Rd., 1-800-34-HOMES, single-family detached, from $190,000s.

The Gardens at Parkview, Standard Pacific Homes, off Corral Hollow Rd., 1-877-786-3722, single family detached, 2,103-2,707 sq ft, 3-5 bedrooms, coming soon, call for prices.

Glenbrook at Glenbriar Estates, WestCo Community Builders, Glenbriar Circle, (209) 833-6400, single-family detached, up to 6 bedrooms, from $140,000.

Kaufman & Broad at Edgewood, Kaufman & Broad, Linne Rd., 1-800-34-HOMES, single-family detached, up to 4,000 sq ft, 3-6 bedrooms, from the $190,000s.

Tracy (Continued)

Lyon Estates and Villas, William Lyon Homes, Inc., off Bryon Rd., (209) 839-1800 or 830-7100, single-family detached, 3-5 bedrooms, from high $100,000s to mid-$200,000s.

Reflections at Hidden Lake, Richmond American Homes, MacArthur Road and Valpico Rd., (209) 830-1884, single-family detached, up to 6 bedrooms, 2,000-2,500 sq ft, call for prices.

The Reserve at Woodfield, Seeno Homes, Corral Hollow at Fieldview, (209) 839-9952, single-family detached, 1,785-3,159 sq ft, 3-6 bedrooms, low $200,000s.

Ryland Junction, Ryland Homes, 1-888-646-6888, single-family detached, up to 2,298 sq ft, 3-5 bedrooms, from high $100,000s.

Sandpiper Cove at Hidden Lake, Pulte Homes, MacArthur Rd., (209) 838-0338, single-family detached, up to 2,366 sq ft, 3-4 bedrooms, mid-upper $200,000s.

Savoy, Award Homes, Byron Rd., (209) 839-9275, single-family detached, 3-5 bedrooms, 1,531-2,130 sq ft, from $200,000s.

The Shores at Hidden Lake, Pulte Homes, MacArthur Rd., (209) 838-0338, single-family detached, 3-5 bedrooms, upper $200,000s.

The Springs at Parkview, Standard Pacific Homes, Corral Hollow Rd., 1-877-786-3722, single-family detached, 2,420-3,416 sq ft, 4-5 bedrooms, coming soon, call for prices.

Summer Lane, Greystone Homes, Corral Hollow Rd., (209) 833-3700, single-family detached, 4-6 bedrooms, from mid-$200,000s.

Westgate, Standard Pacific Homes, Byron Rd., (209) 832-1860 or 833-3324, single-family detached, up to 2,443 sq ft 3-4 bedrooms, from low $200,000s.

CONTRA COSTA COUNTY

Alamo

Stonecastle of Alamo, Suncrest Homes, (925) 977-6927, single-family detached, 4-6 bedrooms, 2,800-4,200 sq ft, from $700,000s.

Stone Valley Oaks, Summerhill Homes, Stone Valley Rd., 1-800-585-0085, single-family detached, 4-6 bedrooms, opening Spring of 2000, call for prices.

Clayton

Diablo Village at Oakhurst, Presley Homes, (925) 672-3673, single-family detached, 3-4 bedrooms, coming soon, call for prices.

Peacock Creek at Oakhurst, Presley Homes, 1105 Peacock Creek Dr., (925) 672-3673, single-family detached, from 5 bedrooms, from $500,000s.

Concord

Crystyl Ranch, Legacy Homes, 5313 Oak Point Ct., (925) 687-3522, single-family detached, 2,400 to 3,400 sq. ft, mid-$400,000s.

Holly Creek, DeNova Homes, Bailey Rd. & Myrtle Dr., (925) 691-9600, single-family detached, 4-5 bedrooms, 2,700-3,200 sq ft, from high $400,000s.

Danville

California Meadows, Kaufman & Broad, 43 Lily Ct., (925) 736-8327, single-family detached, up to 6 bedrooms, from $400,000s.

Campbell Place, Pacific Union Homes, Campbell Pl. off Glasgow Cir., (925) 743-0238, single-family detached, 4-6 bedrooms, from $800,000s.

The Crossings, Davidon Homes, Old Blackhawk Rd. off Sycamore Valley, (925) 648-3550, single-family detached, 3-6 bedrooms, 3,291-4,282 sq ft, from high $700,000s.

Diablo Ranch Estates, Greystone Homes, Blackhawk Dr., (925) 296-6161, single-family detached, 4,033-4,400 sq ft, from $1,000,000.

Lawrence Estates, Pulte Homes, Lawrence Rd. off Tassajara, (925) 648-9346, single-family detached, 4-5 bedrooms, from mid-$600,000s.

Magee Ranch, Broadmoor Development Co, 100 Magee Ranch Rd., (925) 837-8900, single-family detached, from 4 bedrooms, from $1,365,000.

Ryland Cottages, Ryland, La Gonda Way, (925) 837-7150, single-family detached, up to 2,320 sq ft, 3-4 bedrooms, from high $300,000s.

San Michele, Braddock and Logan, Lawrence at Camino Tassajara Rd., (925) 648-9418, single-family detached, 5-6 bedrooms, 3,325-3,743 sq. ft., from $700,000s.

Shadow Creek Manor, Camino Tassajara off Crow Canyon Rd., (925) 736-7369, single-family detached, 4-5 bedrooms, from high $500,000s.

Victoria Place, Davidon Homes, Old Blackhawk Rd. off Sycamore Valley, (925) 648-3550, single-family detached, 3-6 bedroom, 3,853-5,046 sq ft, from $921,990.

El Sobrante

Hillcrest, Laurelwood Homes, Hillcrest off San Pablo Dam Rd., (510) 758-8888, single-family detached, 3-5 bedrooms, 2,344-2,665 sq ft, from $350,000.

Woodridge Terrace, DeNova Homes, Baroque Dr. off San Pablo Dam Rd., (510) 222-2662, single-family detached, 3-4 bedrooms, 1,768-2,132 sq ft, from high $200,000s.

Hercules

Belleterre, Schuler, Titan Way off Hercules Ave., (510) 741-9165, single-family detached, 4 bedrooms, from $306,880.

Lafayette

Reliez Valley Highlands, Davidon Homes, Hidden Pond off Reliez Valley, (925) 370-2272, single-family detached, 3-6 bedrooms, 3,504-3,800 sq ft, from $733,000-$978,990s.

Martinez

Brittany Hills, Catellus Residential Group, Morrello to Brittany Hills Dr., (925) 372-4040, single-family detached, 3-5 bedrooms, 2,350-3,076 sq ft, from mid-$300,000s.

California Vistas, Kaufman & Broad, 137 Loire Ct., (925) 370-8893, single-family detached, 4-6 bedrooms, from mid-$300,000s.

Meadows, Young California Homes, Arthur Rd. off Pacheco Blvd., (925) 372-7900, single-family detached, 4-5 bedrooms, from mid-$200,000s.

Milano, Silverwing Developers, Arnold Dr., (707) 265-6311, single-family detached, 3-4 bedrooms, from $296,340.

Moraga

Sonsara, Taylor Woodrow Homes, Moraga Way, (925) 314-2700, single-family detached, 3-4 bedrooms, from $836,000.

Pleasant Hill

Grayson Ridge Estates, Lennox Homes, Grayson and Buttner Rd., (925) 284-0415, single-family detached, 3,000-4,000 sq ft, 5 bedrooms, from upper $600,000s-upper $700,000s.

Grayson Woods, Davidon Homes, Grayson off Taylor Blvd., (925) 274-0800, single-family detached, 3-6 bedrooms, 2,212-3,135 sq. ft., from low $500,000s-low $600,000s.

Village Square, Delco Bldrs., Hookston Rd., (925) 952-4595, single-family detached, 3-5 bedrooms, mid-$300,000s.

Richmond

Lakeview, SCS Development, east of Research and Lakeside Drives, 1-877- 391-HOME, single-family detached, 1,291-1, 636 sq. ft., up to 4 bedrooms, low $200,000s.

San Ramon

Cambrio, Braddock and Logan, Crow Canyon Rd. and Porter, (925) 314-9743, townhomes, 3-4 bedrooms, 1,827-2,000 sq. ft., high $300,000s.

Crown Ridge, Standard Pacific, 15 Bruin Ct, (925) 829-1873, single-family detached, 3-4 bedrooms, from upper $400,000s.

San Ramon (Continued)

Lyon Manor & Plantation, William Lyon Homes, Bolinger Canyon Rd. to Cobblestone Dr., (925) 362-9111, single-family detached, 3-5 bedrooms, 2,281-3,564 sq. ft., from $500,000s.

The Bridges at Gale Ranch, Shapell, Bolinger Canyon Rd. east of Hwy. 680, (925) 735-0300, single-family detached, 1,679-3,800 sq. ft., 3-5 bedrooms, from low $400,000s.

Walnut Creek

Briarwood, DeNova Homes, Briarwood off Cherry Ln., (925) 691-9600, single-family detached, 4-5 bedrooms, 2,700-3,100 sq. ft., from low $500,000s.

Larkey Estates, LCI Homes, Geary Rd. at Larkey Ln., (925) 935-9152, single-family detached, 4-6 bedrooms, 2,458-2,800 sq. ft., from $514,900.

Laurel Glen, Delco Bldrs., 2569 Lucy Ln., (925) 975-5205, from mid-$400,000s-mid-$500,000s.

Oak Creek and Shadow Brook Estates, Delco Builders, Northgate Road, (925) 256-9504, from $829,900.

The Vistas at Boundary Oaks, Delco Bldrs., Northgate Rd., (925) 933-2224, single-family detached, mid-$600,000s.

Chapter 15

SANTA CLARA COUNTY *Commuting*

SANTA CLARA COUNTY WILL USHER IN YEAR 2000 by extending the light rail from Santa Clara to Mountain View. In 2001, the light rail should be pushed up to Milpitas and within three or four years down to East San Jose and to Campbell.

The Altamont Commuter Express (trains from Manteca to San Jose) will add a third train in Year 2000. More improvements are coming to freeways and bus and rail service.

Yet as fast as the improvements are made, they seem to overwhelmed by car and population increases. And by habits. A study released in 1999 indicated that about 77 percent of Santa Clara commuters drive solo to work, the highest percentage of Bay Area counties.

The same study concluded that the average Santa Clara commuter drives 14 miles to work and takes 25 minutes to get there. About 18 percent of those interviewed said their commute had gotten better, 30 percent worse, and 52 percent said nothing has changed.

Traffic has turned into one of the biggest headaches for Silicon Valley and the Bay Area. Many people working in Santa Clara commute to Tracy, Manteca and Merced, to Dublin, Livermore and Pleasanton, and to towns in Contra Costa County. So irritating has the traffic become that several of these towns appear close to passing measures that would severely restrict growth.

Some firms have been moving operations out of Silicon Valley. Hewlett-Packard, Intel and Apple have opened plants in Greater Sacramento. Many high-tech jobs can be found in Fremont, Milpitas, San Ramon, Dublin, Livermore, Pleasanton, and cities of San Mateo, notably Menlo Park and South San Francisco (bio tech).

But many firms still want to settle in the original Silicon Valley and want their people to mix and exchange ideas with the brainy and dynamic people the Valley attracts.

If you are going nuts with driving, you might think about other ways of commuting. Alternatives out are there: bus, light rail, train, car-pooling.

Time-saving Strategies

- Buy a good map book and keep it in the car. The editors favor Thomas Guides, which are updated annually. Sooner than later you will find yourself jammed on the freeway and in desperate need of an alternate route. They're out there.
- Listen to traffic reports on the radio. Helicopters and planes give immediate news of jams. Avoid trouble before you get on the road.
- Buy bridge ticket books and, for buses and light rail, flash passes (good for a month) or ticket books. All will save you time and money.
- Join a car pool. RIDES, 1-800-755-7665, will help you find a car pool in your town — no charge. In the typical arrangement, passengers meet at one or two spots and are dropped off in one or two destinations. The pools go all over. All that's needed are passengers and a driver.

  If you want to set up your own pool, RIDES will help you find passengers and finance the lease of a van. Passengers split the cost, which is based on the type of van, mileage and operating expenses. The driver gets a free commute and use of the van.
- Avoid peak hours. If you can leave for work — it gets earlier every year — about 6:30 a.m. and hit the freeway home before 4 p.m., your kids might not greet you, "Hey, stranger."
- Take public transportation. Yes, the car is flexible, so handy, so private. But if other, easier, cheaper ways of commuting are at hand, why ignore them?

Buses

Run by the Santa Clara Valley Transportation Authority. They go all over the county: Gilroy, Milpitas, Palo Alto, San Jose, Los Gatos.

During morning commute hours, express buses travel from Gilroy and Santa Cruz to destinations in Silicon Valley.

Wheelchair access. Stops at Park & Ride lots, Caltrain stations, shopping malls, hospitals, San Jose State University and other colleges, city halls, parks, airports, Fremont BART station. Connections to AC Transit (Alameda County) and SamTrans (San Mateo County) buses.

Dial-A-Ride — bus pickup at door — in south county.

Historic trolleys circle the downtown transit mall, 1.5-mile route. 9 a.m. to 5 p.m. Weekends and holidays.

The transportation authority puts out a handy map. To obtain one and for more information, phone (408) 321-2300; from south county, (408) 683-4151; Los Gatos, (408) 370-9191; from Palo Alto, (800) 894-9908.

Light Rail

From South San Jose (and other neighborhoods) to downtown San Jose to Great America and the city of Santa Clara. A sleek ride. Work is wrapping up on the extension of the line to Mountain View, which is spending about $6 million to build a transit center in its downtown. Scheduled opening is Year 2000.

For the present, about 33 stations. Bus connections at each. The line also provides service to the San Jose neighborhoods of Blossom Valley (Santa Teresa Boulevard and San Ignacio Avenue) and to Almaden (Winfield and Coleman).

Run by Santa Clara Valley Transportation Authority. All tickets sold from machines, none on board. Day passes can be used for bus and light rail. For information, (408) 321-2300. Ask for light-rail brochure.

Caltrain

The old Southern Pacific route, now employed for commute service by the Peninsula Corridor Joint Powers Board, an agency with representatives from San Francisco, San Mateo and Santa Clara counties.

Trains from Gilroy to San Francisco. Stops at Morgan Hill, San Jose, Santa Clara, Sunnyvale, Mountain View, Palo Alto, Menlo Park, Redwood City, San Carlos, Belmont, San Mateo, Burlingame, Millbrae, San Bruno, South San Francisco, San Francisco. Transfers are available for buses from SamTrans, Santa Clara County Transportation Agency and Muni. More trains are being added. Track and stations are being improved, $41 million job. For schedules and more information, call (800) 660-4287.

Amtrak

Amtrak is used more for excursions, especially during ski season, than commuting but for some people it can work as a commute train. Service nationwide and for locals throughout the East and South Bay. Stations in San Jose and Santa Clara. Nice ride. Check the schedule. (800) 872-7245.

BART

In East Bay, the end of the line is in Fremont, right next to Milpitas, but the Santa Clara County Transportation Agency runs a connector bus to that station. For BART schedules and info, (510) 441-2278.

After years of arguing, agreement appears near to connect BART to downtown San Jose.

One number

Universal number for commute information. New effort to make it simple. (408) 817-1717.

Altamont Commuter Express (ACE)

New service. Proving popular. Because housing prices are so high in Silicon Valley and so low in other places, like Central California, many Silicon Valley workers are buying homes in such places as Tracy and Manteca, and eastern Alameda County. This commute train starts in Stockton and stops in Manteca, Tracy, Livermore, Pleasanton, Fremont, Santa Clara, San Jose. Phone 800-411-7245.

Tidbits

- Metering lights have been installed on many access ramps to local freeways and expressways, an effort to keep the flow steady. Some freeways have car pool lanes, a reward for people who double up.
- Highway jobs that appear to have win funding: another lane for Interstate 680, probably high-occupancy, between Dublin and Milpitas. Interstate 680 used to be one of the fast freeways to San Jose; it's much slower now, much of the traffic coming from East Alameda and the San Joaquin Valley.

  From Morgan Hill to San Jose, Highway 101 is to add one north and one south lane.
- On busy routes, some local buses are being run 24 hours a day, a recent innovation.
- Also running 24 hours a day are the light-rail trolleys.

Chapter 16

SANTA CLARA COUNTY

Weather

"HE HAD BEEN suddenly jerked from the heart of civilization and flung into the heart of things primordial. No lazy, sun-kissed life was this ...."

Jack London, in "The Call of the Wild," was describing the great dog, Buck, stolen from the Santa Clara Valley and secreted to Alaska to work as a sled dog. Compared to frigid Alaska, Santa Clara was cream cheese, Jack thought, an arguable proposition, but there was no denying he caught the gist of the local weather, "sun-kissed."

One of Life's Joys

Rarely very hot or cold, always finding its way back to balmy tranquillity.

Although appearing somewhat erratic, the weather proceeds logically, responding to broad patterns and local topography. Easily learned, these patterns will make you somewhat of a weather expert, a reliable source on what to wear, when to have a picnic and when to drive slowly.

For starters, it can be safely said that rain will rarely fall between May and September, that Pacific swimming will be warmer in October than in June, that the San Lorenzo Valley to the south and Berkeley to the north will receive more rain or moisture than the Santa Clara Valley.

Five great actors star in the Bay Area weather extravaganza: the sun, the Pacific, the Golden Gate, the Central Valley and the hills.

The Sun

In the spring and summer, the sun moves north bringing a mass of air called the Pacific High. The Pacific High blocks storms from the California Coast and dispatches winds down the coast. In the fall, the sun moves south, taking the Pacific High with it. The winds slough off for a while, then in bluster the storms. Toward spring, the storms abate as the Pacific High settles in.

The Pacific

Speeding across the Pacific, spring and summer winds pick up moisture and, at the coast, strip the warm water from the surface and bring up the frigid.

Cold water exposed to warm, wet air makes a wonderfully thick fog. In

Average Daily Temperature

Location	Ja	Fb	Mr	Ap	My	Ju	Jy	Au	Sp	Oc	No	Dc
Gilroy	47	52	54	58	62	68	71	71	69	63	54	48
Los Gatos	48	52	54	57	61	66	70	69	68	62	54	48
Mt. Hamilton	44	44	43	48	55	64	71	71	65	58	48	44
Palo Alto	48	51	54	57	61	65	66	67	65	60	53	48
San Jose	49	53	55	59	63	67	70	69	68	63	55	49
San Francisco	49	52	53	56	58	62	63	64	65	61	55	49

Source: National Climatic Data Center, Ashville, NC, 1961-1990

summer, San Francisco, Monterey, Half Moon Bay and Pacifica, among others, often look like they are buried in mountains of cotton.

The Golden Gate

This fog would love to scoot inland to the Santa Clara Valley and Bay shore cities such as Palo Alto and Mountain View. But the coastal hills and mountains stop or greatly impede its progress — except where there are openings. Of the half dozen or so major gaps, the biggest is that marvelous work of nature, the Golden Gate.

The fog shoots through the Golden Gate in the spring and summer, visually delighting motorists on the Bay Bridge, bangs into the East Bay hills and eases down toward San Jose, where it takes the edge off temperatures. The Crystal Springs gap, located northwest of Palo Alto, also allows cooling air into the South Bay.

The Central Valley

Also known as the San Joaquin Valley and located about 75 miles inland, the Central Valley is influenced more by continental weather than coastal. In the summer, this means heat. Hot air rises, pulling in cold air like a vacuum. The Central Valley sucks in the coastal air through the Golden Gate and openings in the East Bay hills, until the Valley cools.

Then the Valley says to the coast: no more cool air, thank you.

With the suction gone, the inland pull on the ocean fog drops off, often breaking down the fog-producing apparatus and clearing San Francisco and the coastline. Meanwhile, lacking the cooling air, the Valley heats up again, creating the vacuum that pulls in the fog.

This cha-cha-cha between coast and inland valley gave rise to the Bay Region's boast of "natural air conditioning." In hot weather, nature works to bring in cool air; in cool weather, she works to bring in heat.

In Santa Clara County, this push-pull phenomenon has a diminutive counterpart. At night, fog will occasionally creep over the coastal mountains only to be burned off the following morning by the robust sunlight.

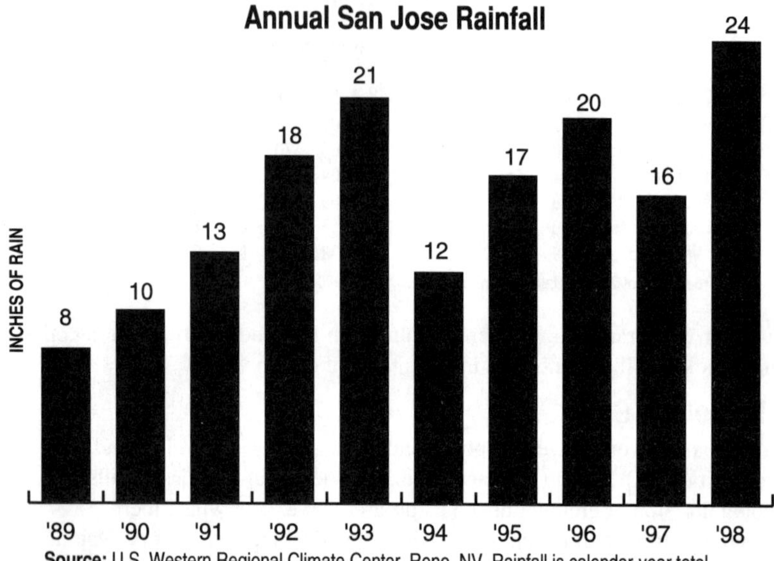

Source: U.S. Western Regional Climate Center, Reno, NV. Rainfall is calendar-year total.

The Hills

Besides blocking the fog, the hills also greatly decide how much rain falls in a particular location. Many storms travel south to north, so a valley that opens to the south (San Lorenzo) will receive more rain than one that opens to the north (Santa Clara).

When storm clouds rise to pass over a hill, they cool and drop much of their rain. Some towns in the Bay Region will be deluged during a storm, while a few miles away another town will escape with showers. Saratoga reports an average annual rainfall of 29 inches, Cupertino 14 inches.

That basically is how the weather works in the Bay Area. Unfortunately for regularity's sake, the actors often forget their lines or are upstaged by minor stars.

Rainfall at San Jose over 10 years (1975-84) demonstrates the mildly erratic nature of Mother Nature. From 12 inches in 1975, rainfall dropped to 7

San Jose Temperature Patterns

Month	Avg. Max.	Avg. Min.	Record High	Record Low
January	58	41	79	22
April	69	47	93	30
July	81	56	108	43
October	74	51	97	31
Year	70	49	108	20

Source: San Jose Municipal Weather Station.

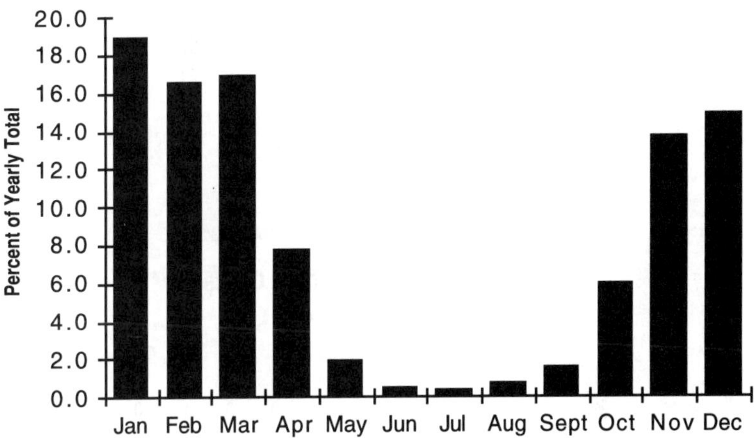

Source: U.S. Western Regional Climate Center, Reno, NV. The chart shows, on average, what percent of the year's total rain falls each month. Rainfall data from the years 1961-1993.

and 9 inches in the drought years of 1976 and 1977 and after bouncing between 16 and 20 over the next five years, zoomed to 33 inches in storm-wracked 1983.

In 1987, a drought began that in subsequent years forced rationing. It ended with the 1992 winter, which soaked all, loaded the Sierra with snow and filled local reservoirs.

Swimming

September and October are often best months to swim in the Pacific. The upwelling of the cold water has stopped. Often the fog has departed. Sunshine glows upon the water and the coast. Almost every year the summer ends with hot spells in September and October.

Sunshine

Like sunshine? You are in the right place. Records show that during daylight hours the sun shines in New York City 60 percent of the time; in Boston, 57 percent; in Detroit, 53 percent and in Seattle, 43 percent. San Jose averages 63 percent.

The gloomiest month: January, 42 percent sunshine. The brightest, the summer months, e.g. July, 83 percent.

Humidity

Heat Santa Clara County does experience but rarely muggy weather. When hot spells arrive, the air usually has little moisture — dry heat. When the air is moist (the fog), the temperatures drop.

Temperatures for Selected Cities

Number of Days Greater than 90 Degrees

City	Ja	Fb	Mr	Ap	My	Ju	Jy	Au	Sp	Oc	No	Dc
Gilroy	0	0	0	0	0	NA	NA	19	11	0	0	0
Los Gatos	0	0	0	0	0	NA	6	12	7	0	0	0
Mount Hamilton	0	0	0	0	0	NA	1	5	2	0	0	0
Palo Alto	0	0	0	NA	0	NA	3	7	3	0	0	0
San Jose	0	0	0	0	0	NA	8	12	8	0	0	0

Source: National Climatic Center, Asheville, N.C. 1998.NA not available. tlw8/30/99

Temperatures for Selected Cities

Number of Days 32 Degrees or Less

City	Ja	Fb	Mr	Ap	My	Ju	Jy	Au	Sp	Oc	No	Dc
Gilroy	1	0	0	0	0	NA	0	0	0	0	0	12
Los Gatos	0	0	3	0	0	NA	0	0	0	0	0	10
Mount Hamilton	6	18	10	14	6	NA	0	0	0	0	3	10
Palo Alto	0	0	0	NA	0	NA	0	0	0	0	0	10
San Jose	0	0	0	0	0	NA	0	0	0	0	0	6

Source: National Climatic Center, Asheville, N.C. 1998. NA not available. tlw8/30/99

Fog

Of the Bay Area's two types of fog, one is more dangerous than the other. The coastal fog often forms well above the Pacific and, pushed by the wind, generally moves at a good clip. In thick coastal fog, you will have to slow down but you can see the tail lights of a car 50 to 75 yards ahead.

Valley or tule fog blossoms at shoe level when cold air pulls moisture from the earth. Found mostly in the Central Valley, tule fog hugs the ground and generally stays put. When you read of 50- and 75-car pileups in the Central Valley, tule fog is to blame.

Occasionally, tule fog is pulled down into the Bay — an effect of the pull of heat on cold air. The ocean being warmer than the land, the Bay Area in winter will occasionally suck in the colder air and fog of the interior — the reverse of the summer pattern.

If you are planning a redwoods excursion to Big Basin in the summer, bring a jacket and an umbrella. Redwoods are creatures of the fog, need it to thrive. Where you find a good redwood stand, you will, in summer, often find fog, cold thick fog, that will usually burn off by noon.

Scorchers

During the summer and fall, the Pacific High will occasionally loop a strong wind down from Washington through the Sierra and the hot valleys,

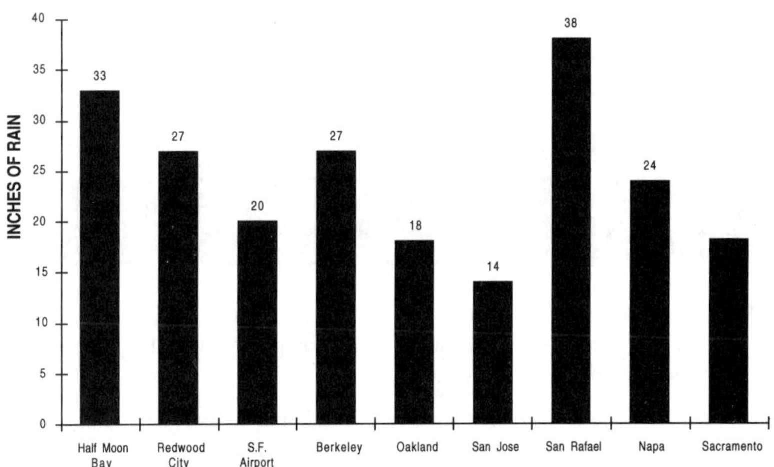

Source: National Weather Service.

where it loses its moisture, and into the Bay Area.

Extremely dry, these northeasters, which are now called "Diablos," will tighten the skin on your face, cause wood shingle roofs to crackle and turn the countryside into tinder. The October 1991 fire that destroyed 2,500 homes and apartments in the Berkeley-Oakland hills and killed 25 was caused by a Diablo. If you buy in the hills, if your home is surrounded with brush and trees, take a look at fire-retardant shingles and fire-prevention tactics.

Storms

Rain is rain, generally welcome all the time in dry California. But some rains are more welcome than others. Storms from the vicinity of Hawaii turn Sierra Nevada slopes to slush and, in the upper elevations, deposit soft snow that sinks under the weight of skis.

Alaskan storms bring snow to the lower mountains and deposit a fine powder, ideal for skiing. Some Alaskan storms occasionally bless the Bay Region with snow on the mountain tops. The air will be crystal clear, with a shiver of cold. Mt. Hamilton and the other mountains, green for the winter, will overnight don a lovely mantle of white.

Allergies

They often kick in during the spring and in October. During the spring, the grasses pop their buds and many trees release pollen. In the fall, the Diablos dry out the trees and cones and pollen fills the air. Hanky time.

Chapter 17

SANTA CLARA COUNTY

Crime

EVERY neighborhood and city in this country suffers from some crime. Even communities surrounded by gates and patrolled by guards will on occasion see domestic violence or pilfering by visitors.

So the question to ask when shopping for a home or apartment is not: Is this neighborhood safe? But rather, how safe is it compared to other places?

In California, crime often follows demographics: High-income neighborhoods generally have low crime, middle-income places middling crime and low-income towns and neighborhoods high crime.

For these guides, we label towns with fewer than 50 crimes per 1,000 residents over a year as low in crime. Towns with 50 to 80 crimes per 1,000 residents are placed in the middling category. Towns with over 80 crimes per 1,000 are labeled high in crime or worrisome. The statistics are supplied by the FBI and the California Dept. of Justice.

In many instances, these figures mislead. You can take probably every high-crime city in the country and find within it low-crime neighborhoods. New York City, to look at its statistics, seemingly is overrun with felons but the City includes Staten Island, generally suburban and probably low to middle in crime.

The same for Oakland, San Francisco, San Diego and Los Angeles. These are not crime cities; they are cities with certain neighborhoods high in crime.

Sometimes the statistics give a false picture. Theft is the most common crime. A city with many stores or a regional shopping mall will often have a high number of thefts — and consequently, a higher crime rate. Number of homicides, in some instances, gives a clearer picture of local crime.

The demographic connection also can mislead. Many peaceful, law-abiding people live in the "worst" neighborhoods. But these neighborhoods also contain a disproportionate number of the troubled and criminally inclined.

Why does crime correlate with income and demographics? In many countries, it doesn't. Japan, devastated after World War II, did not sink into

Crime Statistics by City

City	Population	Rate	Homicides
Campbell	39,871	38	0
Cupertino	47,668	24	0
Gilroy	39,071	53	3
Los Altos	28,488	14	0
Los Altos Hills	8,247	9	0
Los Gatos	30,274	25	0
Milpitas	64,325	35	0
Monte Sereno	3,443	8	0
Morgan Hill	31,896	41	1
Mountain View	75,201	33	0
Palo Alto	61,189	41	3
San Jose	909,062	34	29
Santa Clara	102,682	34	1
Saratoga	31,255	11	0
Sunnyvale	132,940	23	2
Santa Clara Co.	1,715,374	33	44

Crime in Other Northern California Cities

City	Population	Rate	Homicides
Concord	114,521	60	4
Danville	39,881	18	0
East Palo Alto	25,568	53	7
Hillsborough	11,618	7	0
Fremont	203,569	36	9
Monterey	33,103	54	0
Oakland	399,916	93	72
Sacramento	396,163	80	31
San Francisco	790,498	59	58
San Ramon	44,688	21	1
Santa Cruz	55,717	52	2
Scotts Valley	10,698	30	0
Stockton	243,673	72	27
Vacaville	89,403	28	3
Vallejo	112,795	68	6
Walnut Creek	63,944	47	0

Source: California Crime Index from State Dept. of Justice, 1998 data, with population estimates from the 1999 California Dept. of Finance. Rate is all reported willful homicide, forcible rape, aggravated assault, burglary, motor vehicle theft, larceny-theft and arson per 1,000 residents. Homicides include murders and non-negligent manslaughter.

violence and thievery. Many industrialized nations with lower standards of living than the U.S. have much less crime. In 1990, according to one study, handguns killed 10 people in Australia, 22 in Great Britain and 87 in Japan. The count for the U.S. was 10,567.

Sociologists blame the breakdown of morals and the family in the U.S, the pervasive violence in the media, the easy access to guns, and other forces. Any one of these “causes” could be argued into the next century but if you’re

Crime in Other Cities Nationwide

City	Population	Rate	Homicides
Anchorage	255,634	60	23
Atlanta	420,865	139	150
Baltimore	719,587	108	312
Birmingham	275,236	96	108
Boise	156,026	51	4
Boston	555,024	68	43
Chicago	2,765,852	NA	757
Cleveland	496,624	75	77
Dallas	1,077,029	93	209
Denver	525,793	64	69
Des Moines	195,455	86	12
Honolulu	880,272	61	34
Jacksonville	702,545	83	75
Little Rock	183,840	119	34
Milwaukee	628,507	76	122
Miami	391,766	128	103
New York	7,320,477	49	770
New Orleans	488,509	94	267
Oklahoma City	472,046	117	59
Pittsburgh, PA	353,248	58	50
Phoenix	1,172,538	96	175
Portland, OR	473,696	112	46
Reno	166,924	64	13
Salt Lake City	185,553	117	21
Seattle	547,209	104	49
Tucson	485,933	100	50
Washington, D.C.	529,000	98	301

Source: Annual 1998 FBI crime report, which uses 1997 data. Population estimates are based on updated estimates from 1990 census. **Key**: NA (not available).

shopping for a home or an apartment just keep in mind that there is a correlation between demographics and crime.

How do you spot a troubled neighborhood?

Crime is a young person's game, particularly boys and men. In one of its annual studies, the FBI determined that 61 percent of all the people arrested were under age 30. For every female arrested four males were arrested, the same study noted.

Take a look at the academic rankings of the neighborhood school. Very low rankings indicate that many children are failing, that the dropout rate is probably high, that the young people will have difficulty finding jobs — conditions that often breed crime.

In middle-scoring towns, the failures are fewer. In higher scoring towns, fewer still.

Crime in States

State	Population	Rate	Homicides
Alabama	4,319,000	49	426
Alaska	609,000	53	54
Arizona	4,555,000	72	275
Arkansas	2,523,000	47	250
California	**32,268,000**	**49**	**2,579**
Colorado	3,893,000	47	157
Connecticut	3,270,000	40	124
Delaware	732,0000	51	18
Florida	14,654,000	73	1,012
Georgia	7,486,000	58	563
Hawaii	1,187,000	60	47
Idaho	1,210,000	39	39
Illinois	11,896,000	51	1,096
Indiana	5,864,000	45	430
Iowa	2,852,000	38	52
Kansas	2,595,000	46	155
Kentucky	2,908,000	31	228
Louisiana	4,352,000	64	682
Maine	1,242,000	31	25
Maryland	5,094,000	57	502
Massachusetts	6,118,000	37	119
Michigan	9,774,000	49	759
Minnesota	4,686,000	44	129
Mississippi	2,731,000	46	358
Missouri	5,402,000	48	426
Montana	879,000	44	42
Nebraska	1,657,000	43	50
Nevada	1,677,000	61	187
New Hampshire	1,173,000	26	16
New Jersey	8,053,000	41	337
New Mexico	1,730,000	69	134
New York	18,137,000	39	1,093
North Carolina	7,425,000	55	614
North Dakota	641,000	27	6
Ohio	11,186,000	45	523
Oklahoma	3,317,000	55	229
Oregon	3,243,000	63	95
Pennsylvania	12,020,000	34	705
Rhode Island	987,000	37	25
South Carolina	3,760,000	61	314
South Dakota	738,000	32	10
Tennessee	5,368,000	55	511
Texas	19,439,000	55	1,327
Utah	2,059,000	60	60
Vermont	589,000	28	9
Virginia	6,734,000	39	488
Washington	5,610,000	59	241
West Virginia	1,816,000	25	75
Wisconsin	5,170,000	37	205
Wyoming	480,000	42	17
Washington, D.C.	529,000	98	301

Source: FBI 1997 Figures

Crime In Other California Cities

City	Population	Rate	Homicides
Anaheim	306,298	34	18
Bakersfield	230,771	54	20
Fresno	415,381	79	36
Huntington Beach	196,660	30	0
Riverside	254,262	49	17
Los Angeles	3,781,545	49	426
San Diego	1,254,281	43	42
Santa Ana	314,990	38	21
Santa Barbara	91,909	37	2

Source: California Crime Index from State Dept. of Justice, 1998 data, with population estimates from the California Dept. of Finance (Jan. 1, 1999). Rate is all reported willful homicide, forcible rape, aggravated assault, burglary, motor vehicle theft, larceny-theft and arson per 1,000 residents. Homicides include murders and non-negligent manslaughter.

Drive the neighborhood. The signs of trouble are often easily read: men idling around the liquor store, bars on many windows, security doors in wide use.

Should you avoid unsafe or marginal neighborhoods?

For some people, the answer depends on tradeoffs and personal circumstances. The troubled neighborhoods often carry low prices or rents and are located near job centers. Many towns and sections are in transition; conditions could improve, the investment might be worthwhile. What's intolerable to a parent might be acceptable to a single person.

Tradeoffs also apply when choosing really safe neighborhoods.

If you don't have the bucks, often you can still buy safe but you may have to settle for a smaller house or yard. Or the equivalent of North Dakota. The state is quite safe — 6 homicides in 19975, the FBI reported — but when the temperatures drop to 40 below, the sunny but less-safe places may seem a better choice.

Whatever your neighborhood, don't make it easy for predators. Lock your doors, join the neighborhood watches, school your children in safety, take extra precautions when they are called for.

Subject Index

(See Advertising Index for list of advertisers)

Advertisers' Index

To advertise in McCormack's Guides, call 1-800-222-3602

BUY 10 OR MORE & SAVE!

If your order adds up to 10 or more, the price drops to $5.95 per book. You also save on shipping. Fill out form and send with check to: McCormack's Guides, P.O. Box 1728, Martinez, CA 94553. Or fax to (925) 228-7223.

Visa and MasterCard accepted on phone orders.  

1-800-222-3602

Next to title, write in number of copies ordered and total below:

No.	McCormack's Guide Title	Single	Bulk
___	Alameda County 2000	$13.95	$5.95
___	Contra Costa & Solano 2000	$13.95	$5.95
___	Los Angeles County 2000	$13.95	$5.95
___	Marin, Napa & Sonoma 2000	$13.95	$5.95
___	Orange County 2000	$13.95	$5.95
___	Riverside, San Bernardino 2000	$13.95	$5.95
___	Sacramento County 2000	$13.95	$5.95
___	San Diego County 2000	$13.95	$5.95
___	San Francisco & San Mateo 2000	$13.95	$5.95
___	Santa Barbara, Ventura 2000	$13.95	$5.95
___	Santa Clara County 2000	$13.95	$5.95

_________ Books @ $_________ (Price) = $______________

CA sales tax (8.25%) ______________

Shipping* ______________

Total Amount of Order: $______________

*** For orders of 10 or more, shipping is 45 cents per book. For orders of fewer than 10, shipping is $4.50 for first book, $1.50 per book thereafter.**

Paid by (circle one) Check/MC/Visa or Bill Us

Name ____

Company ______________________________________

Address _______________________________________

City ___________________________ State____ Zip________

Phone: (_____)__________ Fax: (_____)______________

☐ **Check here to receive advertising information**

bookinfo@mccormacks.com • www.mccormacks.com